The Complete Manual of Land Planning and Development

William E. Brewer
Charles P. Alter

A RESTON BOOK

PRENTICE HALL, Englewood Cliffs, New Jersey 07632

LIBRARY OF CONGRESS
Library of Congress Cataloging-in-Publication Data

Brewer, William E.
    The complete manual of land planning and development / by William
E. Brewer and Charles P. Alter.
        p.   cm.
    Bibliography: p.
    Includes index.
    ISBN 0-13-162066-5
    1. Municipal engineering--Planning--Handbooks, manuals, etc.
2. Land use--Planning--Handbooks, manuals, etc. 3. Building sites-
-Planning--Handbooks, manuals, etc.   I. Alter, Charles P.
. II. Title.
TD160.B74 1988
333.3--dc19   87-22166
                                                            CIP

Editorial/production supervision:
Gretchen K. Chenenko
Cover design: 20/20 Services, Inc.
Manufacturing buyer: Peter Havens

 © 1988 by Prentice-Hall, Inc.
A Division of Simon & Schuster
Englewood Cliffs, New Jersey 07632

Printed in the United States of America

10 9 8 7 6 5 4 3 2 1

ISBN 0-13-162066-5

Prentice-Hall International (UK) Limited, *London*
Prentice-Hall of Australia Pty. Limited, *Sydney*
Prentice-Hall Canada Inc., *Toronto*
Prentice-Hall Hispanoamericana, S.A., *Mexico*
Prentice-Hall of India Private Limited, *New Delhi*
Prentice-Hall of Japan, Inc., *Tokyo*
Simon & Schuster Asia Pte. Ltd., *Singapore*
Editora Prentice-Hall do Brasil, Ltda., *Rio de Janeiro*

DEDICATION

*This book is dedicated to the students at Bowling Green
State University, Bowling Green, OH, who studied land
planning from 1979 to 1985. Without their help and
encouragement, this book would have never been written.*

Contents

Preface

This book presents land planning information specifically for students, designers, planners, and real estate representatives. It can also serve as a reference guide for engineers who are engaged in land planning and land development activities. The twelve chapters were developed through teaching and practical experience in land planning. The material covers a wide range of land planning subjects used in design considerations, which range from zoning to computer applications.

The text is organized for a one-semester course and requires a basic knowledge of algebra, geometry, and trigonometry upon which the mathematical and general science relationships are developed. The text will enable the reader to develop an economic feasibility analysis using all the necessary components that are required in the development of land. It also contains specific information and training in the preparation of related design construction documents and introduces computer applications as used by the industry.

Acknowledgments

The authors wish to acknowledge the following for their efforts and support in the preparation of this book: Ms. Diane Werder, Reston Publishing Company, for her initial interest, encouragement, and tenacity; Dr. Donald Milks, Ohio Northern University, Ada, OH, and Prof. Theodore Horst, The University of Toledo, OH for their assistance in the review of all the technical information presented. We are indebted to Gretchen Chenenko who guided us through the unfamiliar areas of editing. We also want to acknowledge the contributions of both our families in allowing us the uninterrupted time that was required to prepare this book.

Chapter 1

How To Use
This Book

INTRODUCTION

This book is the result of an acknowledged need on the part of many different individuals who work with land planning and land development. These individuals work in a surprisingly diversified group of professions and include real estate agents, construction contracting personnel, architects, civil engineers, owners/builders, bankers, material suppliers, educators, and students. This chapter will address crucial questions such as the following: who needs this book, why they need it, and how to use this book as the ready reference that it was designed to be.

WHY YOU SHOULD USE THIS BOOK

The need for this reference book became apparent when the authors were searching for an appropriate text for a course dealing with site planning for the construction technology curriculum at Bowling Green State University. Results of the search for a suitable text yielded no appropriate instructional material that treated the variety of subjects adequately as a text. The best text available then was used for this class, and plans were developed to write a workbook-type text that would detail the most important topics to be covered in the site planning class. This initial workbook was written in 1982 and proved to be a very acceptable substitute for the previous text. This book is an extension of the originally conceived workbook and contains additional materials and chapters.

The subject matter is designed to be general in nature with enough technical detail so that the reader can use it as a reference in the future. The goal of this book is to provide an overall reference that will be equally valuable to the architect, engineer, construction contractor, real estate agent, and student or teacher of site planning. Following is a brief description of the subjects covered in each chapter.

Chapter 2: Building and Zoning Regulations.   Deals with a brief history of zoning regulations and discusses their evolution as a land planning tool. Also covered is an identification of symbols and terminology used in land planning, subdivision regulations, and property surveys.

Chapter 3: Land Planning Mathematics.   Focuses on some of the specific mathematics used in land planning, including bearing lines, coordinate geometry, property closure, and calculation of areas by established surveying methods.

Chapter 4: Property Description and Deeds.   Topics covered include how property closures are used; a description of the surveying system as used in the United States, with an explanation of townships, sections, and lot division; and how to read property descriptions accurately.

Chapter 5: Topography.   Addresses types and uses for topographic maps, map scales, key terms needed to interpret topo maps, contour lines, plotting and developing contours, stationing, and plan and profile views of topographic maps.

Chapter 6: Soils.   Topics covered include soil composition, volume calculations, particle size, type of soils, testing procedures, soil classifications, liquid limit, moisture content, plastic limit, soil sampling, and interpretation of soil test data.

Chapter 7: Stormwater Drainage.   Discusses the process used to design and lay out a typical storm drainage system and the calculations needed to determine critical data. Also covered are key terms, drainage structures, pipe sizing, design methods, and use of nomographs.

Chapter 8: Sanitary Sewer Considerations.   Topics covered include a description of different types of sanitary sewers, sewage regulations, sewage flow estimates, the Ten States Standards, design methods, materials, construction methods, and sample design problems.

Chapter 9: Pavement Alignment (Horizontal and Vertical Curves).   An in-depth discussion of aligning pavements both horizontally and vertically with a step-by-step discussion of the calculations needed for both of these pavement alignment curves. An excellent quick reference.

Chapter 10: Pavement Design Considerations.   Topics covered include a history of pavement design, test roads, pavement types, materials, thickness design considerations, and construction techniques.

Chapter 11: Project Cost Feasibility.   Discusses the importance of cost feasibility studies on any size project and how to acquire reliable cost information and use it in a logical manner to conduct cost analysis. The major components of a feasibility study are explained and actual examples of such studies are described.

Chapter 12: Computer Applications.   This chapter describes typical hardware and software that can be used by land planning professionals. It includes a discussion of microcomputer CAD (computer-aided drafting) systems accessible to small firms.

Also discussed are data systems, spreadsheets and programs, and how each of these computer software methods can be used effectively. Examples are included that describe the use of spreadsheets and computer programs that the reader can use immediately for typical land planning calculations. This is an extremely valuable chapter for all types of land planning and land development professionals. Appendices are included with complete programs that can be loaded on to an APPLE IIe, or compatible computer. This same software is also available, on a floppy disk, for both APPLE IIe and IBM PC compatible equipment by writing the authors.

Appendix A: The Solution of Any Triangle.   Contains a computer program for the solution of any triangle. The user is required to know three components of a triangle. The program RUN will yield the remaining three unknowns in the triangle.

Appendix B: Bearing and Distance Program.   This program will yield the bearing and distance between any two points if the coordinates of those points are known. This program will work for any number of sides and is very helpful when calculating property closures and land areas.

Appendix C: Pavement Cost Analysis.   This program calculates the cost of different pavement sections after the user enters specific cost data and is extremely helpful in analyzing the most economical pavement section.

Appendix D: Mathematics Review.   A mathematical review to serve as a reference for land planners and site developers. This appendix contains explanations for basic algebra, angular measurements, and trigonometric functions. A good mathematical background is a necessary tool for doing land planning and site development.

SUMMARY

This reference book is designed to be used easily and quickly by a wide cross-section of individuals who are engaged in land planning activities.

Construction management personnel will find this book a quick reference to use when bidding and managing development projects and/or actual construction. Real estate professionals will appreciate a readable, semi-technical book that will help them to better understand the many steps required in property development. Contractors will be able to use this book to identify ways to save money on all types of projects. Homeowners contemplating the development of a piece of property either as an investment or a home, will find this book extremely informative when planning their project. College and high school educators will be able to use this book as a text and reference book in a variety of different curricular settings to explain the "How To" aspects of land planning concisely and accurately.

Chapter 2

Zoning and Building Regulations

INTRODUCTION

Regulated land development requires the understanding and implementation of local and state building and zoning regulations. Some areas in the United States do not have building and zoning regulations. These areas are usually associated with less populated areas where the land value is usually lower than in regulated areas.

Zoning will be reviewed with considerations as to its history, purpose, legal basis, and land use controls. Building regulation topics will include building codes, subdivision regulations, and standards.

HISTORY OF ZONING

Zoning dates back to England (1593) when parliament passed the Act Against New Buildings. The act was in response to the population increase in London which had reached 120,000. It ruled against the erection of a dwelling within the cities of London or Westminister, or within three miles of their city gates. Punishment for disobeying this act was a fine of five pounds, which was a considerable amount in 1593. The Act was not repealed until 1888 when population had grown to over four million.

In the United States, zoning started in the form of nuisance laws as the population in urban communities increased. Types of nuisance law regulations are recorded in The United States Supreme Court records.

1909—A Boston law was upheld that regulated building heights, with the primary purpose of ensuring that there would be ample sunlight for each property.

1915—The operation of a brickyard was halted because of excessive noise and

odor (*Hadacheck* v. *Sebastian,* 1915). These are but two examples of nuisance laws that still play a major part in the land-use regulations and place controls on junkyards, billboards, pornography, and other uses of land considered to be offensive by a community.

Legally, zoning began in the United States in 1916 with the New York City Zoning Ordinance. This ordinance divided New York City into residential, commercial, and unrestricted land-use districts. The ordinance also mapped out areas according to building heights. Behind any ordinance there is a sponsor or a special interest group. In this case, the special interest group was the Fifth Avenue merchants who wanted the ordinance to protect them from the rapidly growing garment industry.

By 1926, at least 425 municipalities, representing more than half of the urban population in the United States, had enacted some form of zoning ordinances. The police power of the municipalities was the legal basis for the zoning ordinance. The ordinance placed new controls on the use of personal property without offering any compensation because of the controls. The increase in zoning ordinances was a result of inadequate enforcement of nuisance laws and the rapid growth of municipalities.

The New York City Zoning Ordinance was aimed at neighborhood protection, merchants versus industry, while later ordinances were aimed at community protection. Suburban communities used zoning primarily for community protection. The early arguments for zoning were all related to the needs of cities and villages. Some communities attempted to use zoning for segregation based on social or economic factors. In Euclid, Ohio (1924) a zoning ordinance was declared unconstitutional because it attempted to regulate entry into the community by imposing social and economic requirements.

Zoning laws allowed for variances, or exceptions, in special circumstances. In the early 1960's, planned unit development variances were introduced. Under these variances, developers were required to provide detailed plans and specifications in the form of record surveys and plat plans. These variances have lead to a formal project-to-project review.

Through the years zoning has changed greatly. In the past communities had adopted restrictive zoning ordinances resulting in limited development. The introduction of broad administrative discretion on zoning variances helped to overcome restrictive zoning issues. In 1976, the United States Supreme Court declared that all communities could require a public referendum on zoning change. (*City of Eastlake, Ohio* v. *Forrest City Enterprises*). This enables citizens to overrule any administrative decision on zoning.

CURRENT TRENDS IN ZONING

Since the emphasis today is on the development of the neighborhood within the community as a basis for land-use planning, professional planners are engaged in a major reappraisal of the possibilities for zoning. Since World War II, zoning ordinances have concentrated much of their effort on suburban development. As seen from this urban point of view, zoning is accomplishing its aims of the protection of high-quality

neighborhoods. However, in the last 30 years suburban communities have been growing at the expense of the downtown areas of many major cities. For many reasons
this trend is now slowing, and the need for new types of zoning ordinances and new
techniques for land-use planning together with the public policy to implement them
have become necessary.

One of the most significant departures from traditional zoning practice has been
the emergence of special zoning districts that have been used to create a separate zoning
ordinance for an inner-city area. The best known example of the special zoning district
is the Historic Preservation district. In these special areas an effort has been made
to preserve the original architectural design of a particular area. Federal funds have
been allocated to encourage the redevelopment of valuable neighborhoods and commercial areas in the inner city. Whether the Special Zoning district concept succeeds
as a tool for cities or merely camouflages the more major problems in cities remains
to be seen.

Zoning exists as a vibrant force in the planning methods used to develop property in urban areas. At its best, zoning is a reflection of the current economic, social,
and individual concerns of a community. Because each community has its own individual priorities and concerns, there can never be a model zoning ordinance or "how
to do it" manual on zoning. With this in mind, this chapter provides an overview
of zoning concerns as they exist today and how these typical zoning concerns can
be blended with fresh approaches to urban zoning and land-use planning.

ZONING AND RELATED LAND-USE CONTROLS

Zoning is defined as the use of land-use controls to protect the rights of the individual
property owner and the rights of others within the community. Zoning allows community residents to control how their environment and public services are used. In
essence, community zoning powers provide a collective property right to maintain
the neighborhood and business environment and the right to the public services that
compliment that environment.

There are usually four basic types of zones, which depend on how the land is
to be used. The most common terminology for these zones is residential, commercial, industrial, and agricultural. Areas where only housing for residences is permitted
are classified as residential. There are separate divisions of residential zoning designed
to control the density of population. These separate divisions are represented by the
following symbols.

- R1—single family residencies
- R2—duplexes that may be mixed with single family units
- R3—apartment complexes and condominiums

Areas designed for business (with the businesses primarily consisting of retail
establishments) are zoned commercial. As was with residential zoning, commercial

zoning also is divided into separate divisions. The symbols for these separate divisions are

- C1—for neighborhood shopping areas. Examples would be banks, grocery stores, barber shops, and other small retail businesses.
- C2—restricted office areas, this classification would encompass offices for medical clinics, schools, and specialized retail shops.
- C3—the "catch-all" classification that includes most types of commercial businesses; fast food restaurants, bars, gas stations, garages, and some light manufacturing with less than 10,000 square feet of interior space.

The third major classification for zoning is industrial. It is also separated into divisions

- M1—covers most types of manufacturing
- M2—allows heavy industrial operations. Examples would be chemical plants, junk yards, and other businesses that employ more than 1500 people.
- M3—is for planned industrial parks. This is similar to shopping centers under commercial zoning. Planned industrial parks provide space that is commonly maintained and usually includes parking areas. The emphasis in these parks is on efficiency and convenience.

See Fig. 2-1 for an example of zoning.

Zoning establishes a uniform, consistent guide for the land's use. Residential zoning can regulate such things as lot sizes, building lines, property widths, and maximum building heights. Properly enforced, zoning will protect one's rights and the rights of others within a community.

ZONING SYMBOLS

A general set of symbols has been developed for land development drawings and plans. These symbols are as illustrated in Fig. 2-2 and are defined as follows:

- R/W (right of way)—The portion of the subdivision that is allocated for public use. This area, maintained by the community, contains the street, sewers, water lines, and other utilities. Usually, for residential subdivisions, the right of way width is 60 feet.
- C/L—(center line)—References the center line of the right of way and usually references the center line of the street. It should be noted that the center line of the street may not always be the same as the center line of the right of way.
- P/L (property line)—Designates the ownership line for a parcel of property. The property line for a lot usually consists of four lines; front, two sides, and

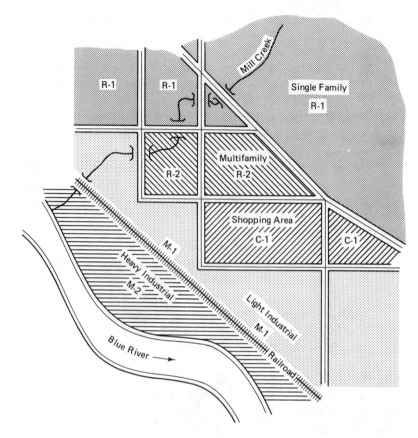

Figure 2-1 Zoning map.

rear lot lines. See Fig. 2-3. The property line towards the street is a common line with the right-of-way line.

- B/L (building line)—Refers to the building line of the structure that is to be built on the lot. See Fig. 2-3. No portion of a structure can be built beyond this designated line. Typical building line locations are 35 feet back from the front property line and 25 feet back from the side property line if a corner lot exists.

- Lot number—References the lot within a subdivision. This number helps describe and identify the property within a subdivision. For example, one could own Lot 4, in Orchard Dale Estates. This would be lot number 4 in a subdivision recorded as Orchard Dale Estates.

PURPOSE OF ZONING

One of the main purposes of zoning is to put land to its best possible use. Some areas do not have zoning ordinances because of a variety of factors, chief among them

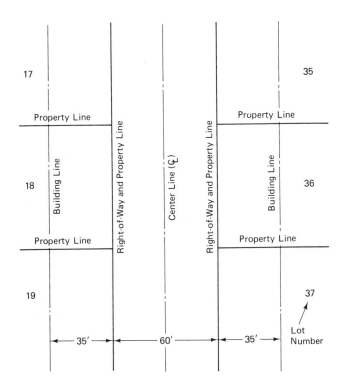

Figure 2-2 Plat symbols.

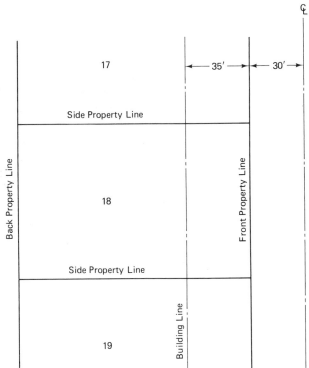

Figure 2-3 Typical lot—property lines.

being the apparent lack of economic development potential of the land. In Ohio, for example, out of 88 counties only 77 have zoning ordinances. The counties that do not have zoning regulations are located in southeastern Ohio, which has been traditionally underdeveloped and has high levels of poverty. At present, there is little need for zoning resolutions in these counties.

Personnel who might enter the construction profession should have a clear understanding of what zoning is and how it is used to create livable areas within urban centers. A major concern of zoning resolutions is to protect the land and use it in the best manner. Good planning for land use includes economic considerations, social factors, and the physical characteristics of the land. It is important to determine the total estimated cost of the project before the project is undertaken. Economics is the underlying factor in any land development project.

Social factors that are of concern in zoning are centered on who the people are that are expected to live in a development. The income levels of these individuals provides a guide to the types of housing that will be constructed. In the past, defacto segregation occurred in many new developments because of exclusionary practices of developers. This condition has largely disappeared; however, it is still a significant aspect of land planning.

The best use of the physical characteristics of the land is another primary concern in determining the uses of the land. Hills, streams, trees, vegetation, and the natural lay of the land should all be considered to produce the most pleasing design. Natural factors can be used to create a unique setting for whatever use the land may have.

Still, another important concern of zoning is the protection of property values. As discussed earlier in the History of Zoning, one of the initial purposes of zoning was the protection of high-quality neighborhoods. Central to this purpose is the protection of property values. In this context, a developer can stipulate the type and quality of housing that will be constructed in a subdivision. The subdivider may require that each house in a development have at least a certain minimum square footage of interior space and blend with other structures in the subdivision with respect to exterior, building height, and building-line set backs. These types of zoning regulations are designed to protect the rights of the people who own the property now and in the future.

To accomplish the purposes of zoning a local government has three types of powers on which the legal basis for zoning is built. These powers are taxation, police power, and eminent domain.

Property taxation has a concrete value to local governments because the property is stationary and, with the exception of annexation by a larger government, it will provide a steady source of revenue. In some states property taxes are primarily used for the support of schools.

Police power refers to the right of the local government to enforce the laws of the land. It is with the police power right that local governments may enforce health regulations, pollution control, building codes, subdivision regulations, and housing codes.

Eminent domain refers to the right of the local government to take possession of property in the public's interest. This power is used to acquire right of ways for the construction of public and transportation systems. This power can be easily abused by local planning commissions and can create much controversy. Today it appears that planning commissions are much more conscious of their obligation to protect high-quality neighborhoods that may previously have been uprooted in the name of the public interest.

BUILDING CODES

Building codes are concerned with the health, welfare and safety in regard to buildings, construction, and property. Building codes are concerned with how a structure will be built in contrast with zoning, which is concerned with the use of a piece of property and what is to be built on it. State building codes apply to three types of zoning; R3 (three (or more) family units), industrial, and commercial. Local building codes govern R1 (single-family units) and R2 (two-family units) zoning. State laws require that local building codes be at least as strict as the state's building code.

Model building codes are now used in the place of many separate state building codes. The Building Officials & Code Administrators International, Inc. (BOCA) and the International Conference of Building Officials (ICBO) are the two largest model code groups. Their purpose is to write uniform building codes based on the most up-to-date information. These two model code groups are in direct competition with each other to sell their version of modern building codes to states and communities within the states that accept these codes.

SUBDIVISION REGULATIONS

In most cases, raw land that is being developed for a subdivision is land that has previously been zoned agricultural. Regulations for subdivisions are important because they guide the way in which the land may be developed, especially in cases where land has only been used for farming.

The original land-use surveys, which were conducted in the early 19th century, were developed to facilitate the devlopment of land that previously was unused. For example, northwestern Ohio in the early 19th century was known as the Black Swamp and was an area largely covered by virgin forests and swamp lands. The original surveyors and land planners had to organize a manageable system for land uses and development. Therefore, Ohio, and other states employed the rectangular system of survey and the land was laid out in approximate squares, with each side being 6 miles long. These squares, known as townships, were then divided into 36 sections, which are 1 mile on a side. Land was originally sold in sections. A true section is 1 square mile, which contains 27,878,400 square feet. An acre of land contains 43,560 square feet. Therefore, a section would contain

$$\frac{27,848,400 \text{ sq ft}}{43,560 \text{ sq ft/A}} = 640\text{A}$$

The original sectional survey system also functioned as the model for the countys' road systems. Many county roads existing today are on the original section lines that were laid out in a county. This rectangular system of survey was also responsible for the locations of each county seat within the 88 counties in Ohio. A county seat was located so that a man on horse back could ride to the county seat and return home on the same day. Because of this requirement, county seats were usually located near the center of the county.

To help develop the land, two types of subdivision classifications have been created: minor subdivisions and major subdivisions. A minor subdivision is defined as a subdivision that contains five lots or less. A major subdivision is defined as having more than five lots and will usually require an adjustment to the existing road system, sewer system, utilities, and so on.

A minor subdivision, five lots or less, is usually a division or split of some portion of a section. The minor subdivision must be located along a dedicated right of way, which is usually a county road. It must not require road improvements by the county or conflict with any other land development or zoning regulations.

A major subdivision, more than five lots, requires more information and engineering work than the minor subdivision. The developer must produce a detailed plan for the subdivision prior to starting actual land development construction. This detailed plan includes: boundary survey, preliminary plat, final plat, engineering drawings for all streets, sewer, and water lines. The final plat will be used for the sale of the property (lots) and the assignment of property taxes. All boundary dimensions for all lots, streets, and so on, must fit, mathematically, for the final plat to be accepted by the governing subdivision agency. The boundary survey (see Fig 2.4) is made by a registered surveyor and is a detailed map of the boundary for the property to be developed. The preliminary plat and preliminary engineering construction estimates make up part of the cost feasibility considerations for proceeding with the project.

After the boundary survey has been completed, a preliminary plat, which is a preliminary plan of what the developer intends to do with the land, is prepared. See Fig. 2–5. Upon approval of the preliminary plat, which is usually done by a local planning board, a final plat can be produced.

The final plat is frequently delayed until a favorable cost feasibility for the land's development has been received. The final plat is the final plan for the proposed subdivision and includes the exact dimensions of the lots, roads, sanitary sewers, water lines, storm sewers, and all other utilities, and any other information that the local planning board requires. See Fig. 2–6.
The final plat must duplicate the boundary survey's information and define the individual properties within the subdivision.

The local planning board must be able to control the minimum standards for a subdivision in order to protect its right to maintain the right of way and the property of the taxpayers of a county. Minimum standards for a subdivision include

- street widths—the minimum width of streets to allow parking on one or both sides of a street. Minimum, for residential, is usually 25 feet measured back-

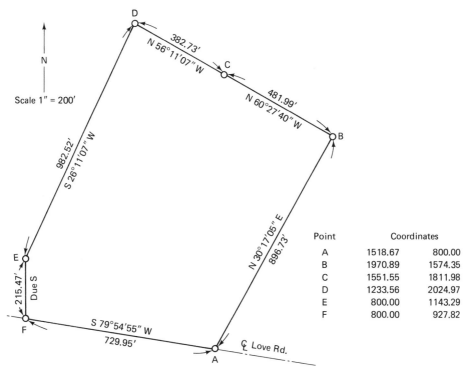

Point	Coordinates	
A	1518.67	800.00
B	1970.89	1574.35
C	1551.55	1811.98
D	1233.56	2024.97
E	800.00	1143.29
F	800.00	927.82

Figure 2-4 Boundary survey.

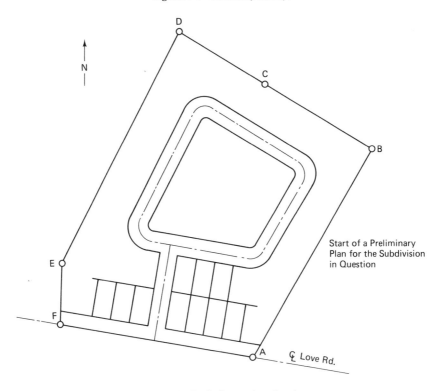

Start of a Preliminary
Plan for the Subdivision
in Question

Figure 2-5 Preliminary plat planning.

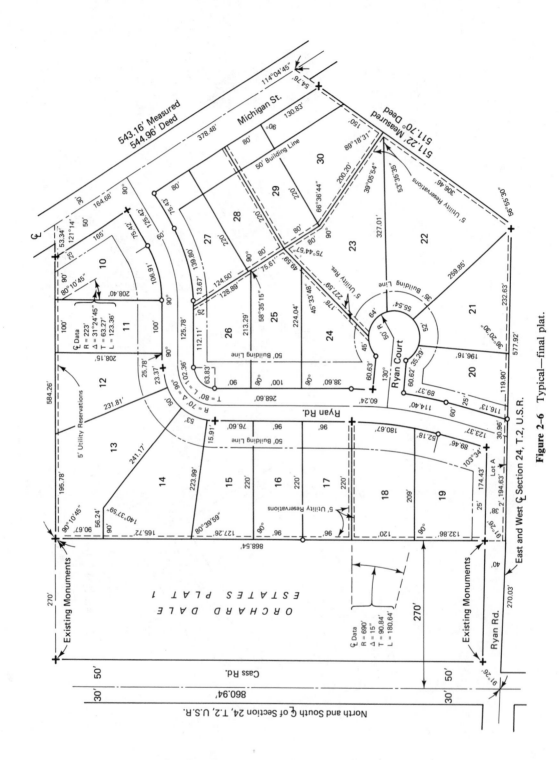

Figure 2-6 Typical—final plat.

14

to-back of the curbs. See Fig. 2-7. The pavement's geometrics must allow for the entrance of emergency vehicles into the subdivision. Suggested minimum turn radius, at street intersections, is 25 feet measured to the back of the curb.

- construction of pavement—the pavement's line (location), grade (vertical rise or fall), construction methods, construction materials, and final rideability are regulated by the subdivision's minimum standards.
- sanitary sewers—both material and construction method are regulated as well as the design.
- storm sewers—similar to sanitary sewer's minimum standards. All aspects of the storm drainage system can be set forth in the minimum standards including the amount of runoff a sewer can handle.
- water supply—this is also covered by minimum standards. The water supply must be of high enough quality to supply all the residents of a planned subdivision. This is of concern in areas where water will be supplied by individual wells.
- fire hydrant locations—fire protection is a key element in the planning of any subdivision, therefore, the locations of fire hydrants is a major concern of a local planning board. Minimum standards can include location and manufacturer.

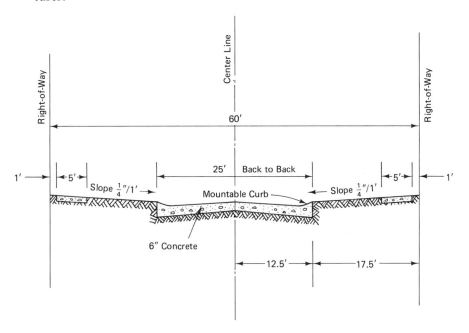

Figure 2-7 R/W cross section.

PROBLEMS

2–1. Zoning dates back to what country and what year? This early zoning regulation is known as what act?

2–2. Early zoning laws in the United States were the result of what community concern?

2–3. How are zoning regulations enforced?

2–4. Early New York City zoning ordinance was developed because of what concern?

2–5. What United States Supreme Court ruling, in 1976, had an effect on zoning?

2–6. What is meant by *Historic Preservation District?*

2–7. Define zoning.

2–8. What are the basic types of zones?

2–9. Define each of the following symbols:

    (a) R 1   **(d)** M1

    (b) R 3   **(e)** M3

    (c) C 2   **(f)** C3

2–10. What can residential zoning regulate?

2–11. Define each of the following symbols:

    (a) R / W   **(c)** C/L

    (b) P / L   **(d)** B/L

2–12. List items that a developer can stipulate in a subdivision.

2–13. What are the major concerns of building codes?

2–14. Name the two major model building codes in the United States.

2–15. A *section* of land contains how many acres?

2–16. What are the two types of subdivisions? Define each.

2–17. Define each of the following:

    (a) boundary survey

    (b) preliminary plat

    (c) final plat

    (d) engineering drawings

2–18. List items that may be included in minimum subdivision standards.

2–19. Explain the advantages and disadvantages of zoning.

Chapter 3

Land Planning Mathematics

INTRODUCTION

This chapter deals with the mathematics used in land planning. The specific sections relative to bearing lines, coordinate geometry, property closure, and areas explain calculation methods and their applied uses. This chapter should be read in the order presented. Upon completion of this chapter, the reader should be able to calculate bearings of lines, distances between property points, determine if the property actually closes, calculate acreage of property, and understand the use of coordinate geometry in land planning.

BEARINGS OF LINES

The bearing of a line is important to land planners because it helps with the required land calculations and the writing of legal descriptions. It is a reference to the lines' direction from a designated reference. This designated reference is either north or south and can be either true north or true south or the assumed north or south direction. It is similar to a bearing (direction) one would use in the navigation of a ship or airplane except the line will be referenced from either north or south. The selection of north or south as the designated reference depends on which quadrant the line lies in. The lines illustrated in Fig. 3-1: A-B, A-C, A-D, and A-E would have bearing directions of

- A–B south east (SE)
- A–C north east (NE)

- A–D north west (NW)
- A–E south west (SW)

It should be evident, from Fig. 3–1, that the bearing of a line will consist of line direction, NE, SE, and so on, and some angular measurement from either north or south. Therefore, one should note that the angular measurement <u>will always be less than 90°</u>. If the bearing angle for line A–B was 90°, then the bearing of line A–B would be referenced as N 90° E, S 90° E, or due E. The bearing angle for lines in a due north or due south direction is 0°.

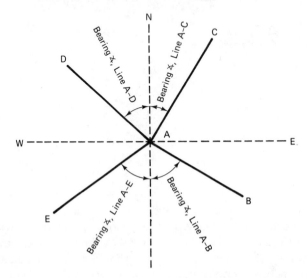

Figure 3–1 Bearing angle direction.

The next consideration is how to calculate bearing of lines for a given property layout. In surveying terms the given property would be referenced as a closed traverse, meaning that all the sides and angles, if laid out on paper or in the field, would close the figure. Property closure calculations will be discussed later in this chapter. Fig. 3–2 shows a closed traverse consisting of the interior angles. The distances between the points will be discussed later. Bearings for the lines (direction) will be computed from the information shown. The interior angles are as noted in Table 3–1. (For changing angles for degrees, minutes, and seconds to decimal form, see Appendix D)

The first consideration, when working with line bearings, is to check that the interior angles will add up to the proper sum for the figure to be considered "closed." In Appendix D it was referenced that the sum of the interior angles, for any closed figure, would equal

$$\angle = (N - 2)180°$$

where, N represents the number of sides.
In this case, there are seven sides. Therefore,

$$\angle = (7 - 2)180° = 900°$$

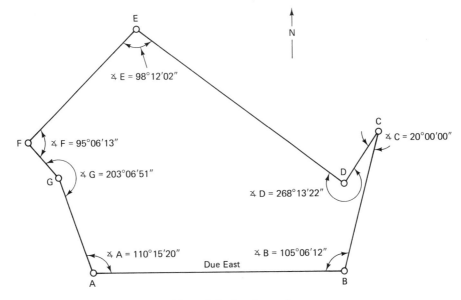

Figure 3-2   Interior angles.

TABLE 3-1   INTERIOR ANGLES

Point	Interior angle	Decimal form (degrees)
A	110° 15 ′20 ″	110.25556
B	105° 06 ′12 ″	105.10333
C	20° 00 ′00 ″	20.00000
D	268° 13 ′22 ″	268.22278
E	98° 12 ′02 ″	98.20056
F	95° 06 ′13 ″	95.10361
G	203° 06 ′51 ″	203.11417
	900° 00 ′00 ″	900.00000

The summation of the interior angles must equal 900° for a seven sided figure or the figure will not close. Summation of the interior angles shown in Fig. 3-2 yields 900°; therefore one may proceed to calculate the line bearings. Note that the line bearing for line A–B was referenced as due east. To determine the line bearing of the next course (line) B–C, follow these steps. (The terms course and line are interchangeable.)

1. At point *B* draw reference coordinate lines. See Fig. 3–3. It is very important to construct the reference coordinates to help visualize the angles to be used in the calculation of the bearing angle value.

2. Draw the bearing angle as noted by two double lines.

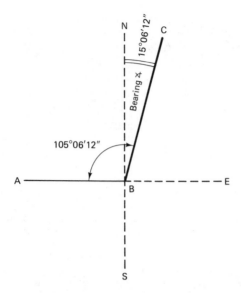

Figure 3-3 Bearing angle calculation.

3. Calculate the bearing angle value by determining its relation to the given interior angle and the referenced points. In this case the value is 15° 06′12″.

4. Finally give the line direction as discussed previously. The direction for line B–C is NE. Therefore, the bearing of line B–C would be N 15° 06′12″ E.

5. Determine the bearing of the next course (line) by repeating steps 1 through 4.

Each bearing line value for the shape shown in Fig. 3–2 will now be determined as outlined in the preceding steps. In Fig. 3–4 the line B–C is extended beyond point C to help identify the bearing angle value of line C–D. The bearing angle value, in this case, is equal to the interior angle plus the bearing angle value of line B–C. Note in Fig. 3–4 that opposite angles of two intersecting lines are equal. The bearing of line C–D is, therefore, S 35° 06′12″ W.

The bearing line value for line D–E in Fig. 3–5 illustrates a calculation when an interior angle is obtuse, greater than 180°. The bearing angle value is the difference between 360° and the sum of the interior angle and the bearing value of line C–D. The bearing of line D–E is N 56° 40′26″ W.

Figure 3–6 shows that the bearing line angle value of E–F can be derived by subtracting the bearing angle value (56° 40′26″) of D–E from the interior angle (98° 12′02″). The bearing of line E–F is S 41° 31′36″ W.

The bearing angle value for line F–G, as shown in Fig. 3–7, is derived by subtracting the bearing angle value (41° 31′36″) of E–F and the interior angle value (95° 06′13″) from 180 degrees. The bearing of line F–G is S 43° 22′11″ E.

To calculate the bearing angle for line G–A, as shown in Fig. 3–8, add bearing angle value for F–G (43° 22′11″) to 180° and subtract interior angle (203° 06′51″). The result is the angle value of line G–A (20° 15′20″). The direction is SE. Therefore, the bearing of line G–A is S 20° 15′20″ E.

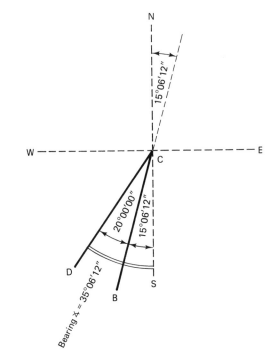

Figure 3–4 Bearing angle calculation.

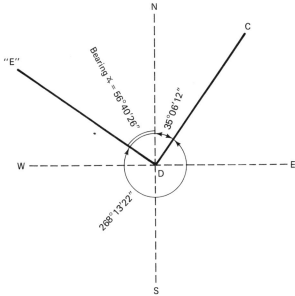

Figure 3–5 Bearing angle calculation.

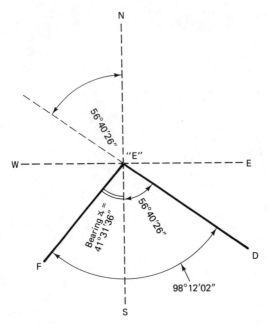

Figure 3-6 Bearing angle calculation.

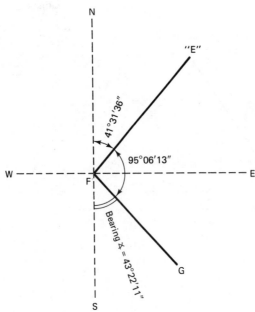

Figure 3-7 Bearing angle calculation.

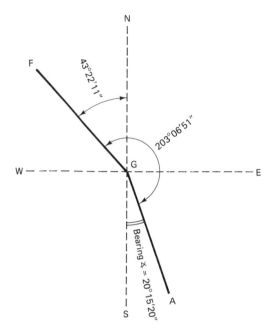

Figure 3-8 Bearing angle calculation.

To be sure that all bearing angle values have been calculated correctly, a final check should be made on the first course. Therefore, repeat steps 1 through 4 for point *A*. See Fig. 3-9.

The bearing angle value for line A–B checks!!! The bearing for line A–B is N 90° 00′00″ E or due E.

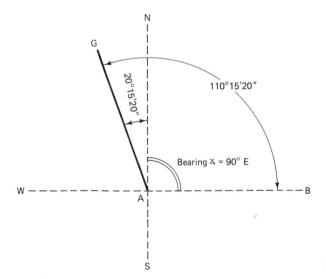

Figure 3-9 Bearing angle calculation.

The example just completed should illustrate the importance of making a reference sketch at the point in question. The bearings for all the lines just calculated are rewritten here in table form as Table 3–2.

TABLE 3–2 BEARING
ANGLES

Line	Bearing angle
A–B	due E
B–C	N 15° 06′12″ E
C–D	S 35° 06′12″ W
D–E	N 56° 40′26″ W
E–F	S 41° 31′36″ W
F–G	S 43° 22′11″ E
G–A	S 20° 15′20″ E

PROPERTY CLOSURE

A line will have both direction (bearing) and length. The line's length will be referenced as distance. If the bearings of the lines check for bearing closure, the figure still may not close because of incorrect distances. This section, property closure, will demonstrate how to determine if the recorded bearings and distances actually close. The values calculated will be used later to help determine the actual acreage for the property in question. For this example, consider the property as shown in Fig. 3–10. The sum of the interior angles should add up to

$$\angle = (N - 2)180° = 360°$$
$$\angle A = 78° 41′24″$$
$$\angle B = 132° 16′26″$$
$$\angle C = 85° 36′04″$$
$$\angle D = \underline{63° 26′06″}$$
$$358° 119′60″ \text{ or } 360° 00′00″$$

The sum of the internal angles check for closure. Note the distances that are recorded for each line.

A–B = 360.56′
B–C = 412.31′
C–D = 632.46′
D–A = 707.11′

Knowing the line bearing angle, direction and distance will enable breaking the figure down into right triangles for easier land closure and acreage calculations. Consider line A–B in Fig. 3–11.

Labels will be applied to the easterly and northerly directions from point *A* to point *B*. These labels will be *departures* and *latitude* respectively. These distances,

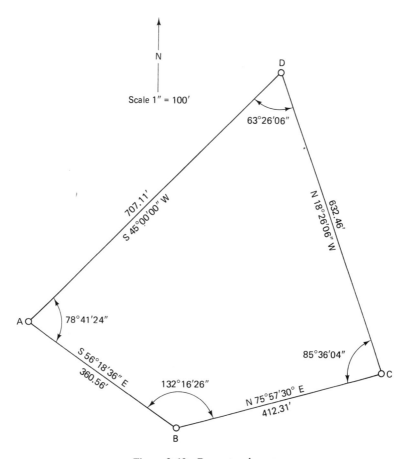

Figure 3–10 Property closure.

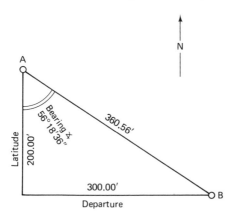

Figure 3–11 Latitudes and departures.

departure and latitude, can be calculated with the use of the trigonometric functions; sine and cosine. As referenced in Fig. 3–11, the values for the departure and latitude can be calculated by

$$\text{Departure (A–B)} = 360.56' \times \sin 56° \, 18'36'' = 300.00'$$
$$\text{Latitude (A–B)} = 360.56' \times \cos 56° \, 18'36'' = 200.00'$$

The departure's direction would be east, the same as the direction stated in the bearing. The latitude's direction would be south. A general rule can be written for the value of the departure or latitude for any line.

$$\text{Departure} = \text{Distance} \times \sin \text{(Bearing Angle)}$$
$$\text{Latitude} = \text{Distance} \times \cos \text{(Bearing Angle)}$$

Applying these equations to the remaining lines in Fig. 3–10 will produce the results shown in Table 3–3.

TABLE 3–3 LATITUDES AND DEPARTURES

Line	Latitude		Departure	
	N +	S −	E +	W −
A–B	—	200.00	300.00	—
B–C	100.00	—	400.00	—
C–D	600.00	—	—	200.00
D–A	—	500.00	—	500.00

Note that the direction for the departures and latitudes are as noted on the line's bearing. When making numerous calculations it is easier and more accurate to keep track of the results by developing a "table form" for the results. This will be especially true when making land development calculations. A standard calculation table is shown in Table 3–4. This table is arranged in an order that facilitates the calculations required. The values in the first ten columns from the left have been discussed, but will be summarized here.

- line (col. 1)—identification of the line in question, such as A–B, B–C.
- bearing (col. 2)—direction and bearing angle value, such as S 56° 18′36″ E.
- decimal equivalent (col. 3)—the decimal form of the bearing angle value.
- dist. (col. 4)—the distance from one reference point to another; expressed in feet.
- cos (col. 5)—the cosine of the bearing angle.
- sin (col. 6)—the sine of the bearing angle.
- latitude (N) or (S) (col. 7 or 8) = Distance × cos (Bearing ∠)
      col. 7 or 8 = col. 4 × col. 5
- departure (E) or (W) (col. 9 or 10) = Distance × sin (Bearing ∠)
      col. 9 or 10 = col. 4 × col. 6

TABLE 3-4 CALCULATION FORM

Line	Bearing	Decimal Equiv.	Distance	cos	sin	Latitudes N+	Latitudes S−	Departures E+	Departures W−	DMD	Double Areas +	Double Areas −
(1)	(2)	(3)	(4)	(5)	(6)	(7)	(8)	(9)	(10)	(11)	(12)	(13)

TABLE 3-5 CALCULATION FORM EXAMPLE

Line	Bearing	Decimal Equiv.	Distance	cos	sin	Latitudes N+	Latitudes S−	Departures E+	Departures W−	DMD	Double Areas +	Double Areas −
A–B	S 56-18-36	56.3099	360.56	.554701	.832050		200.003	300.004		300.00		60,000
B–C	N 75-57-50	75.9633	412.31	.242535	.970143	100.00		400.00		1000.00	100,000	
C–D	N 18-26-06	18.4350	632.46	.948680	.316228	600.004			200.002	1200.00	720,000	
D–A	S 45-00-00	45.0000	707.11	.707107	.707107		500.002		500.002	500.00		250,000
						700.004	700.005	700.004	700.004		820,000	310,000
										−	310,000	
										2	510,000	
											255,000	sq ft
											5.85	A
(1)	(2)	(3)	(4)	(5)	(6)	(7)	(8)	(9)	(10)	(11)	(12)	(13)

28

This table form (Table 3–4) will now be applied to the traverse as shown in Fig. 3–10 to calculate closure for this figure. See Table 3–5.

The values for the latitudes (N +, S −) and departures (E +, W −) are calculated as previously described and recorded in the table. The northerly and southerly values are added and compared to each other. The easterly and westerly values are also added and compared. If the northerly (N +) and the southerly (S −) values are equal and the easterly (E +) and the westerly (W −) values are equal, as shown in Table 3–2, then the figure (traverse) is considered closed.

If the figure does not close (northerlings not equal to southerlings, and easterlings not equal to westerlings) then adjustments must be made to sides, angles, or both to accomplish closure. These mathematical adjustments are not included as part of this text.

AREAS—DOUBLE MERIDIAN DISTANCE

The calculation of the area of a closed figure (traverse) is relatively easy if the latitude and departure for each side of the figure are known. Consider the figure as shown in Fig. 3–10 and the calculations as previously recorded in Table 3–5 and now recorded, in part, in Table 3–3. The calculation method is known as the *double meridian distance* (DMD) method. The general rules for determining the DMD of a line are

1. Always start with the most westerly point in the figure. For the figure in this example, the most westerly point is point *A*. It is important to start at this point to assure that the DMD values, col. 11, will always be positive (+).

2. The value (DMD) of the first course (side), line A–B for the figure in this example, is equal to the departure of the course. In this case the value is 300.00′ as referenced in Table 3–5.

3. The value (DMD) of the next course (side) and all the remaining courses (sides), is equal to the algebraic sum of the
   (a) departure of the previous course
   (b) DMD of the previous course
   (c) departure of the course itself
   For the figure in question the DMD values for lines B–C, C–D, and D–A are

$$\begin{aligned}
B–C &= (\ 300.00 + 300.00 + 400.00) = 1000.00\,' \\
C–D &= (1000.00 + 400.00 - 200.00) = 1200.00\,' \\
D–A &= (1200.00 - 200.00 - 500.00) = \ \ 500.00\,'
\end{aligned}$$

   These values are also recorded in Table 3–5.

4. A check can be applied to the DMD calculations by considering the last course (side). The DMD for the last course, if all calculations have been made correctly, will be equal to the departure of the last course but of opposite sign. For the figure in question, the DMD of the last course (D–A) is + 500.00′. The departure of this course (D–A) is − 500.00′. This confirms that the DMD calculations have been made correctly.

The values for col. 11, Table 3-5, are generated from information contained in col. 9 and 10.

Once the DMD values have been determined and checked, the double areas (col. 12 and 13) can be calculated. The values for the double areas are determined by multiplying the DMD value by the latitude of the course. This generates a double area (square feet). The sign (+ or −) is determined by the sign (+ or −) of the latitude because the DMD values are all positive (+) if calculated correctly. See Table 3-5 for values for the double areas. The calculation by columns would be

$$\text{col. 7 or 8} \times \text{col. 11} = \text{col. 12 (+) or 13 (−)}$$

The values in each column, col. 12 (+) and col. 13 (−), are added and the results are written in the table as shown. For this example these values are 820,000.00 square feet and 310,000 square feet respectively. The negative (−) total is subtracted from the positive (+) total and results in 510,000 square feet. Since this value represents a double area, it needs to be divided by 2. This value, 255,000 square feet represents the number of square feet in the closed figure as referenced in Fig. 3-10. To calculate the number of acres (A), divide the area expressed in square feet by 43560. One acre contains 43,560 square feet. Therefore the referenced figure contains 5.85 A. See Table 3-5 for the proper recording of these calculations and results.

COORDINATE GEOMETRY

Having completed property closures with considerations for line bearings and distances, the subject of coordinate geometry offers still another and a more powerful tool for use by the land planner. Consider assigning an address to all points in Fig. 3-10. This address would reference a point from some given point, for example, from some origin. This would be similar to referencing a point on a checker board if one would reference distances from the lower left-hand corner. See Fig. 3-12.

The point being referenced would have an address of 3,4 as referenced from the lower left-hand corner 0,0. If the reference point 0,0 was the origin of a coordinate system, then the distance, 3, would be in an easterly direction and the distance, 4, would be in a northerly direction. The address of a point is always referenced as the easterly distance followed by the northerly distance, or 3,4. It is important to have the origin (0,0) so located that all points, in the figure being considered, lie in the first quadrant. This will result in all easterly and northerly distance being positive (+).

Consider again the figure in Fig. 3-10. If coordinates for point A were assigned, for example, 1100.00,1100.00. The origin (0,0) would be 1100.00 feet west of point A and 1100.00 feet south of point A. The coordinates of the other points in the figure can easily be determined since the easterly and northerly distances are actually the latitudes and the departures for each line being considered. See Fig. 3-13.

The coordinates for point B are 1400.00,900.00 and are calculated by either subtracting or adding the northerlings (latitude) and the easterlings (departures) to the coordinate values of point A.

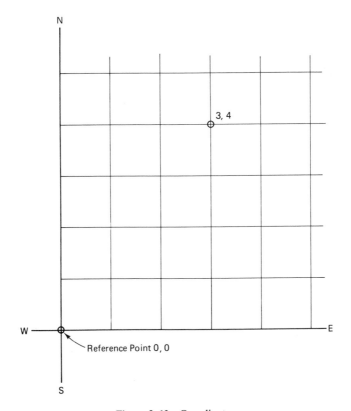

Figure 3–12 Coordinates.

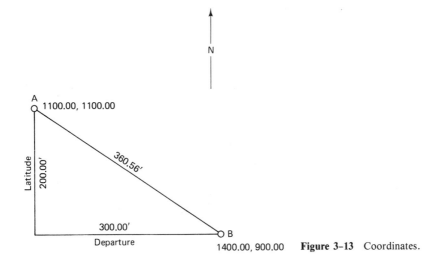

Figure 3–13 Coordinates.

Easterling (*B*)   = 1100.00 + 300.00 = 1400.00
Northerling (*B*) = 1100.00 − 200.00 =   900.00

Similarly, the coordinates for points *C* and *D* can be found by simply adding or subtracting the latitudes or departures. See Fig. 3–14.

Easterling (*C*)   = 1400.00 + 400.00 = 1800.00
Northerling (*C*) =   900.00 + 100.00 = 1000.00

Easterling (*D*)   = 1800.00 − 200.00 = 1600.00
Northerling (*D*) = 1000.00 + 600.00 = 1600.00

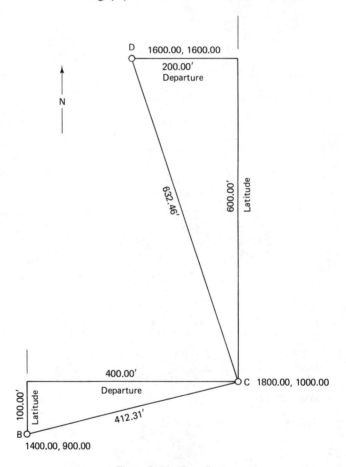

Figure 3–14   Coordinates.

Using the same procedure, the coordinates for point *A* can be checked. See Fig. 3–15.

Easterling (*A*)   = 1600.00 − 500.00 = 1100.00
Northerling (*A*) = 1600.00 − 500.00 = 1100.00

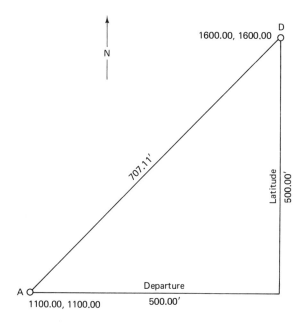

Figure 3–15 Coordinates.

Therefore, if one knows the coordinates of all the points in a figure, the latitudes and departures can be readily found by simple addition and subtraction. The coordinates of the points also allows one to readily calculate distances and line bearings between points. For example, if the distance and line bearing from point *A* to point *C* were desired (see Fig. 3–10) these values can quickly be calculated. See Fig. 3–16.

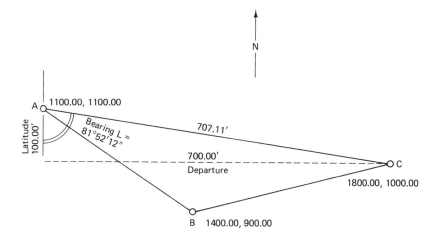

Figure 3–16 Coordinates.

The distance between point A and point C can be found by Pythagorean theorem

$$c^2 = a^2 + b^2$$
$$c^2 = 100.00^2 + 700.00^2$$
$$c = 707.107 \text{ feet}$$

The bearing angle can be found by

$$\tan \angle = 700.00/100.00 = 7.000000$$
$$\angle = 81.869898° = 81° 52'12''$$
$$\text{Bearing} = \text{S } 81° 52'12'' \text{ E}$$

PROBLEMS

3-1. For Fig. 3–17, calculate the missing angle C.

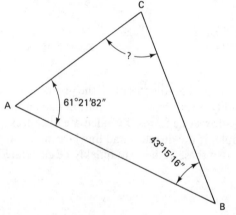

Figure 3-17

3-2. If line A–B, in Fig. 3–17, has a bearing of S 21° 31'16'' E, what are the bearings for lines B–C and A–C?

3-3. For Fig. 3–18, calculate the missing angle E.

3-4. For Prob. 3–3, calculate all line bearings and directions starting with point A and proceeding in a counter-clockwise direction.

3-5. For the coordinates listed in Table 3–6, calculate and draw all interior angles, bearings of lines, and all distances between the reference points.

3-6. For the figure described in Prob. 3–5 calculate closure of the figure.

3-7. For the figure described in Prob. 3–5 calculate the enclosed area in acres.

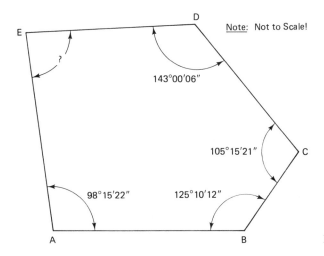

E

D

Note: Not to Scale!

143°00'06″

?

105°15'21″   C

98°15'22″   125°10'12″

A   B   **Figure 3–18**

TABLE 3–6

Reference point	N	E
A	7187.96	8777.77
B	7305.21	8965.14
C	7516.06	8815.37

3–8. For the coordinates listed in Table 3–7, calculate and draw all interior angles, bearings of lines, and all distances between the reference points.

TABLE 3–7

Reference point	N	E
A	1595.96	1752.91
B	1543.21	2137.82
C	1786.37	2294.31
D	1995.96	1752.91
E	1795.96	1687.58

3–9. For the figure described in Prob. 3–8 calculate the enclosed area in acres.

Chapter 4

Property Description and Deeds

INTRODUCTION

In order for property to be developed, for whatever use it is intended, it is necessary for site developers to have accurate, detailed property descriptions of the proposed development site. Usually, this information is supplied by the owner of the property and may involve a new survey of the property or reference to an existing survey. This process involves calculating the bearings of the property lines, the lengths of the property lines, setting of coordinates and determining the total area (acreage) contained within the described boundary.

PROPERTY CLOSURE

From the data received from the property survey or resurvey one can determine: bearings of property lines, lengths of property lines, and establishment of coordinates. Using this information it is possible to determine if the property in question actually closes. A property is considered *closed* when all distances and stated line bearings, if actually traversed (travelled), would bring one back to the beginning point. (The mathematics of closing a property were discussed in general in Chapter 3, Land Planning Mathematics.) This closure information will be used for writing the property's description.

PROPERTY DESCRIPTION

Property descriptions are an integral part of site planning and development. Therefore, it is necessary for the site planner to have a knowledge of the United States Survey System in order to be able to read and understand property descriptions.

The United States System of Public Lands was inaugurated in 1784; in 1812 the General Land Office was established to direct public lands surveys. Since 1812 most of the United States has been surveyed into rectangular control tracts. This was done to facilitate the development of land and to be able to accurately locate and describe the land. Even though this rectangular control tract survey system is nearly complete, there are variations that occur within this system in certain sections of the country. These variations are the result of private claims and land grants based on other survey systems prior to the introduction of the control system.

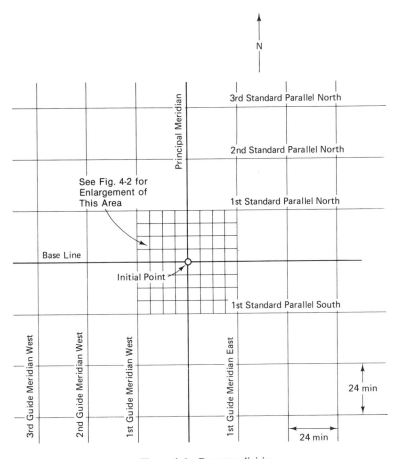

Figure 4–1 Property division.

Briefly, the survey system is based on a division of the lands into 24-mile *control squares* referenced from a north–south line (meridian) and an east–west line (parallel). The principal meridian was determined originally by astronomical observations. See Fig. 4–1. The north–south lines of the squares follow the longitudinal lines of the earth. The east–west lines follow the earth's latitude lines. There is a correction factor that is used to allow for the earth's curvature in these lines.

Each of the 24 mile control squares is further divided into 16 towns, or townships, that are as close to 6 miles square as possible. See Fig. 4–2. The reference for township with respect to their parallel and meridian reference is town (tier) and range respectively. For example, for the township shown in Fig. 4–2, the town-range reference would be "township 4 north, range 1 west of the principal meridian." This is usually shortened to read "T.4N., R.1W., P.M." In turn, each township is divided into 36 sections that are 1 mile square, each containing 640 acres (1 acre = 43,560 sq. ft.). See Fig. 4–3.

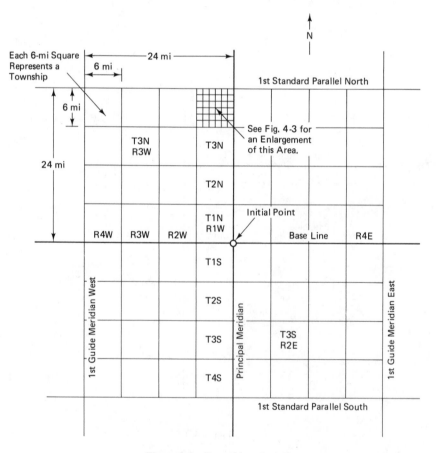

Figure 4–2 Township orientation.

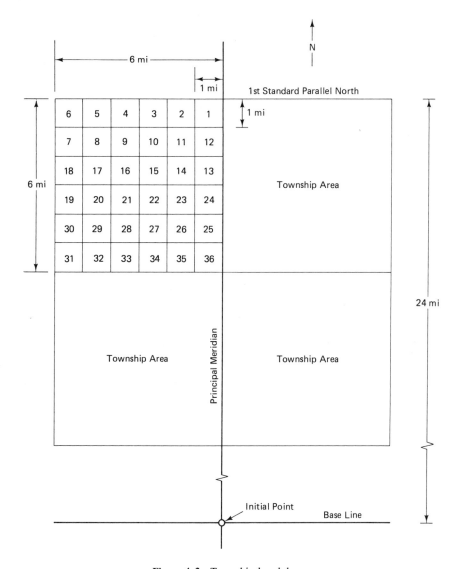

Figure 4–3 Township breakdown.

The sections of a township are numbered 1 to 36, beginning with section 1 in the northeast corner of the township, proceeding west along the northern tier and continuing east, and in the same manner to number all the sections. The section, or part of a section is generally the largest tract of land with which the site planner will be concerned.

A sample section property description is as follows; "T.4N.,R.1W., County of McComb, State of Michigan, being more particularly described as: the SW 1/4 of the NE 1/4 section 32, containing 40 acres." T.4N. tells us that the land being described is in township 4 North, the fourth tier of 6-mile townships north of base line. R.1W. tells us that it is the first township west of the referenced meridian (principal meridian). The property description then proceeds to locate the property more specifically within section 32 by saying that it is the 40 acres in the southwest quarter of the northeast quarter of the section.

The subdivision of land into a suburban development requires a calculated plat, where all control corners are marked with designated monuments and all property lines are given bearings and dimensions to hundredths of a foot. The procedure for drawing plats is controlled by local, county, and state laws. The drawn plat is recorded with the county and contains the subdivision name, lot numbers, and references to the property's description. Most political subdivisions have standard subdivision regulations that a subdivider is required to follow. These subdivision regulations usually include approval procedures for all subdivision work.

DEEDS

A deed is used in the sale and transfer of property. Information contained in a deed should include: name of property owner, line bearings, distances along each property line, and if it borders any road or highway. The deed description should run *to* and *from* each property point (corner points). For example, (see Fig. 4–4) this property would be described as commencing at a point, *A,* in the center line of Love Lane, station 16 + 95.92, thence travelling in a due east direction a distance of seven hundred and twenty-one and sixty-eight hundredths (721.68) feet, along the center line to a point (B), station 24 + 17.60, thence in a direction north 30°-00′-00″ west a

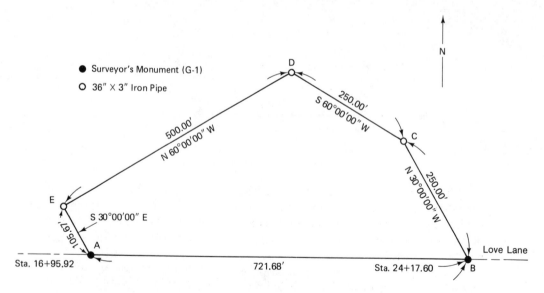

Figure 4-4 Property survey.

distance of two hundred and fifty (250.00) feet to a point (C), thence in a direction north 60°-00′-00″ west a distance of two hundred and fifty (250.00) feet to a point (D), thence in a direction south 60°-00′-00″ west a distance of five hundred (500.00) feet to a point (E), thence in a direction south 30°-00′-00″ east a distance of one hundred and five and sixty-seven hundredths (105.67) feet to the point of beginning (A). Points (A) and (B) are referenced by surveyor's monuments (Type G-1) while all other points are referenced by 36″ × 3″ iron pipes.

All property sales or transfers must be recorded with the proper governmental authority: state, county, or city. The deed description is used for the calculation of property tax. The land is usually taxed at a different rate than any structures that are on the land. Different states and counties have different tax formulas for calculating the property (land) tax. Any land change, whether it is subdividing, building, use, and so on could result in a different tax assessment.

PROBLEMS

4-1. For the figure described in Prob. 3-5, write a property description. *Note:* Line A-B is the centerline (C/L) of Cass Road and all corners are marked in the field with iron pipes.

4-2. For the figure described in Prob. 3-8, write a property description. *Note:* Line A-B is the center line (C/L) of Scottwood Avenue and all corners are marked in the field with iron pipes.

4-3. For the coordinates shown in Fig. 4-5, write a property description. (All bearings and distances will have to be calculated.) *Note:* Line A-B is the center line (C/L) of Glendale Avenue and all corners are marked in the field with iron pipes.

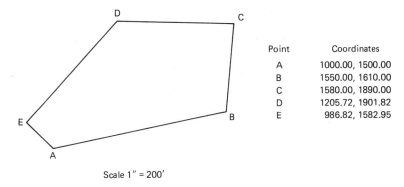

Point	Coordinates
A	1000.00, 1500.00
B	1550.00, 1610.00
C	1580.00, 1890.00
D	1205.72, 1901.82
E	986.82, 1582.95

Scale 1″ = 200′

Figure 4-5

Chapter 5

Topography

INTRODUCTION

Cartography is defined as the art or practice of drawing maps and charts or otherwise graphically delineating relative positions, elevations, and features of a region. Features of a region, or area of land, include hills, valleys, rivers, canals, lakes, bridges, roads, and cities. Topographic maps furnish a detailed representation of all the natural and man-made features on particular sections of land. Topographic maps depict the true "lay of the land."

Topographic drawings combine mechanical drawing with considerable free hand drawing to pictorially express large amounts of information as efficiently as possible. To produce an efficient topographic map it is necessary to use symbols and specific topographic terms that have been developed to communicate the characteristics of the land. A topographic map should be developed when considering the possible purchase of land or alternate uses of land. See Fig. 5-1 for an example of a typical topographic map.

TYPES OF TOPOGRAPHIC MAPS

There are many types of topographic maps, but the three major types are culture, relief, and hydrographic. A culture topographic map represents features that are man made. The features that culture maps describe include highways, railroads, bridges, fences, towns, cities, houses, and any lines that show private property ownership.

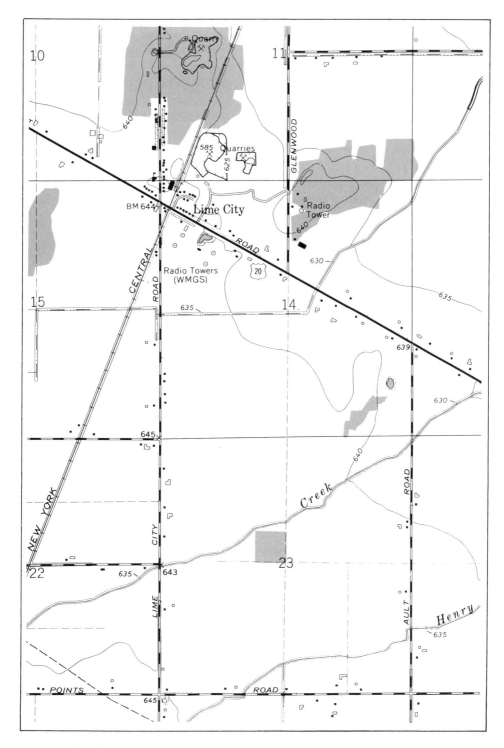

Figure 5-1 Topography map. (Reprinted with permission of U.S. Geological Survey.)

Relief topographic maps show the contrast between uneven natural surfaces, such as mountains, hills, valleys, and plateaus. Relief maps describe these contrasts between uneven surfaces by use of a combination of symbols and letters. Hydrographic topographic maps depict the depths of oceans, lakes, and rivers and are usually used for navigational and commercial purposes. Navigational charts, which indicate depth in fathoms (1 fathom equals 6 feet), are an example of a hydrographic map. Other types of maps consist of the following:

City maps have been used successfully to control the growth of cities. They provide accurate information for land developers and planners, who use this information to better judge how to develop an urban area. Aerial photographs have proven to be of significant advantage in mapping out new developments and in redesigning the geometrics of roads.

General engineering maps are used by engineers to draw preliminary sketches of proposed development areas and to draw final plans. The scale to which these maps are drawn depends on the area being described. A large area may be drawn on a scale of 1 inch = 500 feet or more, while a smaller area would be drawn to a scale of 1 inch = 50 feet or less.

Building site maps are used to show the locations and size of all buildings in a particular area. The position and size of walks, driveways, patios, yards, and so on are included in plans of the building site. Apparent compass orientation is shown on a building site map with all elevations.

Golf course layout maps show the actual topographic features of the land and a pictorial view of what a particular golf course will look like. Usually a scale of 1 inch = 50 feet is used to show as much detail as possible for each proposed golf hole.

Landscape maps are used to show the types and locations of vegetation for a development. A landscape map will also show position of the building on a particular lot and the contour of the land in relation to the building. The landscape architect needs this information to control the placement of vegetation on a particular site.

General topographic maps are prepared to describe large areas, such as drainage systems, flood control projects, and dams. These maps are not as accurate as smaller scaled maps because of their larger scale.

Underground survey maps are used to locate underground utilities in areas of high population density or in areas where utility poles and electric lines would detract from the appearance of the land. The designer needs to know the exact locations of the existing sewers, water lines, gas lines, and so on to place new underground utility lines economically and safely.

A *survey plan* is a drawing that shows the exact size, shape, and elevations for a particular property. The survey can be used to confirm or establish the legal description of a piece of property. A lot description could include the lot's dimensions, tree locations, corner elevations, contour lines, streams, ponds, rivers, street, and utility lines. See Fig. 5–2.

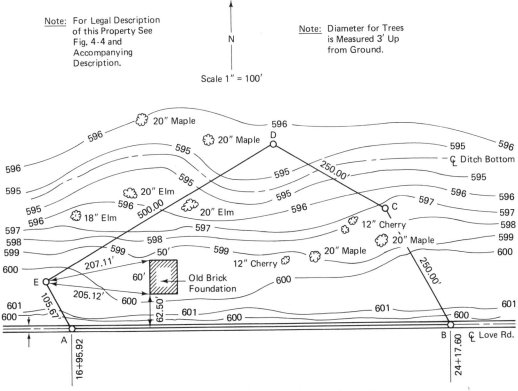

Figure 5-2 Survey and topography map.

SCALES FOR MAPS

A *map scale* is defined as the constant ratio between the actual dimension of objects and distances on the ground and the representation of these dimensions and distances on the map. A map scale is the proportion that a map has to what it is representing. The choice of a particular map scale will depend on the purpose of the map, the size of the drawing, and the accuracy that is desired. More detail can be shown with a smaller scale. For example, a map scale where 1 inch = 10 feet will show more detail than a scale where 1 inch = 100 feet. Naturally, the 1 inch = 10 feet will result in a larger drawing.

An engineer's scale is used for topographic maps. It is graduated into units of 1 inch which are subdivided into various fractions that are multiples of 10—10, 20, 30, and so on. This subdivision makes the engineer's scale very convenient for setting off dimensions expressed in decimals. An engineer's scale can be used in drawing maps to various scales: 1 inch = 10 feet, 1 inch = 50 feet, 1 inch = 500 feet,

1 inch = 5 miles, and so on. In rugged or mountainous country, a map scale should be selected that will clearly show as much detail as possible.

The engineer's scale should be distinguished from the architect's scale, which is graduated differently. The architect's scale allows for scales such as 1/16 inch = 1 foot, and 1/8 inch = 1 foot. The architect's scale is primarily used for the drawing of plans for building and structures. See Fig. 5–3.

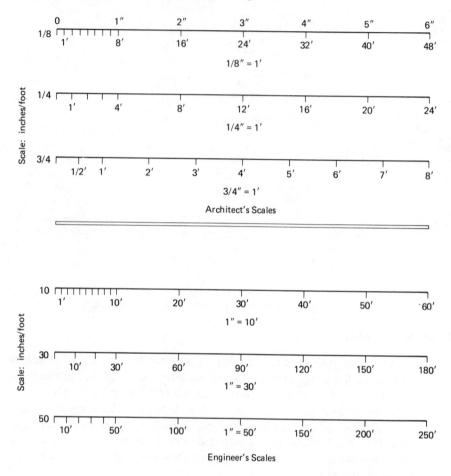

Figure 5-3   Scales.

DEFINITION OF TERMS

Topographic maps require a knowledge of distances as measured and drawn to some scale and laid out to some particular geometric reference system. The ability to visualize an area that a topographic map represents is very important to the land planner. The use of topographic maps allows for the development of both plan and elevation views.

The *plan* view represents the horizontal arrangement of the land; the *elevation* view represents the vertical or profile of the land. One of the most popular methods for describing the topography of land is by the use of contour lines. Contour lines represent imaginary level (horizontal) planes that pass through the land. All equal elevation points, above or below a known reference point, are contained on the same level (horizontal) plane. To fully understand the use and development of topographic maps, contour lines, and so on, familiarity with the following terms is necessary:

Datum Any level surface to which elevations are referred (for example mean sea level). Also called the datum plane of reference. For example, one would express an elevation as 651.00 feet above datum, sea level.

Elevations The vertical distance from the datum to the plane being referenced.

Benchmark Usually abbreviated B.M. and is a permanent object, natural or artificial, bearing a marked point whose elevation, above or below the adapted datum, is known or assumed. Usually above or below sea level.

Mean Sea Level The average height of the surface of sea for all stages of the tide. (Assumed to be zero.)

Plan View A drawing or diagram showing the arrangement of a piece of land from a horizontal or top view.

Profile A side view or cross section of a drawing that shows its outline between contours.

Interpolation The process of spacing the contour proportionally between plotted elevations on a grid. This process can be done by estimation, mental calculations, or arithmetical computations.

THE CONTOUR LINE

Contour lines are two-dimensional symbols used to represent a three-dimensional area. Contour lines were first used by Cruquius, a Dutchman, in 1730 to represent the bottom configuration of a river. It was a natural extension to represent dry land surface with these same lines or contours. Nevertheless, it was not until the late 19th century that contour lines became a common method of depicting terrain on survey maps.

A contour line, an imaginary level plane, connects all points of equal elevation. If a hill could be sliced off with level horizontal lines at uniform levels or intervals, the result would be contour lines. The contour interval is the vertical distance between the contour planes. It may be a one-foot interval for flat terrain, 2 to 20 feet for normal terrain and 20 to 100 feet for mountainous terrain. The closer the contour lines are together, the steeper the sides of the hill or valley. In mountainous terrain, a true vertical face would be noted as one line. The contour lines would lie upon each other. See Fig. 5–4.

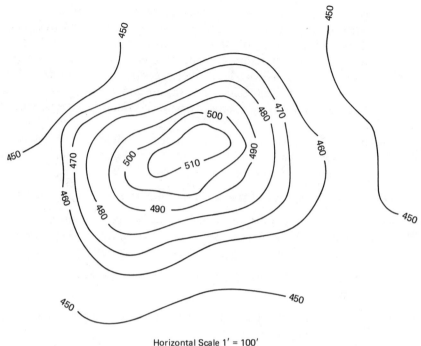

Horizontal Scale 1' = 100'

Figure 5-4   Hill contours.

CHARACTERISTICS OF CONTOUR LINES

The following general characteristics are common for all contour lines:

1. All points on a contour line have the same elevation. A contour line connects all points of equal elevation.

2. Every contour line closes on itself somewhere, either within or beyond the limits of the map. In the latter case, the contour will run to the edge of the map and the loose end should be labelled.

3. Within a series of closed contour lines the smallest is either a summit or a depression.

4. Contour lines cannot cross or merge with one another on the map, as they represent different elevations of the ground. The only exceptions to this are rare cases such as caves, vertical cliffs, overhangs, and natural bridges.

5. Contours that are equally spaced indicate a uniform sloping surface.

6. The horizontal distance between contour lines is inversely proportional to the slope. The steeper the slope, the closer the contour lines are together.

PLAN VIEW OF CONTOUR LINES

The plan view of contour lines, as used in a topographical map, allows the viewer to look down on the property or area in question. The contour lines graphically describe the surface of the property. See Fig. 5–4. The shape of the line labelled *490* represents where a plane, 490 feet above some reference plane, usually sea level, meets the existing ground for the area being considered. The closed contours, as shown, represent a hill, approximately 50 feet high. The reference contours *450* do not form a complete contour because this contour plane and the existing ground meet outside the area being considered. If the shape were a pit, the contour map would appear similar to Fig. 5–4 except the contour elevations would be different. See Fig. 5–5.

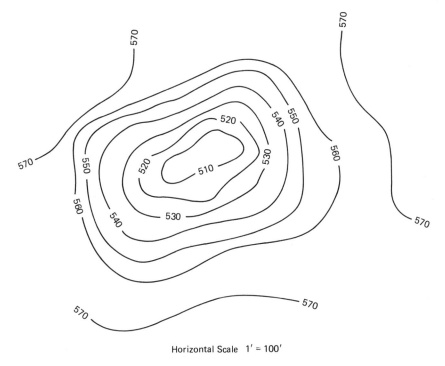

Horizontal Scale   1′ = 100′

Figure 5-5   Pit contours.

PLOTTING AND DEVELOPING CONTOURS

One of the most common methods for plotting contour lines of an area for a topographic map is by use of the grid system or coordinate map. A map scale is selected that will show sufficient detail of the terrain of the property; a grid system using 50-foot intervals would be common for a typical residential or commercial site. The grid is superimposed upon the property and laid out on the property by standard

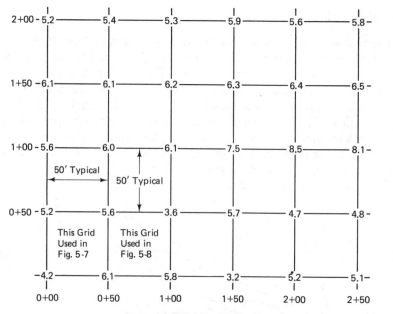

Note: Add 600.00 to All Elevations

Figure 5–6   Typical 50-foot grid.

surveying methods. The intersections of the grid lines are where the actual field elevations, to the nearest one tenth (0.1) of a foot for ground, are recorded. See Fig. 5–6.

The grid's sides are usually laid out in "station" distance from a reference coordinate. The elevation of one-foot contour lines, for this example case, are estimated and drawn for each grid square. Since the method of "tracing contours" is approximate, it is recommended that contour points, which are used to establish contours, also be estimated. For example, if we start on each grid side we can locate the number of one-foot contours that cross each side (see Fig. 5–7). This has to be done for each grid square. Side A–B has one contour crossing; 605.00 approximately 0.2 the distance from point A to point B. There are no contours crossing line B–C. Both corners, B and C, are near the same elevation, 605.2 and 605.6 respectively. The line C–D contains *one* contour (606.00) and is located nearer D than C since it (606.00) is 0.4 feet higher than C and only 0.1 feet lower than D. The line A–D contains two contours, 605.00 and 606.00.

The diagonal should also be checked. Line A–C has only one contour crossing (605.00) and line B–D also has one contour crossing (606.00). All grid squares are similarly analyzed and contour lines are drawn for each grid. Sometimes it is difficult to determine if the grid contains a valley (depression) or a hill (ridge). To help eliminate this confusion, it is recommended that the *lower diagonal sets precedent*. This means that where there could be a low or high diagonal, the lower diagonal would be the one used (see Fig. 5–8). In Fig. 5–8, the grid contains a valley (depression) running from 3.6 to 3.2 and the ground slopes *down* from the other corners.

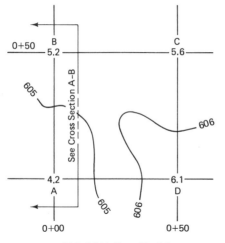

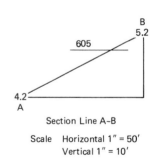

Section Line A–B

Scale   Horizontal 1″ = 50′
             Vertical 1″ = 10′

This Grid is From Fig. 5-6

Figure 5–7   Grid and contour details.

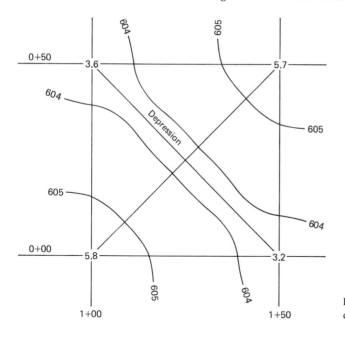

Figure 5–8   Detail of grid showing diagonals.

PROFILE FROM CONTOUR LINES

Profiles are cross sections of a plan view of a topographic map and represent the contour lines on a vertical section. Profiles can easily be constructed from contour lines by (1) drawing the desired section line on the contour plan view or topographical map, (2) scaling the horizontal distances between the contour lines, and (3) plotting these same horizontal distances. If a different scale is desired for the profile, then the scaled horizontal distances would have to be plotted to the new desired scale. The contour elevation is plotted as the vertical height. The horizontal and vertical scales do not have to be the same. When all points have been located they are usually connected, drawn free hand. See Fig. 5–9. A relatively accurate profile of the contours on the plan view has now been constructed.

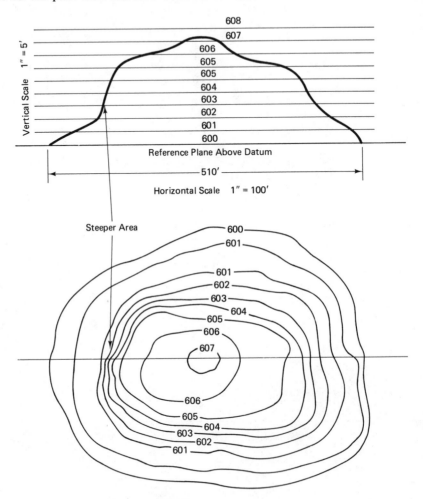

Figure 5-9 Profile plot.

USE OF CONTOUR LINES

Contour lines and the understanding of these lines have many uses in engineering, construction, and design. The plotting of the profile from a contour map, for example, assists in the design of pavement grades, drainage (runoff) characteristics, and

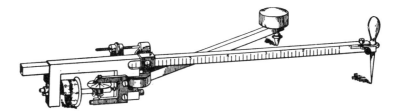

Figure 5-10   Planimeter. (From Charles B. Breed, *Surveying,* 2nd ed., p. 363. Reprinted by permission of John Wiley & Sons, Inc., © 1957.)

determination of excavation quantities. Earth quantities can be easily calculated from a contour map with the use of a planimeter. See Fig. 5-10. The planimeter allows for rapid calculation of the contour plane area. With this information, the volume of earth between two planes can be easily calculated. For example, in Fig. 5-4 the area of contour plane 490 is 30,000 square feet and the area of contour plane 500 is 16,000 square feet. Therefore the volume of earth contained between these two planes can be found by

$$V = \frac{1}{2} (\text{area } 490 + \text{area } 500) \times \begin{array}{c} \text{Vertical distance} \\ \text{between planes} \end{array}$$

$$V = \frac{1}{2} (30,000 + 16,000) \times 10$$

$$V = 230,000 \text{ cu ft}$$

Examples of other contour applications will be discussed in other chapters.

PROBLEMS

5-1. Define the following terms:
   (a) topography
   (b) engineer's scale
   (c) architect's scale
   (d) contour line
   (e) datum

5-2. Define the following terms:
   (a) elevations
   (b) benchmark
   (c) mean sea level
   (d) plan view
   (e) profile
   (f) planimeter

5-3. For the figure shown in Fig. 5-11, redraw (1 inch = 50 feet) and sketch in all one-foot contour lines.

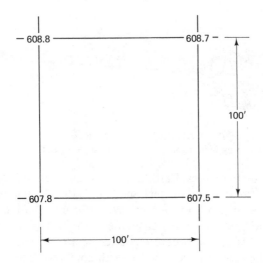

Figure 5–11

5-4. For the 50-foot grid shown in Fig. 5–12, redraw and sketch all one-foot contour lines.

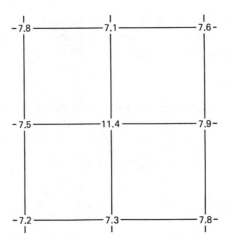

Figure 5–12

5-5. In Fig. 5–13, a 50-foot grid has the elevations as shown. Redraw the grid (1 inch = 50 feet) and sketch in all one-foot contour lines.

5-6. In Prob. 5–4, what is the volume (cubic feet) of earth between reference elevation planes 8.0 and 9.0?

5-7. In Prob. 5–4, what is the volume (cubic yards) of earth between reference elevation planes 9.0 and 10.0?

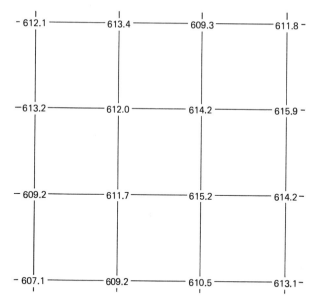

Figure 5-13

Chapter 6

Soils

INTRODUCTION

One of the most important considerations in site development planning and actual construction is the need for an understanding of soils. The majority of construction problems can be traced back to either a lack of soil knowledge or a misinterpretation of soil information. Knowledge of soils is necessary for all site developers, whether they are planning residential, commercial, industrial, or marine projects. This chapter will review specific soil informational tests and how this information should be used in land planning.

COMPOSITION

Soil can be visualized as a collection of particles interspersed with open spaces called voids. See Fig. 6–1. The particle size, for a typical soil, will range from very small particles, .001 mm to 19.05 mm (3/4 inch) usually. The chemical makeup of these particles could consist of clay, nonclay, or combinations of clay and nonclay particles. Some common mineral names for these nonclay particles are quartz, calcite, dolomite, and gypsum. Similarily, some common mineral names for clay particles are kaolinite, vermiculite, mica, chlorite, and alumina. Silt particles are larger than clay particles but considerably smaller than sand particles, usually 0.003 inches in diameter or less. Silt can consist of fresh ground rock that has not had a chance to break down into minerals, which make up clay soils. Clay soils are considered to be plastic soils; silt soils are not. Plastic soils can be readily molded. Silt soils become plastic when combined with clay.

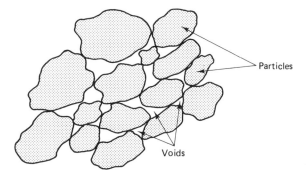

Figure 6-1 Particles and voids.

Many industries make use of particle sizing information in the manufacture of their products, which might include concrete, glass, or ceramics. The number and size of the voids is directly related to the soil's particle size, shape, and packing. Packing is the consideration for how the particles are arranged. For example, if the particle shape were spherical, it would be rather easy to make volume and void calculations. Consider the condition where a single sphere is placed in a one-cubic-foot box. See Fig. 6-2. The volume of the sphere is found by the equation

$$V = \frac{4}{3} \pi R^3$$

where,

$$V = \text{volume of sphere}$$
$$R = \text{radius of sphere}$$

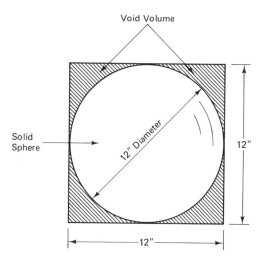

Figure 6-2 One sphere in a box.

Therefore, the volume of the sphere would be

$$V = \frac{4}{3} \pi R^3$$

$$V = \frac{4}{3} \pi (6)^3$$

$$V = 904.78 \text{ cu in.}$$

Now consider the same box filled with eight spheres. See Fig. 6–3. These spheres represent a vertical packing. Again, calculate the volume of the spheres.

$$V = \frac{4}{3} \pi R^3$$

$$V = \frac{4}{3} \pi (3)^3 \times 8$$

$$V = 904.78 \text{ cu in.}$$

It is very interesting to note that the solid volume for each situation, either one or eight spheres, was the same. This would be true for any number of spheres with the same diameter and with a vertical packing. Since the volumes are the same, the voids will also be the same.

Volume of voids = Volume of box − Volume of spheres
Volume of voids = 1728 cu in. − 904.78 cu in.
Volume of voids = 823.22 cu in.

For the one-cubic-foot box filled with the spheres, in this example, 52.36% was solid material while 47.64% was voids. Naturally, the percent of voids could be reduced by a different packing arrangement or the addition of smaller sized particles, or both.

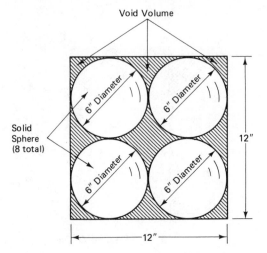

Figure 6–3 Eight spheres in a box.

If the example box were weighed, one would discover that the weight per cubic foot would be the same for the one sphere and the eight spheres, assuming the spheres are of the same material. This weight per cubic foot is known as the *density* of the material. See Table 6–1 for the density of various materials.

TABLE 6–1 MATERIAL DENSITIES

Material	Density (lb/cu ft)
Wood	50
Water	62.4
Soil	85–110
Concrete	150
Steel	500

TESTING PROCEDURES

There have been numerous tests developed, by various agencies, for the testing of soils. Tests as defined by two agencies, American Society for Testing and Materials and the American Association of State Highway and Transportation Officials, will be reviewed. Before delving into specific tests and testing procedures, a brief review of the two agencies, ASTM and AASHTO, is presented.

The American Association of State Highway and Transportation Officials (AASHTO) is an organization consisting of representatives from all the state highway and transportation departments in the United States. They have compiled tests and specifications for all construction-related materials. The American Society for Testing and Materials (ASTM) was founded in 1898 and is a scientific and technical organization consisting of volunteers who assist in writing standards. It is the world's largest source for these types of standards. The work by these agencies allows for rapid technical communications between engineers and designers. Without such organizations, technical communications would be very difficult and would certainly result in higher design and construction costs.

The most frequent soil information desired for design purposes is classification, bearing capacity, density (in place), and soil/mixture relationship. See Table 6–2 for test reference titles; see Table 6–3 for a cross reference for the desired tests

TABLE 6–2 AASHTO AND ASTM SOIL TESTS

Type of test	AASHTO no.	ASTM no.	Title
Classification	T-88		Mechanical Analysis of Soils
Bearing capacity	T-235		Bearing Capacity of Soil for Static Load on Spread Footing
	T-221		Repetitive Static Plate Load Tests of Soils

(cont.)

TABLE 6-2 (cont.)

Type of test	AASHTO no.	ASTM no.	Title
Classification	T-88		Mechanical Analysis of Soils
Bearing capacity	T-222		Nonrepetitive Static Plate Load Test of Soils
Density	T-191		Density of Soil-In-Place by the Sand-Cone Method
	T-238		Density of Soil and Soil-Aggregate In-Place by Nuclear Methods (Shallow-Depth)
	T-205		Density of Soil In-Place by the Rubber-Balloon Method
Moisture	T-99		Moisture-Density Relations of Soils Using a 5.5# Rammer and a 12-in. Drop
	T-180		Moisture-Density Relations of Soils Using a 10# Rammer and an 18-in. Drop
Classification		D-2487	Classification of Soils for Engineering Purposes
		D-3282	Classification of Soils and Soil-Aggregate
Bearing capacity		D-1194	Test for Bearing Capacity of Soil for Static Load on Spread Footings
		D-1195	Repetitive Static Plate Load Tests of Soils
		D-1196	Nonrepetitive Static Plate Load Tests of Soils
Density		D-2937	Test for Density of Soil In-Place by the Drive-Cylinder Method
		D-2922	Tests for Density of Soil and Soil-Aggregate in Place by Nuclear Methods
		D-2167	Test for Density of Soil in Place by the Rubber-Balloon Method
		D-1556	Test for Density of Soil in Place by the Sand-Cone Method
Moisture		D-698	Test for Moisture-Density Relations of Soils, Using 5.5# Rammer and 12-in. Drop
		D-1557	Test for Moisture-Density Relations of Soils, Using 10.0# Rammer and 18-in. Drop
		D-1558	Test for Moisture-Penetration Resistance Relations of Fine-Grained Soils

TABLE 6-3 CROSS REFERENCE BETWEEN AASHTO AND ASTM SOIL TESTS

Type of test	AASHTO reference number	ASTM reference number
Classification	T-88	D-2487
		D-3282
Bearing capacity	T-235	D-1194
	T-221	D-1195
	T-222	D-1196
Density	T-191	D-2937
	T-238	D-2922
	T-205	D-2167
		D-1556
Moisture	T-99	D-698
	T-180	D-1557
		D-1558

between AASHTO and ASTM. These tables show the large number of test procedures available through AASHTO and ASTM. Specific use of the information generated by these tests will be discussed later in this and other chapters.

CLASSIFICATION

The two methods of soil classification that will be reviewed are: ASTM D2487, Classification of Soils for Engineering Purposes, and ASTM D3282, Classification of Soils and Soil-Aggregate Mixtures for Highway Construction Purposes. The ASTM D2487 method will be considered first. This method requires that a soil sample be tested to determine its

- liquid limit (LL) (ASTM D423)
- plastic limit (PL) (ASTM D424)
- particle size (ASTM D1140)
- particle-size analysis of soils (ASTM D422)

The liquid limit (LL) (ASTM D423) is the boundary between the liquid and plastic state of a soil. The actual test consists of placing a prepared soil sample in a liquid limit device and grooving the sample with a grooving tool (see Fig. 6-4). The liquid limit test (LL) and the plastic limit test (PL) are sometimes referred to as the Atterberg Limits, named after the Swedish chemist, A. Atterberg, who devised the tests.

The crank handle is turned at the rate of two turns per second to bring the separated soil sample into contact over a length of about one-half inch, and the number of cup drops required are recorded. The moisture content of the sample is determined and the results of at least three samples are then plotted. The graph shows the number

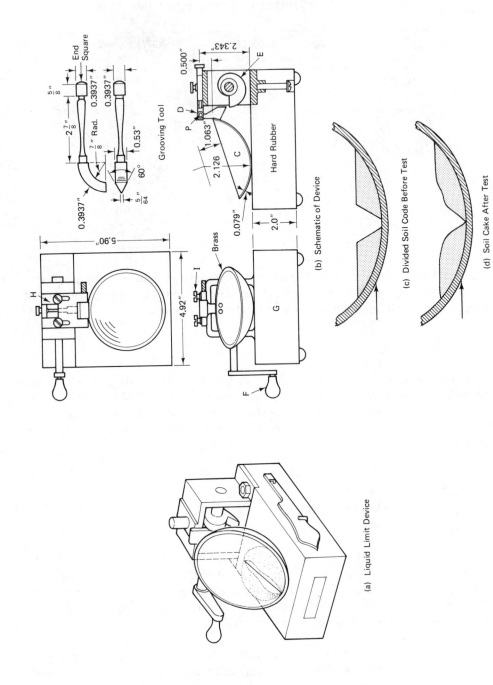

Figure 6-4 Liquid limit apparatus. (From American Society for Testing and Materials, Part 19, *Soil and Rock; Building Stones; Peats*. Copyright ASTM. Reprinted with permission.)

(a) Liquid Limit Device

(b) Schematic of Device

(c) Divided Soil Code Before Test

(d) Soil Cake After Test

of drops versus the percent moisture. The (LL) is the percent moisture content that corresponds to 25 drops of the cup. This value will later be used for the soil's classification.

The (PL) (ASTM D424) is the boundary between a soil's plastic and semisolid state. The actual tests consist of taking a soil sample and rolling it into a thread, 1/8 inch in diameter, without breaking it into pieces. See Fig. 6–5. The percent moisture content at which this 1/8-inch-diameter thread occurs is the plastic limit (PL). This value will also be used later for the soil's classification. It should be noted that granular (sandy) soils will not meet this test requirement of a 1/8-inch thread without breaking into pieces. In the case of sandy soils, the PL test should be performed before the liquid limit test. If the soil sample does not meet the requirements for a plastic limit test, the plastic limit and the liquid limit will both be reported as nonplastic (NP). If the (LL) is equal to or less than the (PL) the soil is also recorded as (NP).

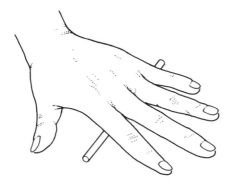

Figure 6–5 Plastic limit test.

TABLE 6–4 SIEVE SIZES

Sieve size*	Measurement (mm)
3 in.	75.00
2 in.	50.00
$1\frac{1}{2}$ in.	38.1
1 in.	25.00
3/4 in.	19.00
3/8 in.	9.50
#4	4.75
#10	2.00
#20	0.85
#40	0.425
#60	0.25
#140	0.106
#200	0.075

*Largest sizes are at the top of the table.

Knowing the (LL) and the (PL) allows one to calculate an index, the plasticity index (PI), that will also be used for the soil's classification. The (PI) is calculated by taking the difference between the (LL) and the (PL).

Plasticity index (PI) = Liquid limit (*LL*) − Plastic limit (*PL*)

$$PI = LL - PL$$

The test for particle size of soils is ASTM D422, Particle-Size Analysis of Soils. This test consists of sieving a known amount of soil through a set of sieves. See Table 6–4 for sieve sizes. The sieve number represents the number of openings per lineal inch. For example, a #40 sieve will have 40 openings per one inch or approximately 1600 openings per square inch. If the soil sample is made up of material almost entirely passing the #4 (4.75 mm) sieve, the results could be reported as a certain percent retained on each succeeding sieve as Fig. 6–6 illustrates.

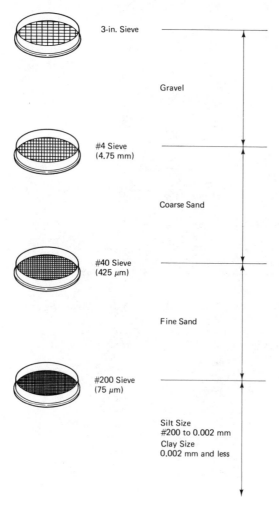

Figure 6–6 Gradation of soils.

The percentage of soil retained or passing each sieve will be used in the classification of the soil, as it is with the (LL) and the (PL). The actual soil classification is accomplished by using soil classification charts. See Figs. 6–7, 6–8, and 6–9.

Let us now suppose that soil samples have been acquired from the field and returned to the lab. The prescribed tests reveal the information as shown in Table 6–5. Table 6–5 shows the test results for three soil samples, #1287, #1288, and #1289 (soil sample reference numbers). Each soil sample shown will be classified according to ASTM D2487, Classification of Soils for Engineering Purposes, and ASTM D3282, Classification of Soils and Soil-Aggregate Mixtures for Highway Construction Purposes. The classification by ASTM D2487 would be as follows:

Soil Sample #1287 (Fig. 6–7). This soil is *coarse grained* since more than 50% of the sample is retained on the #200 sieve. It would also be classified as sands since more than 50% of the coarse fraction passes the #4 sieve.

The percent passing the #200 sieve is greater than 12%; therefore classification is either SM (silt sands, sand-silt mixtures) or SC (clayey sands, sand-clay mixtures). To determine the classification, further examination, using the right side of Fig. 6–7 and the plasticity chart, is required. For an SM classification the Atterberg limits plot below the A line. In this case, the (PI) is 7 and will plot above the A line value of 6.57. (The equation for line A is $PI = 0.73 (LL - 20)$.) Therefore the soil is classified as SC, clayey sands, sand-clay mixtures.

Soil Sample #1288 (Fig. 6–7). This soil is *fine grained* since more than 50% of the sample passes the #200 sieve. It would also be classified as silts and clays with a (LL) of less than 50% and the classification will either be ML (inorganic silts, very fine sands, rock flour, silty, or clayey fine sands), CL (inorganic clays of low to medium plasticity, gravelly clays, sandy clays, silty clays, or lean clays), or OL (organic silts and organic silty clays of low plasticity). Using the plasticity chart, the plot of (LL) 39, versus (PI) 14, reveals that the soil should be classified as a CL.

Soil Sample #1289 (Fig. 6–7). The soil is again fine grained since more than 50% of the sample passes the #200 sieve. It is also classified as silts and clays with a liquid limit of greater than 50% and the classification will either be MH (inorganic silts, micaceous or diatomaceous fine sands, or silts and elastic silts), CH (inorganic clays of high plasticity, fat clays), or OH (organic clays of medium to high plasticity). Using the plasticity chart, the plot of the (LL) 76, versus the (PI) 21, reveals that the soil should be classified as a MH or OH. Final classification, either MH or OH, would be determined by visual inspection of the sample.

Now, using the same data, Table 6–5, the samples will be classified by ASTM D3282, Classification of Soils and Soil-Aggregate Mixtures for Highway Construction Purposes.

Soil Sample #1287 (Fig. 6–8). The soil is classified as granular materials, with less than 35% of the sample passing the #200 sieve. The soil will be classified as the A–2 family because the #200 sieve allows up to 35% passing. The A–1–b classification does not fit since more than 50% passed the #40 sieve. To determine which A–2 classification to use, the conditions for the liquid limit and the plasticity index must

MAJOR DIVISIONS			GROUP SYMBOLS	TYPICAL NAMES
COARSE-GRAINED SOILS — More than 50% retained on No. 200 sieve *	GRAVELS — 50% or more of coarse fraction retained on No. 4 sieve	CLEAN GRAVELS	GW	Well-graded gravels and gravel-sand mixtures, little or no fines
			GP	Poorly graded gravels and gravel-sand mixtures, little or no fines
		GRAVELS WITH FINES	GM	Silty gravels, gravel-sand-silt mixtures
			GC	Clayey gravels, gravel-sand-clay mixtures
	SANDS — More than 50% of coarse fraction passes No. 4 sieve	CLEAN SANDS	SW	Well-graded sands and gravelly sands, little or no fines
			SP	Poorly graded sands and gravelly sands, little or no fines
		SANDS WITH FINES	SM	Silty sands, sand-silt mixtures
			SC	Clayey sands, sand-clay mixtures
FINE-GRAINED SOILS — 50% or more passes No. 200 sieve *	SILTS AND CLAYS — Liquid limit 50% or less		ML	Inorganic silts, very fine sands, rock flour, silty or clayey fine sands
			CL	Inorganic clays of low to medium plasticity, gravelly clays, sandy clays, silty clays, lean clays
			OL	Organic silts and organic silty clays of low plasticity
	SILTS AND CLAYS — Liquid limit greater than 50%		MH	Inorganic silts, micaceous or diatomaceous fine sands or silts, elastic silts
			CH	Inorganic clays of high plasticity, fat clays
			OH	Organic clays of medium to high plasticity
Highly Organic Soils			PT	Peat, muck and other highly organic soils

Figure 6-7 ASTM D2487 Soil Classification. (From American Society for Testing and Materials, Part 19, *Soil and Rock; Building Stones; Peats.* Copyright ASTM. Reprinted with permission.) *Continued on page 67.*

CLASSIFICATION CRITERIA

Classification on basis of percentage of fines

Less than 5% Pass No. 200 sieve — GW, GP, SW, SP
More than 12% Pass No. 200 sieve — GM, GC, SM, SC
5% to 12% Pass No. 200 sieve — Borderline Classification requiring use of dual symbols

$C_u = D_{60}/D_{10}$ Greater than 4

$C_z = \dfrac{(D_{30})^2}{D_{10} \times D_{60}}$ Between 1 and 3

Not meeting both criteria for GW

Atterberg limits plot below "A" line or plasticity index less than 4	Atterberg limits plotting in hatched area are borderline classifications requiring use of dual symbols
Atterberg limits plot above "A" line and plasticity index greater than 7	

$C_u = D_{60}/D_{10}$ Greater than 6

$C_z = \dfrac{(D_{30})^2}{D_{10} \times D_{60}}$ Between 1 and 3

Not meeting both criteria for SW

Atterberg limits plot below "A" line or plasticity index less than 4	Atterberg limits plotting in hatched area are borderline classifications requiring use of dual symbols
Atterberg limits plot above "A" line and plasticity index greater than 7	

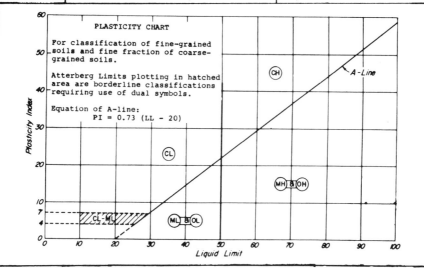

PLASTICITY CHART

For classification of fine-grained soils and fine fraction of coarse-grained soils.

Atterberg Limits plotting in hatched area are borderline classifications requiring use of dual symbols.

Equation of A-line:
$PI = 0.73 (LL - 20)$

Visual-Manual Identification, See ASTM Designation D 2488

Figure 6-8 ASTM D3282 Soil Classification.

General Classification	Granular Materials (35% or less passing No. 200)							Silt-Clay Materials (More than 35% passing No. 200)			
Group classification	A-1-a	A-1-b	A-3	A-2-4	A-2-5	A-2-6	A-2-7	A-4	A-5	A-6	A-7-5, A-7-6
Sieve analysis, % passing:											
No. 10 (2.00 mm)	50 max	...	...								
No. 40 (425 μm)	30 max	50 max	51 min								
No. 200 (75 μm)	15 max	25 max	10 max	35 max	35 max	35 max	35 max	36 min	36 min	36 min	36 min
Characteristics of fraction passing No. 40 (425 μm):											
Liquid limit			...	40 max	41 min	40 max	41 min	40 max	41 min	40 max	41 min
Plasticity index	6 max	6 max	N.P.	10 max	10 max	11 min	11 min	10 max	10 max	11 min	11 min[a]
Usual types of significant constituent materials	Stone Fragments, Gravel and Sand		Fine Sand	Silty or Clayey Gravel and Sand				Silty Soils		Clayey Soils	
General rating as subgrade	Excellent to Good							Fair to Poor			

Figure 6-8 ASTM D3282 Soil Classification. (From American Society for Testing and Materials, Part 19, *Soil and Rock; Building Stones; Peats*. Copyright ASTM. Reprinted with permission.)

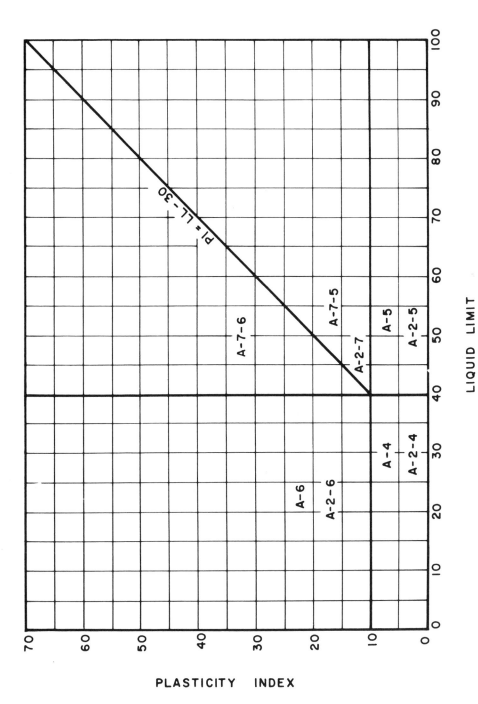

Figure 6-9 ASTM D3282 Soil Classification. (From American Society for Testing and Materials, Part 19, *Soil and Rock; Building Stones; Peats.* Copyright ASTM. Reprinted with permission.)

TABLE 6–5 SAMPLE SOIL ANALYSIS

Sample number															
	1 in.	3/4 in.	3/8 in.	#4	#10	#40	#60	#100	#200	.05	.005	.002	.001	LL	PI
1287	100	90	80	72	67	56	44	34	24	21	11	7	4	29	7
1288	—	100	99	98	97	96	91	80	71	63	34	25	18	39	14
1289	—	—	—	—	100	99	96	92	80	73	41	31	23	76	21

Percent of sample passing various size sieves

be observed. The (LL) conditions reveal a classification of either A-2-4 or A-2-6 because the maximum value of the (LL) could be 40%. The classifications A-2-5 and A-2-7 do not fit since the minimum (LL) value is 41%. The soil is now classified as an A-2-4 since the (PI) must be less than 10. In this example it was 7. An A-2-6 classification requires a minimum (PI) value of 11.

Soil Sample #1288 (Fig. 6–8). Going through this chart again reveals a general classification of silt-clay material, more than 35% passing the #200 sieve. The soil falls into the A-4 to A-7 classifications. Using the (LL) value of 39 places the sample classification as either an A-4 or A-6 and the (PI) value of 14 makes the classification an A-6 soil.

Soil Sample #1289 (Fig. 6–8). Percent passing the #200 sieve is 89% and this makes the classification a silt-clay material. Classification could again be A-4 through A-7. The (LL) value of 76% makes the classification either an A-5 or A-7. The (PI) value of 21 places the classification in the A-7 category. To determine which A-7 classification it is, A-7-5 or A-7-6, one must use Fig. 6–9. Plotting the (LL) 76% versus the (PI) 21 on Fig. 6–9 gives a final classification of an A-7-5.

To summarize the classifications of these three soil samples, see Table 6–6. These soil classifications reveal a number of engineering/construction related characteristics about the soil as sampled. The designer/engineer/contractor can use this information in a number of ways to help in the construction of buildings, streets, sewers, and other related activities.

TABLE 6-6 SOIL CLASSIFICATION RESULTS

ASTM test	Soil reference number		
	#1287	#1288	#1289
D-2487	SC	CL	MH or OH
D-3282	A-2-4	A-6	A-7-5

INTERPRETATION OF SOIL TEST DATA

Knowledge of soil classifications and the tests that are used to make these classifications provides very powerful tools for the design engineer and contractor. When structural trouble develops on a project, it usually starts with the bearing soils. This is either a result of no soil data or a misinterpretation of the soil data.

The classification information, either by ASTM D2487 or ASTM D3282, can be used for a number of engineering-construction related decisions or activities, or both. See Table 6-7 for construction characteristics of soils. This table lists soil group classification symbols, the estimated bearing capacity of the soil in pounds per square foot, drainage capacity, frost heave potential, volume change as a result of excavating and suitability for backfilling. In Chapter 10, Pavement Design Considerations, soil classification information will be used to help determine adequate pavement thicknesses for major pavement materials.

TABLE 6-7   CONSTRUCTION CHARACTERISTICS OF SOILS

Group symbol	Estimated bearing capacity (psf)	Drainage capability	Frost heave potential	Volume change	Backfill potential
GW	8000	Excellent	Low	Low	Best
GP	6000	Excellent	Low	Low	Excellent
GM	4000	Good	Medium	Low	Good
GC	3500	Fair	Medium	Low	Good
SW	5000	Good	Low	Low	Good
SP	4000	Good	Low	Low	Good
SM	3500	Good	Medium	Low	Fair
SC	3000	Fair	Medium	Low	Fair
ML	2000	Fair	High	Low	Fair
CL	2000	Fair	Medium	Medium	Fair
OL	400	Poor	Medium	Medium	Poor
MH	1500	Poor	High	High	Poor
CH	1500	Poor	Medium	High	Bad
OH	remove	No good	Medium	High	No good
Pt	remove	No good	—	High	No good

Source: S.W. Nunnally, *Managing Construction Equipment,* © 1977, p. 14. Adapted by permission of Prentice-Hall, Englewood Cliffs, NJ.

PROBLEMS

6-1. Define the following terms:
   (a) ASTM
   (b) AASHTO

6-2. Define the following terms:
   (a) liquid limit
   (b) plastic limit
   (c) Atterberg limit
   (d) plasticity index
   (e) gradation (soils)

6-3. Define the following terms:
(a) classification (soils)
(b) density
(c) bearing capacity
(d) sieve sizes
(e) percent passing (weight)

6-4. What AASHTO and ASTM tests are used for the following soils tests? (Give title and designated reference number in answer.)
(a) classification
(b) bearing capacity
(c) density
(d) moisture

6-5. Classify (ASTM and AASHTO) the soil samples in Table 6-8.

TABLE 6-8

Sample number	Percent of sample passing various size sieves														
	1 in.	3/4 in.	3/8 in.	#4	#10	#40	#60	#100	#200	.05	.005	.002	.001	LL	PI
1115	100	87	82	72	61	52	41	34	20	19	8	5	3	31	6
1116	—	100	99	95	92	91	90	79	65	52	31	23	17	42	13
1117	—	—	—	—	100	95	92	91	75	62	39	28	19	80	19

6-6. For the soils listed in Problem 6-5, describe their
(a) estimated bearing capacity
(b) drainage capacity
(c) frost heave potential
(d) volume change
(e) backfill potential
   (*Hint:* See Table 6-7.)

Chapter 7

Stormwater
Drainage

INTRODUCTION

In land planning, especially in the United States, stormwater drainage is critical and must be studied. A specific parcel of land may not be usable because of its location in regard to stormwater runoff. Stormwater drainage is concerned with channeling runoff in a safe, controlled manner to protect land areas from erosion and flooding. In the United States the average rainfall for many cities is approximately 35 inches or more per year. This 35 inches of rain can result in 20% to 50% runoff, which is water flowing across the land to some ditch, creek, or lake. This chapter will present an introduction to the process of laying out stormwater drainage systems and the required calculations used in designing the systems.

RAINFALL

Rainfall records have been kept for many years and it has been found that rains of great intensity occur less frequently than rains of lesser intensity. Another finding has been that the intensity of a rainfall is greatest at the early part of the rain and becomes less intense with the duration of the rain. Very intense thunder storms usually occur over a small area. Most major cities, the U. S. Weather Bureau, and the U. S. Department of Agriculture have records and other available data concerning the intensity, duration, and frequency of rainfall. These data are usually presented in the form of maps itemizing the regional rainfall of the United States in terms of one-hour rainfall, in inches, that could be expected in 2, 5, 10, and 25 years. See Fig. 7–1.

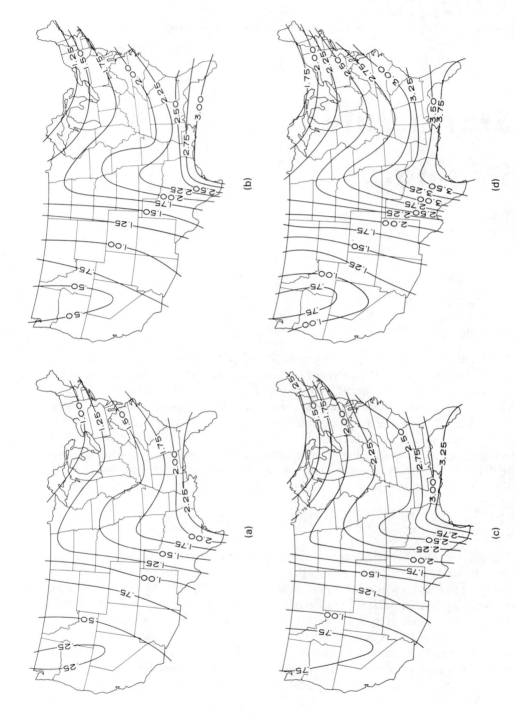

Figure 7-1 Rain intensity maps: (a) 2-year storm, (b) 5-year storm (c) 10-year storm, (d) 25-year storm. (one--hour rainfall in in./hr.). (From D. L. Yarnell, "Rainfall Intensity-Frequency Data," *U.S. Dept. of Agriculture Miscellaneous Publication 204*, U.S.D.A., Wash. D.C., 1935. Reprinted with permission.)

For example, in northern Ohio a 2-inch rainfall per hour would be expected once every 10 years. These intensity values and the total or mean annual rainfall give a good indication of the total volume of runoff that must be handled by the storm-water drainage system.

RUNOFF

Runoff is that portion of the precipitation that finds its way into natural or artificial channels either as surface flow during the storm period or as subsurface flow after the storm has subsided.

The quantity of runoff will be directly dependent on a number of factors in the watershed area. The factors that affect the runoff are

(a) The surface condition of the watershed. Different surface types result in different amounts of runoff. See Table 7–1. This table shows the amount of expected runoff (runoff coefficient, C), for the different possible surface types. Loose gravel would have a runoff coefficient of 0.30 or 30%.

(b) The condition of the surface material in regard to being dry or saturated. Naturally, during a long rain the runoff coefficient C will change because the soil becomes saturated with water and the runoff will increase.

(c) The extent and kind of vegetation. Long grassed areas will have less runoff than areas that are mowed short.

(d) Topography of the area in the watershed. Long steep slopes increase runoff.

(e) The characteristics of the stormwater drainage system to be used.

TABLE 7–1 RUNOFF COEFFICIENTS C

Type of drainage areas or surfaces	Runoff coefficients, C
Roofs	0.95
Pavements, concrete or bituminous concrete	0.75–0.95
Pavement, macadam or surface-treated gravel	0.65–0.80
Compacted gravel	0.70
Loose gravel	0.30
Sandy soil, cultivated light growth	0.15–0.30
Sandy soil, woods or heavy brush	0.15–0.35
Gravel, bare or light growth	0.20–0.40
Gravel, woods or heavy brush	0.15–0.35
Clay soil, bare or light growth	0.35–0.75
Central business districts	0.60–0.80
Dense residential	0.50–0.70
Suburban residential	0.35–0.60
Rural areas, parks, and golf courses	0.15–0.30

Source: From H.M. Rubenstein, *Site and Environmental Planning,* p. 135. Copyright © 1980, John Wiley & Sons, Inc. Reprinted by permission of John Wiley & Sons, Inc.

The size of the inlets, culverts, pipes, and ditches directly affect the runoff of the rain water.

Surface drainage is accomplished by the grading of the soil to carry stormwater away to the drainage inlets. An underground stormwater drainage system then conveys the stormwater to ditches, streams or lakes. The actual size of the stormwater drainage system is based on the quantity of stormwater that reaches the drainage inlets that allow entrance into the underground system.

There have been many methods developed to determine the quantity of runoff. However, to help simplify this determination the *rational method* will be used. To employ this method, for determining the quantity of runoff for a given area, it is necessary to know the size of the runoff area (acres), the average amount of rainfall (in./hr), and the land surface conditions for determination of the runoff coefficient C. The rational method can be expressed by Equation 7–1

$$Q = CIA \qquad\qquad [7\text{–}1]$$

where,

Q = the quantity of stormwater runnoff from a given area in cubic feet per second (cfs).

C = the coefficient of runoff as listed in Table 7–1.

I = the average intensity of rainfall for a duration and location and given as inches per hour (in./hr).

A = the area of the watershed in acres (A).

This rational method is generally used for drainage areas less than 5 square miles. Equation 7–1 will calculate the volume of water for a given area at some average rainfall intensity. For example, if the watershed area consisted of 4.75 A, average rainfall of 1.2 in./hr and was located in a dense residential area ($C = 0.60$, Table 7–1), the quantity of runoff could be determined to be 3.42 cfs by using Equation 7–1.

$$Q = CIA$$
$$Q = 0.60 \times 1.2 \times 4.75$$
$$Q = 3.42 \text{ cfs}$$

(*Note:* Equation 7–1 is an empirical formula. The units for I and A, in./hr and A, will not check out for the units of Q, cfs.)

DRAINAGE STRUCTURES

For stormwater considerations there are four basic types of drainage structures that will be considered: gutter inlets; curb inlets; combination inlets, which contain both curb and gutter inlets; and manholes.

A curb inlet has an opening in the curb that allows stormwater to flow from the street's gutter into the sewer pipe. See Fig. 7–2.

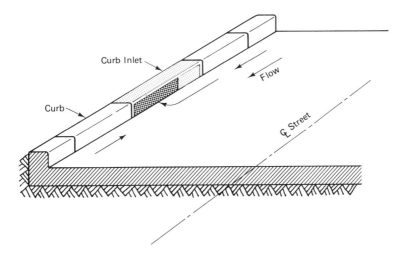

Figure 7-2 Curb inlet.

A gutter inlet consists of an open grate in the gutter of the street. See Fig. 7-3. The gutter inlet's openings (grating) can vary in size, but are usually less than one inch in width because of the danger to bicycle riders.

Figure 7-4 illustrates the combination curb and gutter inlet or combination inlet, which is very popular. The determination for the use of either type of inlet should be based on engineering judgment in regard to availability of grates, safety to the public, satisfactory flow, and cost.

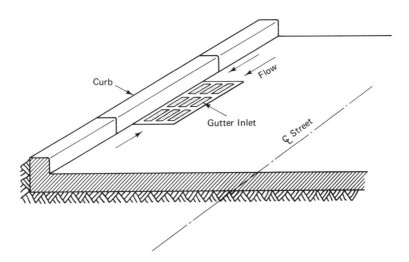

Figure 7-3 Gutter inlet.

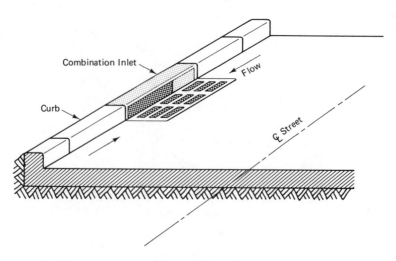

Figure 7-4   Combination inlet.

Stormwater manholes are required wherever there is an abrupt change in grade, a change in pipe size, a junction of several pipes, or a change in horizontal direction. The structure must also be able to provide convenient access to the sewer for maintenance with a minimum restriction to the stormwater's flow. See Fig. 7-5. The spacing of the manholes is usually 300 feet to 400 feet. For larger size pipe, over 4 feet in diameter, 500-foot intervals have been used.

The construction of all stormwater drainage structures requires the use of good materials and good construction practices. Replacement or untimely maintenance of these structures is very expensive and can cause dangerous traffic situations.

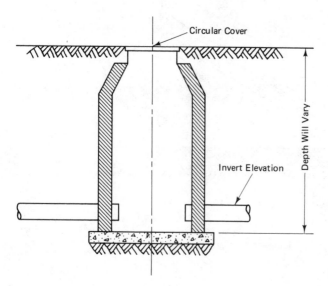

Figure 7-5   Manhole.

PIPE

Pipes are used to connect the drainage structures together into a stormwater drainage system. The system is designed so the stormwater will flow through the drainage system by gravity. To accomplish this, connecting pipes are constructed so that the pipes slope from high point in the system to the lowest point. This lowest point is the final discharge point and is usually a ditch, creek, river, or some body of water.

The pipe could be made from a number of materials that includes clay (vitrified), concrete, steel, or plastic. Most stormwater pipes are circular in cross section. See Fig. 7-6.

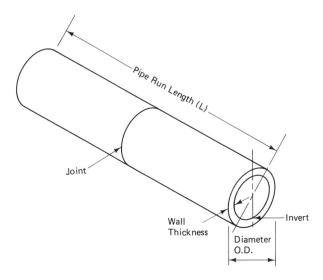

Figure 7-6 Pipe.

The circular shape must be large enough to accompany the quantity of stormwater, Q, anticipated for the system. The determination of this correct pipe size will be discussed in the section on design methods.

The selection of the pipe material should include a number of engineering construction considerations:

- roughness of the pipe's inside wall
- pipe strength requirement
- resistance to acids, alkalis, solvents, and so on
- joint watertightness
- durability, life expectancy
- availability in the sizes required
- cost of materials and construction

The roughness of the pipe's inside surface will affect the ability of stormwater to pass through the pipe. Rougher surfaces slow the stormwater's flow. There have been many studies to determine the roughness of the inside of pipes. A common reference to roughness is Manning's Roughness Coefficient, n. This coefficient is a function of the pipe's composition, slope, and the cross-sectional area of flow of the pipe. See Table 7-2.

TABLE 7-2 MANNING ROUGHNESS COEFFICIENTS, n VALUE

Stormwater structure composition	n values
Pipe	
Concrete pipe 24 in. and under	0.013
Concrete pipe over 24 in.	0.012
Cast-iron pipe, uncoated	0.013
Galvanized corrugated metal pipe (riveted)	0.024
Galvanized corrugated metal pipe with paved invert	0.021
Open channels, lined	
Concrete pavement	0.015
Asphalt pavement	0.015
Concrete bottom, sides as indicated	
Random stone in mortar	0.017–0.020
Riprap	0.020–0.030
Rubble masonry	0.020–0.025
Gravel bottom, sides as indicated	
Concrete	0.017–0.020
Random stone in concrete	0.020–0.023
Riprap	0.023–0.033
Brick	0.014–0.017

Source: From H.M. Rubenstein. *Site and Environmental Planning*, p. 135. Copyright © 1980, John Wiley & Sons, Inc. Reprinted by permission of John Wiley & Sons, Inc.

DESIGN METHODS

The design of a stormwater drainage system requires a collection of specific information regarding the stormwater drainage area to establish pipe sizes and elevations for adequate flow. The required information, using the rational method, consists of

- size of area in acres, A
- runoff coefficient, C
- rainfall intensity in inches/hour, I
- design velocity of stormwater in the pipe, v
- roughness coefficient, n
- length of pipe run between drainage structures, L
- drainage layout drawing

All these items have previously been discussed with the exception of the design velocity and the drainage layout drawing. The design velocity is expressed in feet per second (ft/sec). Studies have shown that the best velocity, for self cleaning purposes, is 2.5 ft/sec. This velocity will keep material, sand, and leaves in suspension. Therefore, for most stormwater designs, a velocity of 2.5 ft/sec will be used.

The drainage layout drawing consists of a drawing showing all drainage structures and connecting pipes. See Fig. 7-7. The drainage structures should be labeled as referenced in Fig. 7-7. The abbreviations are as follows:

- MH—manhole
- I—inlet
- HW—headwall

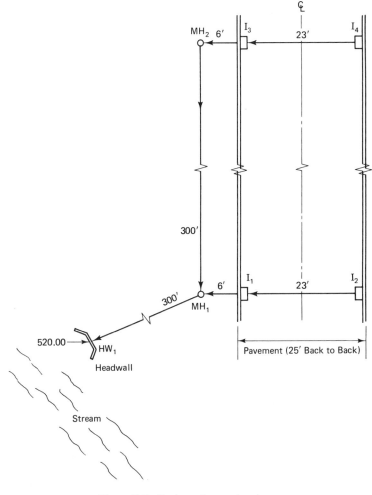

Figure 7-7 Drainage layout drawing.

The subscripted numbers are used for identification.

Since there are a number of quantities to record for the design of the storm-water system, it is best to create a table for these recordings. See Table 7-3. The use of this table will help with organizing, recording, and computations.

The column references, in Table 7-3, are as follows:

Column 1—Line References.   References the drainage line from one drain-age structure to another. The lowest elevation should be listed first. See Table 7-4. This drainage calculation table has been filled in using the drainage layout drawing as shown in Fig. 7-7.

Column 2—Area.   The area to be drained into each inlet, *A*. This area can be determined by scaling the dimensions off the layout drawing.

Column 3—Runoff Coefficient, C.   Values as listed in Table 7-1.

Column 4—Rainfall Intensity, I.   Values as determined from rainfall intensi-ty maps, Fig. 7-1.

Column 5—Quantity of Stormwater, Q.   Value is calculated by using Equa-tion 7-1.

$$Q = CIA$$

Column 6—Flow Velocity in Pipe, v.   Given as 2.5 ft/sec for self cleaning.

Column 7—Manning's Roughness Coefficient, n.   Value, for example prob-lem will be 0.015.

Column 8—Inside Pipe Diameter, D.   Value will be determined by use of a nomograph. See Fig. 7-8.

Column 9—Slope of Pipe.   Slope as expressed as fall per one foot. Value will be determined from nomograph, Fig. 7-8.

Column 10—Length of Pipe, L.   Length of pipe run from drainage structure to drainage structure as shown on drainage layout drawing and expressed in feet.

Column 11—Increment of Change in Elevation.   Value for the pipe's change in elevation; computed by multiplying col. 9, slope, by col. 10, length.

Column 12 and Col. 13—Elevation of Pipe.   The elevation of the pipe's low end, col. 12, and the pipe's high end, col. 13. This elevation is for the pipe's invert. See Fig. 7-9.

The starting elevation is usually the lowest point in the drainage system and would be the final discharge point. This elevation is used to determine the other eleva-tions in the system. This is accomplished by adding or subtracting the increment of change to the previous invert elevation of the preceding pipe.

TABLE 7-3 DRAINAGE CALCULATION TABLE

Column

1	2	3	4	5	6	7	8	9	10	11	12	13
											Elevation	
Line	A (area in acres)	C	I (in./hr)	Q (cfs)	v (ft/sec)	n	D (in.)	Slope	L (ft)	IC (ft)	Low	High

TABLE 7–4 DRAINAGE CALCULATION TABLE (GIVENS LISTED FOR PROBLEMS)

Column

1	2	3	4	5	6	7	8	9	10	11	12	13
Line	A (area in acres)	C	I (in./hr)	Q (cfs)	v (ft/sec)	n	D (in.)	Slope	L (ft)	IC (ft)	Elevation	
											Low	High
$HW_1–MH_1$												
$MH_1–I_1$												
$I_1–I_2$												
$MH_1–MH_2$												
$MH_2–I_3$												
$I_3–I_4$												

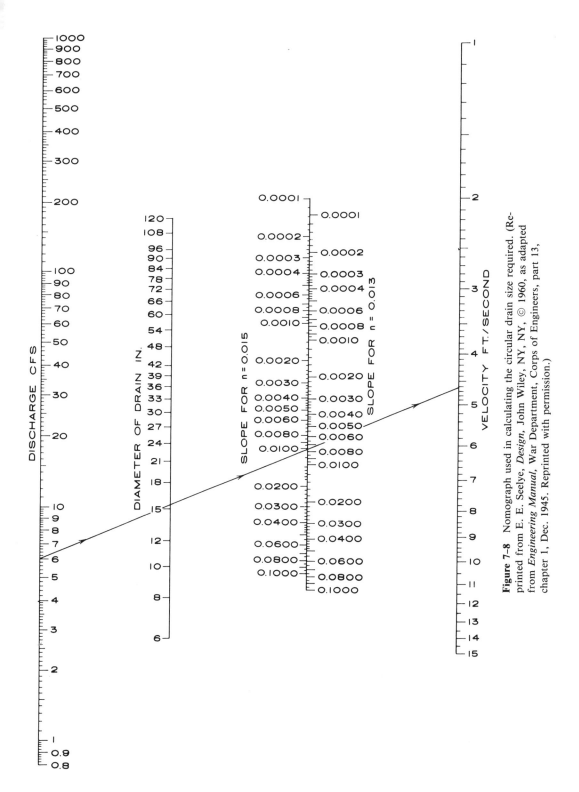

Figure 7-8 Nomograph used in calculating the circular drain size required. (Reprinted from E. E. Seelye, *Design*, John Wiley, NY, NY, © 1960, as adapted from *Engineering Manual*, War Department, Corps of Engineers, part 13, chapter 1, Dec. 1945. Reprinted with permission.)

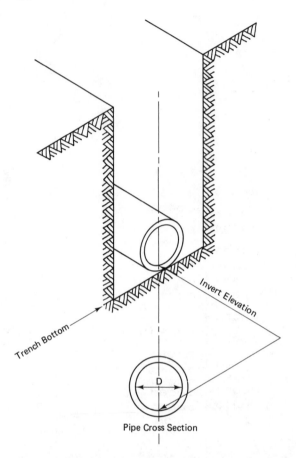

Pipe Cross Section

Figure 7-9   Invert elevation on pipe.

Design Example

To best illustrate the use of the drainage calculation table and design nomograph, consider the following problem. See Fig. 7-7.

Given

$$\text{Area of drainage into each inlet} = 2.0\ A$$
$$C = 0.71$$
$$I = 2.30\ \text{in./hr}$$
$$v = 2.5\ \text{ft/sec}$$
$$n = 0.015$$

Find

1. all pipe sizes
2. all pipe slopes
3. invert elevations for the low and high ends for all pipes

Solution

1. Enter values known into the drainage calculation table. See Table 7-5.

TABLE 7-5 DRAINAGE CALCULATION TABLE (DATA LISTED FOR PROBLEM)

Column

1	2	3	4	5	6	7	8	9	10	11	12	13
											Elevation	
Line	A (area in acres)	C	I (in./hr)	Q (cfs)	v (ft/sec)	n	D (in.)	Slope	L (ft)	IC (ft)	Low	High
HW$_1$–MH$_1$	—	0.71	2.30		2.50	0.015			300		520.00	
MH$_1$–I$_1$	2.0	0.71	2.30		2.50	0.015			6			
I$_1$–I$_2$	2.0	0.71	2.30		2.50	0.015			23			
									—			
MH$_1$–MH$_2$	—	0.71	2.30		2.50	0.015			300			
MH$_2$–I$_3$	2.0	0.71	2.30		2.50	0.015			6			
I$_3$–I$_4$	2.0	0.71	2.30		2.50	0.015			23			

TABLE 7-6 DRAINAGE CALCULATION TABLE (QUANTITIES CALCULATED)

Column

1	2	3	4	5	6	7	8	9	10	11	12	13
											Elevation	
Line	A (area in acres)	C	I (in./hr)	Q (cfs)	v (ft/sec)	n	D (in.)	Slope	L (ft)	IC (ft)	Low	High
$HW_1\text{-}MH_1$	—	0.71	2.30	13.08	2.50	0.015	33	0.0012	300		520.00	
$MH_1\text{-}I_1$	2.0	0.71	2.30	6.54	2.50	0.015	24	0.0019	6			
$I_1\text{-}I_2$	2.0	0.71	2.30	3.27	2.50	0.015	18	0.0030	23			
				—								
$MH_1\text{-}MH_2$	—	0.71	2.30	6.54	2.50	0.015	24	0.0019	300			
$MH_2\text{-}I_3$	2.0	0.71	2.30	6.54	2.50	0.015	24	0.0019	6			
$I_3\text{-}I_4$	2.0	0.71	2.30	3.27	2.50	0.015	18	0.0030	23			

TABLE 7–7 DRAINAGE CALCULATION TABLE (COMPLETED DATA)

Column

1	2	3	4	5	6	7	8	9	10	11	12	13
											Elevation	
Line	A (area in acres)	C	I (in./hr)	Q (cfs)	v (ft/sec)	n	D (in.)	Slope	L (ft)	IC (ft)	Low	High
HW_1–MH_1	—	0.71	2.30	13.08	2.50	0.015	33	0.0012	300	0.36	520.00	520.36
MH_1–I_1	2.0	0.71	2.30	6.54	2.50	0.015	24	0.0019	6	0.01	520.36	520.37
I_1–I_2	2.0	0.71	2.30	3.27	2.50	0.015	18	0.0030	23	0.07	520.37	520.44
MH_1–MH_2	—	0.71	2.30	6.54	2.50	0.015	24	0.0019	300	0.57	520.36	520.93
MH_2–I_3	2.0	0.71	2.30	6.54	2.50	0.015	24	0.0019	6	0.01	520.93	520.94
I_3–I_4	2.0	0.71	2.30	3.27	2.50	0.015	18	0.0030	23	0.07	520.94	521.01

2. Calculate values for Q.

$$\text{Col. 5} = \text{col. 2} \times \text{col. 3} \times \text{col. 4}$$

$$Q = C \times I \times A$$

3. Using the nomograph, Fig. 7–8, find slope, col. 9, and pipe diameter, D, col. 8. Record these values in their respective columns. See Table 7–6.

To use the nomograph, locate the value for Q, discharge in cfs, and the value for the velocity, v, in ft/sec. In this example all velocities will be 2.5 ft/sec. Place a straight edge through these two points; Q and V. Read the pipe's diameter and slope from their respective scales. If a pipe size falls between two recorded diameters, use the next larger diameter.

4. Compute the increment of change IC, col. 11.

$$\text{Col. 11} = \text{col. 9} \times \text{col. 10}$$

$$IC = \text{slope} \times L$$

5. Calculate all pipe elevations using the initial discharge elevation of 520.00 as the starting point. See Table 7–7.

The final pipe elevations should result in adequate soil cover over the top of the pipe so that the pipe will not be damaged from traffic loads or environmental conditions. These calculated elevations will be used in the construction drawings for the stormwater drainage system. All sewer lines require *plan and profile* drawings showing the drainage structure's location and elevation, pipe's invert elevation, and the existing ground elevation.

PROBLEMS

7-1. Define the following terms:
   (a) runoff
   (b) rainfall
   (c) coefficient of runoff, C
   (d) intensity (storm), I
   (e) watershed area, Acres
   (f) roughness coefficient, n

7-2. Using the given nomograph (Fig. 7–8), determine the pipe size and pipe slope for the following conditions:
   (a) $Q = 30$ cfs, $n = 0.015$, $v = 2.5$ ft/sec
   (b) $Q = 30$ cfs, $n = 0.013$, $v = 2.5$ ft/sec
   (c) $Q = 6.5$ cfs, $n = 0.015$, $v = 5.2$ ft/sec
   (d) $Q = 11.5$ cfs, $n = 0.015$, $v = 1.75$ ft/sec
   (e) $Q = 22.2$ cfs, $n = 0.013$, $v = 10.3$ ft/sec

7-3. Using the values listed in Fig. 7–7 and the given nomograph (Fig. 7–8), find all pipe sizes, all pipe slopes, and invert elevations in Fig. 7–7. The headwall flow line (HW) has an elevation of 536.71.

Area of drainage into each inlet = 1.5 Acres
$C = 0.71$ $v = 2.5$ ft/sec
$I = 3.50$ in./hr $n = 0.015$

Chapter 8

Sanitary Sewer Considerations

INTRODUCTION

Concerns for the environment in which we live have grown along with technological advancements. The environment is being stressed with the new chemicals available for insect control, plant growth, ice removal, and so on. A land planner must consider the ecological effects of a plan on the environment. For major projects, the planner could be required to develop an environmental impact document. This is certainly to be expected for industrial and commercial developments and possibly for some residential developments.

In many metropolitan areas, stormwater runoff and sanitary sewers have been combined. This has caused numerous pollution problems and made the economical handling of sewage treatment practically impossible. Currently, large sums of federal, state, and local funds are being spent to separate these combined sewer systems.

This chapter will be primarily concerned with the sanitary requirements of new developments. This will include wastes as derived from industrial, commercial, and residential developments. Although this chapter includes information regarding the "design" of sanitary systems, it should be noted that this information is intended only to alert the reader to some of the technical requirements for sanitary sewer systems.

SEWAGE AND REGULATIONS

Sewage consists of any waste water solids that find their way into sanitary sewers and are transported through the sewer system. Domestic sewage is all the sewage that the average city produces, excluding industrial wastes but including water from fac-

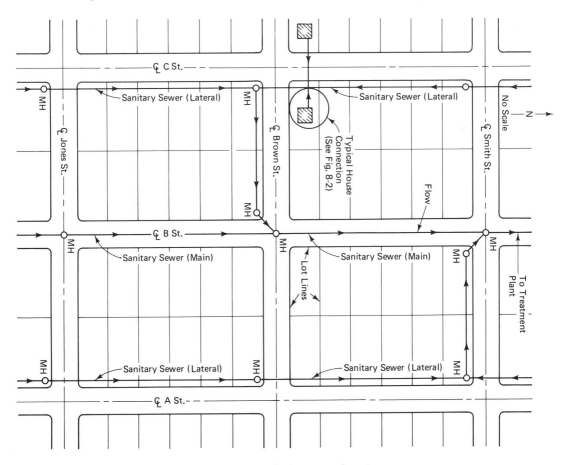

Figure 8-1 Sanitary sewer layout.

tories that is nonindustrial in origin. Chemical or biological waste resulting from some sort of manufacturing process is termed industrial waste water. In some cases, industrial waste water can be processed in municipal treatment plants without special provisions. However, other industrial wastes require considerable pretreatment before going into city sewers.

Raw domestic sewage is gray-colored water. Solids represent only a small amount of the total volume of this type of sewage. Thus, all calculations of sewage flow are computed for water excluding the solid content. The organic material in sewage is in the process of decomposition at all times unless waste is heavily chlorinated or otherwise disinfected. The amount of oxygen contained in the raw sewage is important in regard to the sewage's odor and composition. If the sewage contains a dissolved oxygen content the sewage is nonseptic and does not produce high amounts of foul smelling gases (methane). On the other hand, if sewage is oxygen starved it is considered to be septic and will emit foul-smelling gases. For this reason it is important to introduce either air containing oxygen or oxygen gas into the sewage to control the production of gases.

The subdivision designer must provide a means for collecting and moving the sewage from the planned subdivision to the sanitary sewage system of the regulating political subdivision. In rural areas where there are no sanitary systems in existence, other sewage handling methods must be considered. These could be septic tanks or subsurface filters, or both, for residential subdivisions. Small sewerage treatment plants could also be required for residential subdivisions, or commercial and industrial developments. Final determination for the sewage treatment system will be by the governmental regulatory authority who has jurisdiction over the area being planned. It is necessary to know who this authority is and what the regulations are prior to design of the development. In all cases, the sewage movement will be via a sewer system consisting of main sewer lines and lateral (connecting) sewer lines. See Fig. 8–1 and Fig. 8–2.

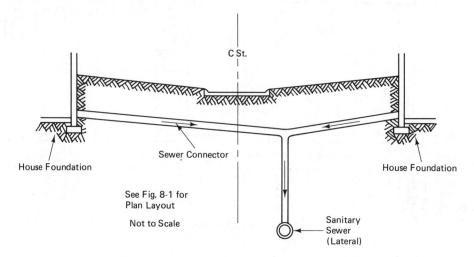

Figure 8–2 Sanitary sewer residential connection.

There have been regulations and standards regarding the distribution and handling of sewage, for many years. One such standard is what is called *Ten State Standards* as published under the title of *Recommended Standards for Sewage Works* by the Health Education Service, Albany, New York.

SEWAGE FLOW ESTIMATES

For all sewage systems it is necessary to estimate the amount of sewage that will be flowing in the system at any given time. The designer must estimate some design period (life) in which the sewer is to function. This design period must take into consideration population growths that would result in an increase of sewage flow. The design period, in many states, ranges from 25 to 50 years.

The sewage flow is directly proportional to the water consumption of the establishment. For residential use it is estimated that 65% of the water used returns to the sewage system. The amount of typical flow has been studied and most standards will list the anticipated flow from the different types of establishments. See Table 8-1.

TABLE 8-1 ANTICIPATED SEWAGE FLOWS

Type of establishment	Unit	Flow (gal/unit/day)
Apartment house	Capita	75
Bowling alley	Lane	75-160
Camp, day	Capita	35
Church	Seat	6
Cottage, summer	Capita	50
Hospital	Capita	200
Hotel	Capita	70
Institution	Capita	100
Laundry, coin	Machine	300
Multiple family residence	Capita	50
Municipality	Capita	100
Office	Employee	20
School	Capita	25
Subdivision, luxury	Capita	150
Subdivision, average	Capita	110
Special considerations		
Mercantile, commercial	Acre	12,000
Industrial	Acre	9,000
Infiltration	Acre	1,250

Source: From *Design and Construction of Sanitary and Storm Sewers,* Water Pollution Control Federation, Wash. D.C., 1970. Reprinted with permission.

The values in Table 8-1 are from the Ten States Standards and are in terms of gallons per unit per day and are based on the average 24-hour discharge rate during a one-year period. Residential flow is based per capita while commercial and industrial flows are based on acreage. A fourth component of sewage flow is infiltration of the system. Storm water can enter a sanitary sewage system through broken pipes and poorly designed and constructed pipe joints. This infiltration amount is usually calculated for the total area of the subdivision. The entire system must be analyzed using these estimated flow values. For anticipated growth, a rule of thumb has been to increase all quantities by a multiple of four.

Where the sewage is flowing to a sewage treatment plant, the sewage flow can be monitored for peak periods. This peak period, in residential subdivisions, would be early morning and late evening. For commercial subdivisions the peak period would be dependent on the type of commercial business. For example, if the commercial business was a car wash, the peak period would probably be in the evening and

Saturday morning or Sunday afternoon. For industrial subdivisions, the peak period would naturally depend on the type of industry and the number of hours (shifts) the industry was working.

DESIGN METHODS

The design of the sanitary sewer pipe sizes is similar to the design of the stormwater pipe sizes as discussed in Chapter 7. The quantity of sewage is first determined along with the desired sanitary sewer line lengths. The system will be at greater depths than the stormwater sewerage system because of the need for longer lines. When adequate depth for gravity fall in the sewer system is not available, lift stations or pressure piping systems, or both, are used. It is better to design the system as a gravity system if possible because of the additional costs that are encountered with lift stations and pressurized systems. Sanitary sewer manholes are placed in the system using the same criteria that were used in Chapter 7 for stormwater sewer systems:

- for grade changes in sewer lines
- for changes in horizontal direction
- for maintenance and inspection
- for spacing, usually at intervals of 500 feet

MATERIALS

Materials used for the sanitary sewer pipe could be concrete, vitrified (clay), or plastic. The factors for determining which pipe material to use are similar to the factors for selecting pipe material for stormwater sewer pipe:

- roughness of the pipe's inside wall
- pipe strength requirements
- resistance to acids, alkalis, solvents, and so on
- joint watertightness
- durability, life expectancy
- availability in the sizes required
- cost of materials and construction

In the sanitary sewer system's design and pipe material selection, joint tightness is more critical than with stormwater sewer's design and pipe material selection. A sewage system does not want to treat storm water that infiltrates the system through the pipe's joints. See Table 8-2 for infiltration rates for various types of joint material.

TABLE 8-2 INFILTRATION THROUGH DIFFERENT TYPES OF JOINTS

Joint material	6-inch diameter claypipe		6-inch diameter concrete pipe	
	Head above flow line (in.)	Average infiltration rate (gpd/in.-dia/mi)*	Head above flow line (in.)	Average infiltration rate (gpd/in.-dia/mi)*
Jute only	3	8,275	3	6,710
	9	71,050	9	52,800
	15	155,250	15	118,000
	21	258,000	21	205,500
	27	356,000	27	278,000
Cement	3	3,360	3	680
	9	15,000	9	4,950
	15	28,700	15	10,450
	21	41,200	21	16,500
	27	53,200	27	22,000
Hot pour	3	1,330	3	0
	9	1,660	9	107
	15	3,410	15	235
	21	4,720	21	419
	27	5,520	27	513
Cold mastic			3	990
			9	1,450
			15	3,210
			21	5,130
			27	7,810
PVC compression joint	3	0		
	9	645		
	15	1,450		
	21	1,850		
	27	2,400		
Rubber gasket			0–27	Negl.

*gpd/in.-dia/mi = gallons-per-day, per inch diameter of pipe per mile in length

CONSTRUCTION METHODS

The selected construction method for the sanitary sewer system is extremely important in regard to cost and the performance of a good operating system. The construction method could be one or a combination of the following methods:

- open trench construction
- tunneling
- jacking

All construction methods will require planning and site preparation. Preconstruction planning includes soil investigation, environmental restrictions, proper equipment selection, and delivery schedules for materials. The site preparation could include clearing and grubbing, removal of unsuitable soils, pavement cuts, traffic detours, and safety barricades.

Open trench construction is where the pipe's placement location is excavated down to the pipe's flow line plus the pipe's wall thickness. If the plans call for bedding, which is placement of support material under the pipe, the trench depth must also be dug deep enough to accommodate this bedding material. The actual trench excavation is accomplished with the use of excavating equipment. The type and size of equipment required will depend on a number of factors such as soil conditions, trench depth requirements, and pipe size. The contractor has a number of equipment types to choose from for excavating: trenching machines, backhoes, clamshells, and draglines.

Safety regulations, in many states, require bracing for trenches or side slope cutbacks for trenches over 5 feet in depth. The amount of side slope cutback is based on the soil conditions encountered. See Fig. 8–3.

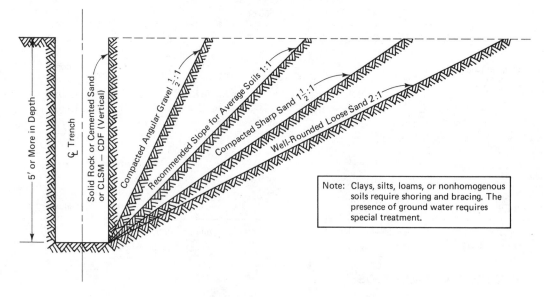

Figure 8-3 Safe trench slope cutbacks.

Upon completion of the pipe's installation, the trench must be backfilled. Trenches that will receive static or dynamic loads should be backfilled in lifts with a selected granular material that will allow for adequate compaction and reduced settlement. Backfill material in the trench is usually compacted with pneumatic or vibratory equipment in lifts of 6 to 12 inches. Each lift should be tested to see that the required density has been achieved. An alternative to this backfill compaction requirement is Controlled-Low-Strength-Material, Controlled-Density-Fill (CLSM-CDF). This specially designed backfill material is poured directly into the trench and around the pipe from a ready-mix concrete truck. The cost of CLSM-CDF's mixes and placement has proven to be more economical than conventional backfilling techniques where compaction is required. For more information on this new backfilling technique, contact the American Concrete Institute, P. O. Box 19150, Redford Station, Detroit, MI 48219 and request the state of the art for Controlled-Low-Strength-Materials by ACI Committee 229.

Tunneling for pipe placement must be considered if the soil is adequate for tunneling, the sewer is deep enough, and the pipe is large enough to pass equipment through. All these conditions are required to make tunneling more economically competitive than open trench construction. The soil condition should be uniform (clay) and the depth should be in the range of 25 feet. The pipe's diameter should be at least 4 feet.

Tunneling can eliminate some environmental concerns that are apparent with open trench construction. Pipe placement, in the tunnel, is usually accomplished by using an oval precast pipe or a cast in place pipe. The oval pipe allows for one section of the pipe to be placed through the pipe sections that have already been placed. See Fig. 8-4.

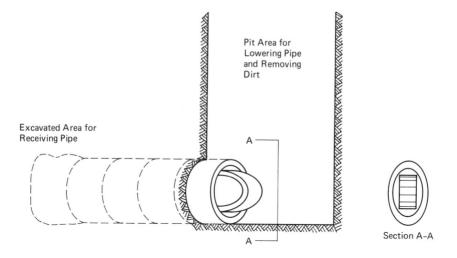

Figure 8-4 Pipe (oval) placement in a tunnel.

Cast-in-place pipe construction in the tunnel is accomplished by drilling material placement holes down to the tunnel and placing a cement/concrete mix around the tunnel liner. CLSM mixes have been used for this cement/concrete mixture. See Fig. 8-5.

Jacking of pipe is used for placement under existing railroads, streets, and structures that could not be open cut. Soil conditions must be acceptable for pipe jacking. The usual range of pipe sizes for jacking is between 3 and 9 feet in diameter. The pipe must be strong enough to withstand the loads exerted on it by the jacking opera-

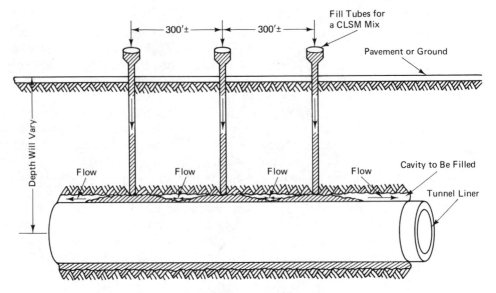

Figure 8–5   Controlled-low-strength-material placement in a tunnel.

tion. The most commonly used materials for such jacking operation are either rein-forced concrete, corrugated metal, or smooth steel pipe.

The jacking procedure consists of digging a jacking pit and placing a cutter edge (shoe) on the leading edge of the first pipe section. As the pipe is jacked (hydraulic) the material inside the pipe is excavated by hand and passed back through the pipe. See Fig. 8–6.

In all these sewer construction methods, the final cost must be calculated prior to method selection. The cost calculation consists of all construction components:

- soil condition
- excavation equipment available
- geographic location (city or rural)
- pipe's size
- pipe's required depth
- availability of pipe

DESIGN EXAMPLE

The actual calculation of the pipe's size (inside diameter) is similar to the calculations made in Chapter 7 for stormwater pipe sizes. The sewage system designer needs to know the total amount of sewage that each sewer line will be required to handle. Most communities set a minimum pipe diameter for house to lateral lines. Consider the following example problem.

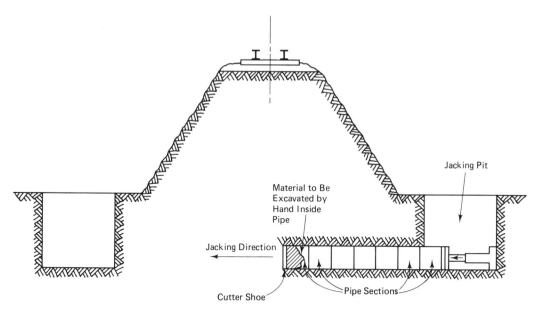

Figure 8-6   Pipe jacking under railroad.

Calculate the total amount of sewage flow for development that contains

Population = 10,000 people
Area   =   420 acres
Industrial =   40 acres
Commerical =   20 acres
Residential =   360 acres

(Note: Use the coefficient 0.65 multiplier by the amount of anticipated flow for a residential per capita component to yield the actual amount of sewage that will reach the sewage system.)

Solution: Using Table 8-1 for flow (gal/unit/day) the solution is as follows:

Residential calculation   (110 gal/capita/day)
    10,000 × 110 × 0.65 =   715,000 gal/day
Commercial calculation   (12,000 gal/A/day)
    12,000 × 20   =   240,000 gal/day
Industrial calculation   (9,000 gal/A/day)
    9,000 × 40   =   360,000 gal/day
Infiltration calculation   (1250 gal/A/day)
    1,250 × 420   =   525,000 gal/day
Total flow   =   1,840,000 gal/day
Total design flow   = Total flow × 4
Total design flow   =   7,360,000 gal/day

The sewage pipe sizes can now be determined by use of a nomograph similar to the one shown in Fig. 7-8.

PROBLEMS

8-1. List at least three areas from which sanitary wastes are derived in a community.

8-2. Define the following terms:
  (a) sewage
  (b) sewer main
  (c) sewer lateral
  (d) Ten State Standards
  (e) lift station

8-3. List the functions of a sanitary sewer manhole.

8-4. List the considerations for the selection of sanitary sewer pipe.

8-5. List construction methods for building sanitary sewers.

8-6. Describe, in detail, the construction methods listed in Prob. 8-5.

8-7. List factors that should be considered when calculating sewer construction components.

8-8. For the following data calculate the total amount of sewage flow. (Use Table 8-1.)

$$
\begin{aligned}
\text{Population} &= 100{,}000 \text{ people} \\
\text{Area} &= 1{,}200 \text{ acres} \\
\text{Industrial} &= 200 \text{ acres} \\
\text{Commerical} &= 100 \text{ acres} \\
\text{Residential} &= 900 \text{ acres}
\end{aligned}
$$

8-9. For the sewage flow calculations in Prob. 8-8, determine pipe size to effectively carry sewage flow. (Use the nomograph as shown in Fig. 7-8.)

Chapter 9

Pavement Alignment— Horizontal and Vertical Curves

INTRODUCTION

The alignment of horizontal and vertical pavements is extremely important in the planning of a subdivision. Horizontal curves will be used to move traffic around corners and will also serve as an esthetic enhancement to the subdivision when used to some degree between intersections. Vertical curves will be used to smooth out grade changes caused by hills and valleys and the requirement for drainage structures. The design of horizontal and vertical curves is primarily mathematical.

The designer should have a good understanding of geometry and trigonometry to fully implement the required horizontal and vertical curve alignment equations in planning subdivision streets. In both curve designs, the approach will be from the designer's approach. Actual field layout techniques for horizontal and vertical curves can be found in surveying references.

HORIZONTAL CURVES

A *horizontal curve* is actually the arc of a circle located between two points on the circle. The tangents to the circle, at these points, represent some reference line. In subdivision planning this line would be the center line of the proposed street. A designer uses horizontal curves primarily for horizontal pavement alignment. The basic design method, used in offices, is to establish the proposed pavement center line using straight lines. Where direction of these lines change, a horizontal curve can be designed to fit the desired curve conditions. Traffic will therefore move

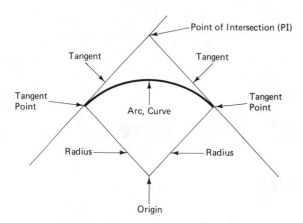

Figure 9-1 Horizontal curve components.

smoothly along the route with the use of a properly designed horizontal curve. See Fig. 9–1.

The design calculations can easily be done on a small hand-held calculator. Prior to the advent of hand-held calculators (1970), the designer had to use trigonometric tables and logarithm tables for solving the related mathematical formulas when doing horizontal curve calculations.

Once the designer has established the desired curve criteria, this information is entered on the construction drawings for bidding and engineering layout of the subdivision. Horizontal curves are used for roads, driveways, bike paths, sidewalks, and in some buildings.

Designing Horizontal Curves

To design a horizontal curve, the designer first establishes reference line criteria: stationing, angle of intersection, tangent direction, and coordinates. See Fig. 9–2.

It is very desirable to use coordinate references for all locations such as the *PI,* and so on. Establishment of coordinate systems was discussed in Chapter 3. Once the designer has the basic information—*PI* location and intersection angle—the desired curve length is established by setting the tangent length. This tangent length will be

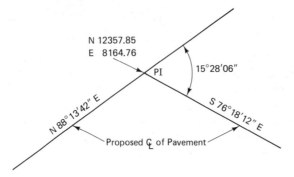

Figure 9-2 Design approach to horizontal curve design.

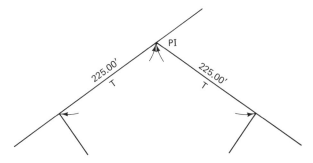

Figure 9-3 Setting of tangent lengths.

used to complete all necessary design calculations. See Fig. 9-3. For example, the tangent length was set at 225.00 feet. The tangent distances are equal. Therefore, the distances along the reference line, from the *PI* to each point of tangency, are equal. Once this tangent distance has been set, the curve mathematics can be completed. See Fig. 9-4.

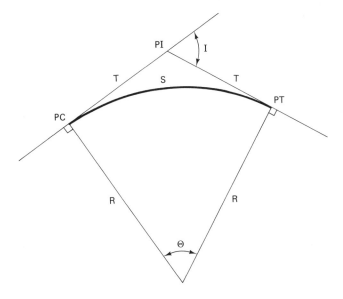

Figure 9-4 Horizontal curve symbols.

where,

PI = Point of intersection of the tangents. This is point established by the designer in the early stages of the planning. It would have stationing and coordinate references.

I = Intersection angle. The value of this angle can be derived from coordinate information and bearing values for the tangent lines. This topic was covered in Chapter 3.

T = Tangent length. The distance set by the designer for the establishment of the curve length.

R = Radius of the circular curve.
S = Arc length of the curve (some texts reference this as L).
Θ = Central angle for the curve.

The values for R, S, and Θ will be calculated from the known values of I, T, and PI location. See Fig. 9–5. From geometry we know that the angle formed by the tangent and the radius drawn to the point of tangency measures $90°$. Or, stated another way, the tangent is always perpendicular to the radius drawn to the point of tangency. Therefore, a right triangle can be constructed with the tangent, T, and the radius, R, as the legs with interior angles of $\Theta/2$ and $90 - I/2$. See Fig. 9–5.

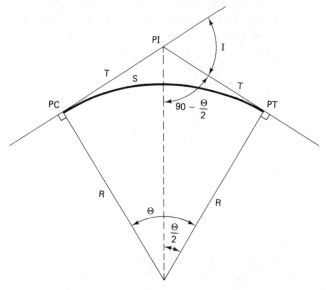

Figure 9-5   Horizontal curve geometry.

It can be shown that the angle of intersection, I, is equal to the central angle, Θ. The sum of the interior angles of any closed figure is equal to 180 times the sum of the number of sides minus two.

$$\text{Sum of interior angles} = 180 (N - 2)$$

In Fig. 9–5, the sum of the interior angles of the referenced four-sided figure is $360°$. Therefore,

$$\Theta + (180° - I) + 90° + 90° = 360°$$
$$\Theta + 360° - I = 360°$$
$$\Theta - I = 0°$$
$$\Theta = I$$

This relationship will prove helpful in calculating the different components for a horizontal curve. In Fig. 9–5 the following trigonometric relations can be derived.

$$\tan \frac{\Theta}{2} = \frac{T}{R}$$

and

$$T = R \tan \frac{\Theta}{2}$$

$$R = \frac{T}{\tan \left(\dfrac{\Theta}{2}\right)}$$

The value for the radius, R, can now be calculated using previously referenced information.

$$R = \frac{T}{\tan \left(\dfrac{\Theta}{2}\right)}$$

Using the previously set value of 225.00 feet for T and $15°28\,'06\,''$ degrees for I.

$$R = \frac{225.00}{\tan \left(\dfrac{15.468333}{2}\right)} = \frac{225.00}{\tan (7.734167)}$$

$$R = \frac{225.00}{.1358126}$$

$$R = 1656.695 \text{ ft}$$

Another geometric relationship that will be used to calculate S (arc length), is the relationship between S, Θ, and R.

$$S = R \times \Theta$$

In this equation, Θ must be in radians. To convert to radians, multiply the angle value, in decimal form, by $\pi/180$. This is a very important and useful relationship to understand since it is extremely helpful in solving horizontal curve relationships. Knowing the radius, R, and the angle, Θ, allows one to find the arc length, S. Therefore,

$$S = R \times \Theta \times \frac{\pi}{180°}$$

$$S = 1656.695 \times 154.6833 \times \frac{\pi}{180°}$$

$$S = 447.250 \text{ ft}$$

The point where the horizontal curve starts is known as the *point of curve, PC,* and is usually referenced to the left in the figures. Its station is found by subtracting the tangent distance, T, from the station of the *PI.* See Fig. 9–6.

The point where the curve meets the tangent, usually on the right of the figure, is known as the *point of tangent, PT.* The stationing is found by adding the arc length, S, to the stationing for the PC. Therefore,

$$17 + 31.93 + 447.25 = 21 + 79.18 \text{ sta. for the } PT$$

Note that the stationing for the PC is found by subtracting T from the *PI* stationing and the stationing for the *PT* is found by adding S to the *PC* stationing.

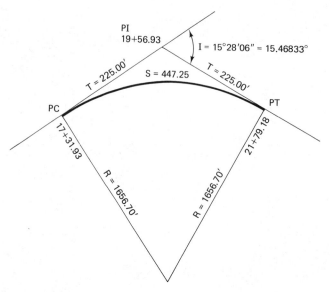

Figure 9-6   Horizontal curve calculations.

$$\text{sta.PC} = \text{sta.PI} - (T)$$
$$\text{sta.PT} = \text{sta.PC} + (S)$$

A common error is to add the tangent distance T to the PI stationing. This is not correct! The PT stationing really states the stationing distance from the PC to the PT along the curve.

The last value to be calculated is the long chord, LC. See Fig. 9-7. The long chord makes a 90-degree angle with the angle bisector from the PI to the origin, O.

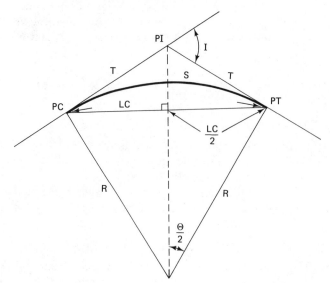

Figure 9-7   Long chord geometry.

Therefore the following trigonometric relationship exists.

$$\sin\left(\frac{\Theta}{2}\right) = \frac{1}{2}\frac{LC}{R}$$

and

$$LC = 2 \times R \times \sin\left(\frac{\Theta}{2}\right)$$

for the values previously given and calculated,

$$LC = 2 \times 1656.695 \times \sin 7.734167$$
$$LC = 2 \times 1656.695 \times 0.1345771$$
$$LC = 445.906 \text{ ft}$$

Note that LC will always be less than S. This is a good check on one's calculations. If S is less than LC then there is a mistake in the calculations.

Let's now work a typical problem together using information presented in this chapter. (It is suggested that you work each part and compare your results with each calculation.)

Horizontal Curve Problem

    Given:

$$PI \text{ @ sta. } 71 + 10.92$$
$$I = 41° \, 10\,'32\,''$$
$$T = 375.92 \text{ ft}$$

    Find:

$$R, \ S, \ PC \text{ sta.}, \ PT \text{ sta.}, \ LC$$

    Solution for PC sta.

$$PC \text{ sta.} = PI \text{ sta.} - T$$
$$= 71 + 10.92 - 375.92 \text{ ft}$$
$$PC \text{ sta.} = 67 + 35.00$$

    Solution for R

$$R = \frac{T}{\tan\left(\dfrac{\Theta}{2}\right)}$$

$$= \frac{375.92}{\tan 20.587777} \text{ (Remembering that } \Theta = I)$$

$$= \frac{375.92}{.3756318}$$

$$R = 1000.767 \text{ ft}$$

Solution for S

$$S = R \times \Theta \times \frac{\pi}{180°}$$

$$= \frac{1000.767 \times 41.175556 \times 3.1415}{180°}$$

$$S = 719.200 \text{ ft}$$

Solution for PT **sta.**

$$PT \text{ sta.} = PC \text{ sta.} + S$$
$$= 67 + 35.00 + 719.20$$
$$PT \text{ sta.} = 74 + 54.20$$

Solution for LC

$$LC = 2 \times R \times \sin\left(\frac{\Theta}{2}\right)$$

$$= 2 \times 1000.767 \times \sin 20.587777$$

$$= 2001.534 \times .351642$$

$$LC = 703.823 \text{ ft (This is less than } S \text{ of } 719.200 \text{ ft)}$$

It should be evident that curve calculations are also possible if the designer initially knew other curve variables such as R, S, Θ instead of T and I.

VERTICAL CURVES

Upon completion of the street pattern layout in the proposed subdivision and the design of all the horizontal curves, the drainage and vertical curves for the pavement must be considered. A *plan and profile sheet* will be used for this design process. Fig. 9–8 illustrates a plan and profile sheet.

The pavement's plan view is plotted on the *plan* section of the plan and profile sheet. A plan and profile sheet is made for every pavement in the proposed subdivision. From the subdivision plan and the initial layout drawing, elevations along the pavement's center line can be plotted on the profile section of the sheet. See Fig. 9–9. With the profile of the existing ground plotted, it is now possible to determine pavement slopes to minimize excessive cut or fill areas in regard to earth movement. See Fig. 9–10 for an example of profile plotting and determination of a pavement's slope.

The minimum grade is 0.50% and the maximum suggested grade is 6%. Percent grade means the rise or fall per 100 feet. For example, 0.50% rises or falls one-half foot in 100 feet. A 6% grade is a rise or fall of 6 feet in 100 feet. The 0.50% grade allows water to move along the pavement's gutter to the inlet structure. Lower slopes, 0.40%, have been used but poor construction can cause "bird baths" along the gutter. It is better to keep the minimum grade at 0.50%. The 6.0% grade is a reasonable maximum grade. Higher percent grades are sometimes used, but it is recommended that 6% be set as the maximum. In some areas that have steep hills, the problem will be too much grade. The designer must figure ways to reduce the grades. In very flat areas, the designer must find ways to increase grades. Both extremes provide a chance to develop some very creative designs.

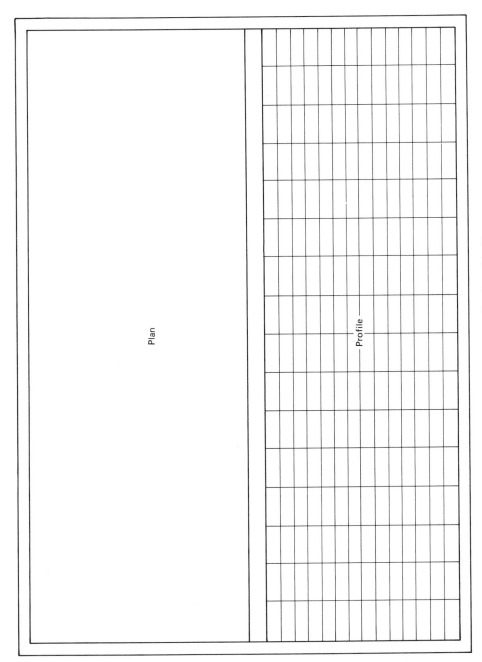

Figure 9–8 Plan and profile sheet (blank).

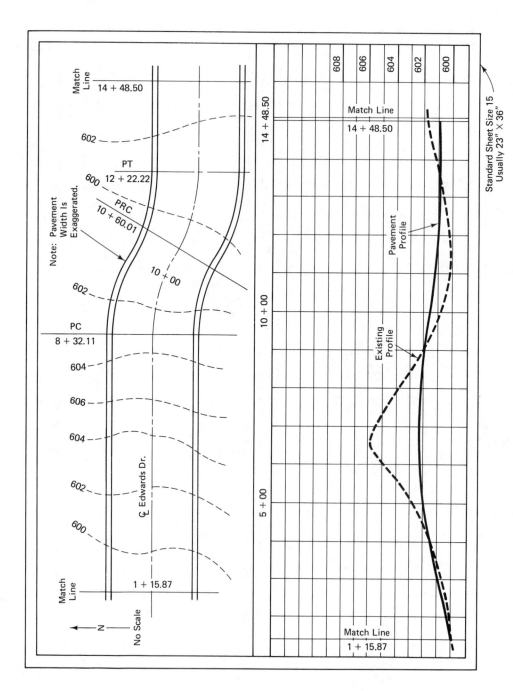

Figure 9-9 Plan and profile sheet (filled in).

112

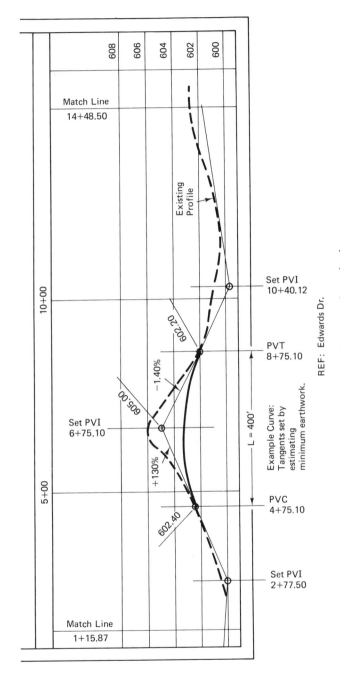

Figure 9-10 Example—slope determination.

113

On the profile sheet, where the slope of the pavement changes from a plus (+) grade to a minus (−) grade, a vertical curve should be designed to reduce an apparent bump. A plus grade signifies a rising grade. A minus grade signifies a falling or dropping grade (when facing in the direction of stationing).

The purpose of the vertical curve is to create a safer, smoother ride. This is what is referred to as *rideability* in pavement construction. The amount of grade change and the relative traffic speed of the vehicle determine the length of vertical curves. In subdivisions there is very little room for long vertical curves and their length is usually determined by available room between vertical curves. See Fig. 9–11 for a vertical curve layout.

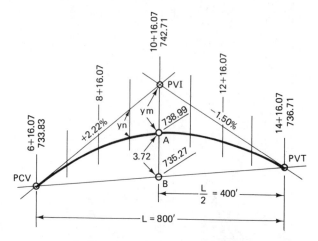

Figure 9-11 Vertical curve calculations.

In Fig. 9–11 there are two percents of grade to be considered. The percent grade, +2.22%, means that the pavement rises 2.22 feet for each 100 feet. The 100 feet is measured in a horizontal direction. Again, the (+) signifies rise in elevation. The percent grade, −1.50%, means that the pavement drops 1.50 feet for each 100 feet and the (−) sign signifies a drop or decrease in elevation. The algebraic sum of the grades is 3.72. Vertical curves should generally be considered when the algebraic sum of the grades is greater than 1.0.

To be able to design a vertical curve it is necessary to understand all the components of the vertical curve and their relationship to each other. These vertical curve components have similar relationships to each other much like the various components of the horizontal curve had to each other. In Fig. 9–11 the references represent

PVC = Point of vertical curve (station).
 PVI = Point of vertical intersection (station).
PVT = Point of vertical tangent (station).
   L = Total horizontal length of vertical curve.
  ym = Vertical distance from the *PVI* to the vertical curve.
   yn = Vertical distance from the tangent to the vertical curve. The number of parts on either side of the *PVI* station will be represented by *n*.
Sta. = Stationing reference for all points on the curve and the *PVC, PVI,* and *PVT.*

(*Note:* All vertical curve reference points will be identified by a station (sta.) and an elevation. In all cases, symmetrical curves will be considered. This means that the distance from the *PVC* to the *PVI* is the same as the distance from *PVI* to the *PVT*. For paving layout in field construction, the vertical curve will have to be laid out at 25-foot or 50-foot intervals.)

Designing Vertical Curves

The vertical curve that will be used for design purposes will be a parabola and not a circular curve as was used for the horizontal curve. From geometry, one knows that a parabola can be represented by the expression

$$y = ax^2$$

In the case of vertical curves, y will represent the vertical distance from the tangents to the curve and x represents the distances along the tangents; a is a constant and will be equal to ym.

The designer starts by establishing the exact station for the PVI and the grades for the proposed curve. This information is derived from the plan and profile sheet. See Fig. 9–9. Once the *PVI* location is known, the curve length can be set. For this initial process, Fig. 9–11 will be used. There are several basic methods that the designer could use. The method outlined here has been widely used and requires only a general understanding of mathematics. The general design steps are as follows:

1. Determine stationing for the *PVI*. In this example,

$$PVI = \text{sta. } 10 + 16.67$$

2. Determine the length of the curve and the stationing for the *PVC* and the *PVT*.

$$
\begin{aligned}
L &= 800 \text{ ft} \\
PVC &= \text{sta. } 6 + 16.67 \\
PVT &= \text{sta. } 14 + 16.67
\end{aligned}
$$

3. Determine the elevation of the *PVI, PVC,* and the *PVT*.

$$
\begin{aligned}
PVI \text{ elev.} &= 742.71 \\
PVC \text{ elev.} &= 733.83 \\
PVT \text{ elev.} &= 736.71
\end{aligned}
$$

This information would be read directly off the profile sheet.

4. Determine the respective slopes for the tangents between the *PVC* and the *PVI*, and the *PVT* and the *PVI*.

$$\frac{\text{elev. } PVI - \text{elev. } PVC}{\dfrac{L}{2}} \times 100 = \frac{742.71 - 733.83}{400} \times 100$$

$$= +2.22\%$$

$$\frac{\text{elev. } PVT - \text{elev. } PVI}{\dfrac{L}{2}} \times 100 = \frac{736.71 - 742.71}{400} \times 100$$

$$= -1.50\%$$

Notice that the slopes sign (+ or −) indicates rise or fall of the grade.

5. Determine the elevation of point *B*.

This point is the midpoint between the *PVC* and the *PVT*. The elevation is quickly determined by adding the elevations of the *PVC* and the *PVT* and then dividing by 2.

$$\text{elev. @ } B = \frac{\text{elev. } PVC + \text{elev. } PVT}{2}$$

$$= \frac{733.83 + 736.71}{2}$$

$$\text{elev. @ } B = 735.27$$

This elevation will be used to calculate the *ym* value.

$$ym = \frac{\text{elev. PVI} - \text{elev. } B}{2}$$

$$= \frac{742.71 - 735.27}{2}$$

$$ym = 3.72 \text{ ft}$$

This value *ym,* the distance from the *PVI* to the curve, will be used to calculate all other elevations along the curve. In the basic parabolic equation, $y = ax^2$, *a* is equal to *ym*.

To simplify the calculation, let's assume that curve data will be required at equal intervals of 100 feet. Therefore curve elevations would be needed at the following points:

$$
\begin{array}{lr}
PVC & 6+16.07 \\
& 7+16.07 \\
& 8+16.07 \\
& 9+16.07 \\
PVI & 10+16.07 \\
& 11+16.07 \\
& 12+16.07 \\
& 13+16.07 \\
PVT & 14+16.07 \\
\end{array}
$$

For ease in calculating and recording all the necessary elevations, a chart or table such as Table 9-1 should be used for this purpose.

Table 9-1 provides spaces for recording the stationing, the tangent elevations, the increment distances, *yn,* between the tangent and the curve, the curve elevations at the station points required, and finally a column for the calculation of the different increments, *yn.* See Table 9-2 for entries of the station elevations required in this example.

The increment distances, *yn,* between the tangents and the curve, can now be calculated. The values between the *PVC* and the *PVI* should be calculated first. Since

TABLE 9-1 VERTICAL CURVE TABLE

Sta.	Tangent elevation	Increment yn	Curve elevation	Calculation for increment yn

the curve will be symmetrical, the increment, *yn,* values between the *PVI* and the *PVT* will be the same as the values between the *PVC* and the *PVI.* Referring to the equation

$$yn = ax^2$$

where

$$a = \text{the value of } ym$$
$$yn = 3.72\, x^2$$

TABLE 9-2 EXAMPLE—VERTICAL CURVE TABLE

Sta.	Tangent elevation	Increment yn	Curve elevation	Calculation for increment yn
PVC 6 + 16.07	733.83			
7 + 16.07				
8 + 16.07				
9 + 16.07				
PVI 10 + 16.07	742.71			
11 + 16.07				
12 + 16.07				
13 + 16.07				
PVT 14 + 16.07	736.71			

The value of x is the distance ratio of the point in question from the *PVC* as compared to the distance from the *PVC* to the *PVI* or $L/2$. In this example the values for x at the respective stations will be as shown in Table 9–3. The increment calculations are as shown in Table 9–4 with the corresponding values entered into the reference table. Note that the increments for stations 7 + 16.07 and 13 + 16.07, 8 + 16.07 and 12 + 16.07, 9 + 16.07 and 11 + 16.07 are the same. It should also be noted

TABLE 9-3 EXAMPLE—INCREMENT CALCULATIONS

Sta.	Tangent elevation	Increment yn	Curve elevation	Calculation for increment yn
PVC 6 + 16.07	733.83			$x = \dfrac{0}{400} = 0.00$
7 + 16.07				$x = \dfrac{100}{400} = 0.25$
8 + 16.07				$x = \dfrac{200}{400} = 0.50$
9 + 16.07				$x = \dfrac{300}{400} = 0.75$
PVI 10 + 16.07	742.71			$x = \dfrac{400}{400} = 1.00$
11 + 16.07				
12 + 16.07				
13 + 16.07				
PVT 14 + 16.07	736.71			

TABLE 9–4 EXAMPLE—INCREMENT VALUES

Sta.	Tangent elevation	Increment yn	Curve elevation	Calculation for increment yn
PVC 6 + 16.07	733.83	0.00		$yn = 3.72 \left(\dfrac{0}{4}\right)^2 = 0$
7 + 16.07		0.23		$yn = 3.72 \left(\dfrac{1}{4}\right)^2 = 0.23$
8 + 16.07		0.93		$yn = 3.72 \left(\dfrac{1}{2}\right)^2 = 0.93$
9 + 16.07		2.09		$yn = 3.72 \left(\dfrac{3}{4}\right)^2 = 2.09$
PVI 10 + 16.07	742.71	3.72		$ym = 3.72$
11 + 16.07		2.09		$yn = 2.09$
12 + 16.07		0.93		$yn = 0.93$
13 + 16.07		0.23		$yn = 0.23$
PVT 14 + 16.07	736.71	0.00		$yn = 0.00$

that while the increments are the same, the curve elevations will not be since there are different slopes involved.

To determine the tangent elevations, add the rise or subtract the fall, as determined by the slope from the *PVC* and *PVT* elevations for each station location required. For example, the tangent elevation of sta. 7 + 16.07 would be

$$\text{Tangent elev.} = \text{elev. } PVC + \left(\frac{\text{slope} \times \text{distance}}{100}\right)$$

$$= 733.83 + \left(\frac{2.22 \times 100}{100}\right)$$

$$= 736.05$$

and for sta. $13 + 16.07$,

$$\text{Tangent elev.} = \text{elev. } PVT + \left(\frac{\text{slope} \times \text{distance}}{100}\right)$$

$$= 736.71 + \left(\frac{1.50 \times \text{distance}}{100}\right)$$

$$= 738.21$$

The tangent elevations for all the other stations are shown in Table 9–5. Finally, the curve elevations at the stations required can now be determined. This is accomplished by subtracting the increments, yn, values from the corresponding tangent elevations. The results of this subtraction are shown in Table 9–6. The table shows the completed curve calculations as required for the selected stationing.

High Point or Low Point on Curve

It may be necessary for the designer to check for the high or low points on the vertical curve. The low point would be very important when considering drainage location for inlets. See Fig. 9–12. Again, only equal tangents will be considered. For equal tangents the high or low point can be determined by

$$x = \frac{L \times G1}{G1 - G2}$$

where,

$$x = \text{distance to low point from } PVC$$
$$L = \text{total length of curve}$$
$$G1 = \text{grade from } PVC \text{ to } PVI$$
$$G2 = \text{grade from } PVI \text{ to } PVT$$

It is very important to use the "+" or "−" signs for $G1$ and $G2$. For the example problem, the high point would be

$$x = \frac{L \times G1}{G1 - G2}$$

$$x = \frac{800 \times 2.22}{2.22 - (-1.50)}$$

$$x = \frac{1776}{3.72}$$

$$x = 477.42 \text{ ft}$$

or at Sta. $10 + 93.49$

TABLE 9-5 EXAMPLE—TANGENT ELEVATIONS

Sta.	Tangent elevation	Increment yn	Curve elevation	Calculation for increment yn
PVC 6 + 16.07	733.83	0.00		$yn = 0$
7 + 16.07	736.05	0.23		$yn = 0.23$
8 + 16.07	738.27	0.93		$yn = 0.93$
9 + 16.07	740.49	2.09		$yn = 2.09$
PVI 10 + 16.07	742.71	3.72		$ym = 3.72$
11 + 16.07	741.21	2.09		$yn = 2.09$
12 + 16.07	739.71	0.93		$yn = 0.93$
13 + 16.07	738.21	0.23		$yn = 0.23$
PVT 14 + 16.07	736.71	0.00		$yn = 0$

The elevation of this point on the curve would be determined by calculating the increment, yn, for sta. 10 + 93.49. In this case x will be the distance from the PVT to sta. 10 + 93.49 because the high point falls between the PVI and the PVT.

$$yn = 3.72 \left(\frac{322.58}{400} \right)$$

$$yn = 2.42 \text{ ft}$$

TABLE 9-6 EXAMPLE—CURVE ELEVATIONS

Sta.	Tangent elevation	Increment yn	Curve elevation	Calculation for increment yn
PVC 6 + 16.07	733.83	0.00	733.83	$yn = 3.72 \left(\dfrac{0}{4}\right)^2 = 0$
7 + 16.07	736.05	0.23	735.82	$yn = 3.72 \left(\dfrac{1}{4}\right)^2 = 0.23$
8 + 16.07	738.27	0.93	737.34	$yn = 3.72 \left(\dfrac{1}{2}\right)^2 = 0.93$
9 + 16.07	740.49	2.09	738.40	$yn = 3.72 \left(\dfrac{3}{4}\right)^2 = 2.09$
PVI 10 + 16.07	742.71	3.72	738.99	$ym = 3.72$
11 + 16.07	741.21	2.09	739.12	$yn = 2.09$
12 + 16.07	739.71	0.93	738.78	$yn = 0.93$
13 + 16.07	738.21	0.23	737.98	$yn = 0.23$
PVT 14 + 16.07	736.71	0.00	736.71	$yn = 0.00$

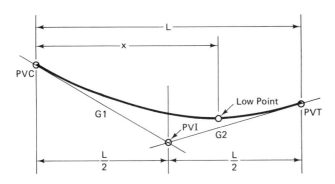

Figure 9-12 Vertical curve low point and high point determination.

The tangent elevation at sta. $10+93.49$ is equal to

$$\text{Tangent elev. @ } 10 + 93.49 = 736.71 + \left(\frac{1.50 \times 322.58}{100}\right)$$

$$= 741.55$$

and the curve elevation at sta. $10+93.49$ is equal to

$$
\begin{aligned}
\text{Curve elev. @ } 10+93.49 &= 741.55 - yn \\
&= 741.55 - 2.42 \text{ ft} \\
&= 739.13
\end{aligned}
$$

The highest point on the curve is at sta. $10+93.49$ and the elevation is 739.13. Checking Table 9–6 reveals that sta. $10+93.49$ falls between $10+16.07$ and $11+16.07$. The elevations of these points are 738.99 and 739.12, respectively. Both are lower in elevation than 739.13.

Now, let's work another example with the curve being placed in a valley. See Fig. 9–13. For ease of calculating we'll set the stations at even values every 50 feet. In actual practice, the *PVI* would probably never fall exactly on an even station. The results of all the necessary calculations are shown in Table 9–7. The calculation for the low point would be

$$
\begin{aligned}
x &= \frac{L \times G1}{G1 - G2} \\
&= \frac{500 \times 0.50}{(-0.50) - 1.86} \\
x &= 105.93 \text{ ft}
\end{aligned}
$$

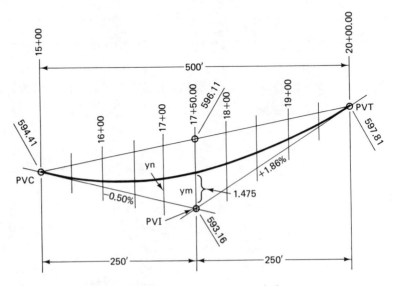

Figure 9-13   Example problem—vertical curve.

TABLE 9-7 EXAMPLE PROBLEM COMPLETED

Sta.	Tangent elevation	Increment yn	Curve elevation	Calculation for increment yn
PVC 15 + 00	594.41	—	594.41	
+ 50	594.16	0.06 ←	594.22	$yn = \left(\dfrac{1}{5}\right)^2 \times 1.475 = 0.06$
16 + 00	593.91	0.24 ←	594.15	$yn = \left(\dfrac{2}{5}\right)^2 \times 1.475 = 0.24$
+ 50	593.66	0.53 ←	594.19	$yn = \left(\dfrac{3}{5}\right)^2 \times 1.475 = 0.53$
17 + 00	593.41	0.94 ←	594.35	$yn = \left(\dfrac{4}{5}\right)^2 \times 1.475 = 0.94$
PVI 17 + 50	593.16	1.475	594.64	
18 + 00	594.09	0.94 ←	595.03	$yn = $ same as 17 + 00
+ 50	595.02	0.53 ←	595.55	$yn = $ same as 16 + 50
19 + 00	595.95	0.24 ←	596.19	$yn = $ same as 16 + 00
+ 50	596.88	0.06 ←	596.94	$yn = $ same as 15 + 50
PVT 20 + 00	597.81	—	597.81	
Low point 16 + 05.93	593.88	0.26	594.14	

The station of the low point would be

$$15 + 00.00 + 105.93 \text{ ft} = 16 + 05.93$$

The curve elevation at the low point would be 594.145. This point, sta. 16 + 05.93 with an elevation of 594.14 would be where curb inlets would be located for adequate drainage.

COMPUTER APPLICATIONS

Elements of horizontal and vertical curves can be readily computed with the use of a computer. This chapter provides a general understanding of the necessary calculations for horizontal and vertical curves. Chapter 12 demonstrates the use of computers using the same example problems that were worked in this chapter.

PROBLEMS

9–1. Define the following terms:
  (a) horizontal curve (as used for horizontal curves)
  (b) vertical curve (as used for vertical curves)
  (c) slope (as used for vertical curves)
  (d) tangent length (as used for horizontal curves)
  (e) point of intersection (as used for both horizontal and vertical curves)
  (f) grade (as used for vertical curves)

9–2. What do the following symbols represent when working with horizontal curves?

(a) I	**(d)** T	**(g)** R
(b) S	**(e)** Θ	**(h)** LC
(c) PC	**(f)** PT	**(i)** PI

9–3. What do the following symbols represent when working with vertical curves?

(a) PVI	**(d)** PVC	**(g)** PVT
(b) L	**(e)** ym	**(h)** yn
(c) Sta.	**(f)** $G1$	**(i)** $G2$

9–4. For a radius, R, of 195.62 ft and a central angle, Θ, of $31°15'25''$, find the arc length, S.

9–5. Find R, S, Θ, LC, PC, PT for the horizontal curve data listed.
  PI = sta. $12+95.26$
  T = 315.92 ft
  I = $32° 16'21''$

9–6. Find R, S, I, LC, PI, PT for the horizontal curve data listed.
  T = 521.16
  Θ = $14° 14'14''$
  PC = sta. $9+61.71$

9–7. Find the curve elevations (100-foot intervals) for the vertical curve data listed.
  PVI = sta. $21+39.76$ and elevation = 916.92
  $G1$ = $+2.25\%$
  $G2$ = -3.14%
  L = 600.00 ft

9–8. Find the curve elevations (50-foot intervals) for the vertical curve data listed.
  PVC = sta. $17+92.21$ and elevation = 752.19
  PVI = sta. $19+92.21$ and elevation = 758.19
  L = 400.00 ft
  $G2$ = $- 2.95\%$

9–9. Find the curve elevations (50-foot intervals) for the vertical curve listed.
  PVT = sta. $21+16.95$, and elevation = 1111.11

$G1$ $= -4.95\%$
$G2$ $= +3.33\%$
L $= 500.00$ ft

9-10. For Prob. 9-7, calculate the elevation of the highest point on the curve and its station.

9-11. For Prob. 9-8, calculate the elevation of the highest point on the curve and its station.

9-12. For Prob. 9-9, calculate the elevation of the lowest point on the curve and its station.

9-13. Draw the solution for the vertical curve as described in Prob. 9-7. Use proper scale so drawing fits onto an 8.5 × 11.0-inch sheet of paper.

9-14. Draw the solution for the vertical curve as described in Prob. 9-8. Use proper scale so drawing fits onto an 8.5 × 11.0-inch sheet of paper.

9-15. Draw the solution for the vertical curve as described in Prob. 9-9. Use proper scale so drawing fits onto an 8.5 × 11.0-inch sheet of paper.

Chapter 10

Pavement Design Considerations

INTRODUCTION

The design of a pavement is of the utmost importance to the developer and the governing regulating authority. If the regulating authority's standards are too high, pavement costs will also be high and result in unrealistic costs to the developer. However, if the paving standards are too low, the community or residents will eventually have to pay for the pavement's repair or even its replacement. For these reasons, it is extremely important that all parties, developer, regulating authority, design engineers and contractors, understand the necessity for good pavement design and construction.

New technology is constantly being developed in regard to pavement design materials and construction. This technology is aimed at building good, serviceable pavements with longer service lives at lower construction costs. All aspects of pavement design, soils, traffic, material and maintenance, must be analyzed for each geographical area and each proposed project. This chapter will consider all these aspects plus construction techniques and cost feasibility for new pavement construction.

HISTORY

The prime concern of early pavements was to keep the vehicles out of the mud. During the early stages of the development of pavement design, design consisted of rule-of-thumb knowledge based on past experience. This was a hit-or-miss approach to pavement design at best. From 1920 to 1940 engineers made an effort to evaluate the structural properties of soil. Even though this information was primarily used for building and bridge foundations, the data that was accumulated provided pavement designers with valuable knowledge. Basically, this knowledge consisted of a soil classification system. Paving engineers were aware that performance of pavements depended on the types of soils upon which the pavement was to be constructed.

Data generated during this period enabled researchers to establish correlations of pavement performance with materials, traffic, and the different types of subgrades. These studies showed that pavements constructed on plastic soils (clay) had a higher degree of distress than those constructed over nonplastic soils. They also demonstrated that frost action and poor drainage were two of the major causes of poor pavement performance. However, even though empirical evidence on pavement design was available, many paving engineers continued to design a constant thickness for pavements over all types of soil.

In the early 1950s, due to increased traffic and axle loads, it became necessary to establish a more rational approach to pavement design. One very effective means that helped establish this rational approach was the development and funding of test roads.

TEST ROADS

The Federal Highway Administration (FHWA) and the American Association of State Highway and Transportation Officials (AASHTO), previously referred to as the American Association of State Highway Officials (AASHO), have been responsible for several test roads in the United States. Several state highway departments have also constructed test roads in order to determine the effect of load and materials on pavements of different design.

The first major test road was the Bates Experimental road, which was constructed in Illinois in 1920. This road was constructed of various materials including brick, portland cement concrete, and asphaltic concrete. The research results on this test road were employed by pavement designers for many years.

The Maryland Test road was the next major test road to be constructed. This test section consisted of a 1.1 mile section of portland cement concrete pavement in 1941. The major conclusions involved the effect of loads on the pumping of rigid concrete sections.

In 1957 the most significant and ambitious road test ever conducted was begun in Ottawa, IL. The AASHO Road test was completed in 1962 and it included both concrete and asphalt pavement sections. A total of six test loops made up the test sections. See Fig. 10–1.

The traffic loads consisted of different axle configurations. See Fig. 10–2. These axle loads varied from no loads, Loop 1, to 48,000 pounds on Loop 6. The trucks were driven by soldiers from the U. S. Army Transportation Corps. The vehicles were driven between 1958 to 1962 to establish an axle count on the pavement sections of 1,114,000 applications on each test loop. The test was conducted almost continuously during the four-year period. The AASHO Road test cost $27,000,000. Although it was a sizeable sum at the time, it is considered a bargain when compared

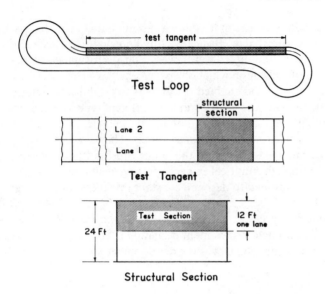

Figure 10-1 AASHO test loops. (From Transportation Research Board Special Report #61, © 1960. Used with permission of Transportation Research Board, Wash., D.C.)

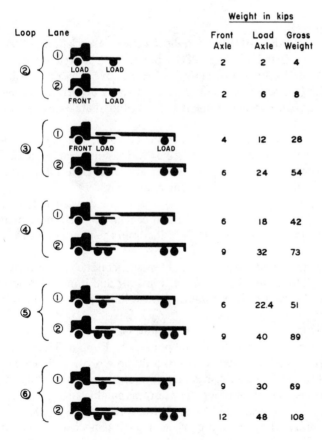

Figure 10-2 AASHO axle loadings. (From Transportation Research Board Special Report #61, © 1960. Used with permission of Transportation Research Board, Wash., D.C.)

to current costs. The results were published by the Transportation Research Board (TRB) in 1962. Major findings dealt with serviceability and the effect of relative pavement thickness on performance for the different construction materials being used. Pavement engineers are now beginning to realize the merits of the data that was generated from this test—some 25 years after the test was completed.

The results of these field test programs have had a major influence on the pavement design concepts that are used today. The performance of prototype pavements that are in service has also had a significant influence on design. Considering that it is difficult, if not impossible, to fully evaluate design concepts in controlled laboratory conditions, it is not surprising that these field tests have had such a significant influence on pavement design.

PAVEMENT TYPES AND MATERIALS

Pavements have traditionally been divided into two broad categories: *rigid* and *flexible* pavements. To a certain extent this is an oversimplification because some flexible pavements can act as rigid pavements and with new concrete-related material designs, concrete pavements could be considered as flexible. The basic difference between these concepts is how the traffic load, or wheel load, is transferred to the subgrade. See Fig. 10–3. This figure represents a typical cross section of a flexible pavement that consists of an aggregate subbase and base, which are sand and stone respectively, with an asphaltic concrete surface course. Note that the curb sections are mountable curbs. This type of curb is primarily used with 25-foot wide pavement for subdivision streets.

The material used in the construction of the flexible pavement is usually designated by the governing political subdivision in which the pavement is to be built and

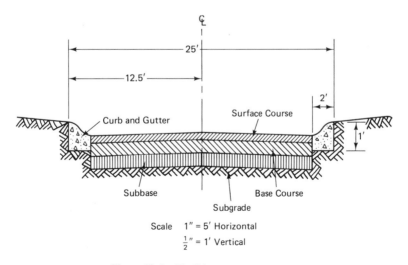

Figure 10–3 Flexible pavement section.

is referenced to AASHTO or ASTM Standards. There are a number of other materials that could be used in a flexible pavement such as asphalt impregnated base, gravel base, stabilized bases, and controlled-low-strength-materials. All these materials must meet prescribed strength and durability reference standards as required by the governing political subdivision.

A rigid pavement cross section is similar to the cross section for the flexible pavement. See Fig. 10–4. A rigid pavement consists of portland cement concrete, coarse and fine aggregates, air-entrainment admixture, and water. The concrete mix design is made to achieve some designated strength. Note that the curb section is an integral part of the pavement's structure and not separate as with the flexible section.

The pavements' thickness, in both flexible and rigid pavements, is a function of the paving materials strength, soil support, and anticipated traffic magnitude and frequency. Pavement thickness will therefore vary between these diverse design func-

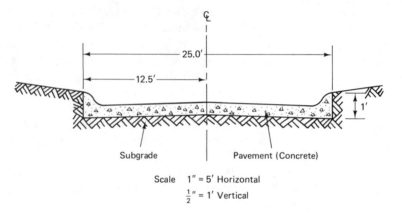

Figure 10-4 Rigid pavement section.

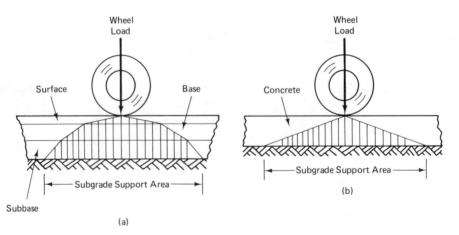

Figure 10-5 Wheel load distribution (a) flexible, (b) rigid.

tions. See Fig. 10–5. This figure shows the transfer of the wheel load to the subgrade for flexible and rigid pavement sections. Note that an increase in the strength of the paving material increases the wheel load's resulting area on the subgrade.

THICKNESS DESIGN CONSIDERATIONS

There are a number of ways to design flexible and rigid pavements. Years ago, many design thicknesses were established by guess work on the part of the designer. Today, because of information generated from the different road tests, pavement thickness design has become more of a science. The pavement design method for flexible and rigid pavements will be based, in part, on the AASHO Road test results. This information is from the AASHO Road test and input from different state agencies as to their use of the AASHO Road test information. The design of pavement thicknesses for both flexible and rigid pavements will be reviewed. The AASHTO material has recently been revised and is contained in a publication entitled *Proposed AASHTO Guide for Design of Pavement Structures, NCHRP Project 20–7/24.* For design considerations in this text only residential, low traffic volumes will be considered. In all cases the pavements will have curb sections.

Rigid Pavement Thickness Design

The thickness design of a rigid pavement requires information in regard to soil, traffic, design life, and concrete. The soil information is as outlined in Chapter 6. Once a soil classification is available, a soil support value can be determined.

Since a residential pavement could be a mile or more in length, soil information should be gathered for the entire proposed length. The soil's support value should be based on the lowest value for support. If there is a definite soil change in the pavement's path, different pavement thicknesses could be used. In actual practice it is usually more economical to use the same thickness throughout the entire pavement project.

There are several soil support references for both flexible and rigid pavements. A flexible pavement's soil support is usually referenced to California Bearing Ratio, *CBR;* the rigid pavement's soil support is referenced to Westergaard's Modulus of Subgrade Reaction, k. Many years ago soil engineers developed a system of indexing a soil in regard to soil support. This index is known as the Group Index, *GI*. It is a number that is dependent on the soil's liquid limit, *LL,* plasticity index, *PI,* and the percentage of soil passing the No. 200 sieve (F). An empirical formula is used to express these relationships.

$$GI = (F - 35) [0.2 + 0.005 (LL - 40)] + 0.01 (F - 15) (PI - 10)$$

where,

$$F = \text{percentage passing No. 200 sieve}$$
$$LL = \text{liquid limit}$$
$$PI = \text{plasticity index}$$

This equation can also be expressed as a nomograph. See Fig. 10-6. The AASHO Road test developed still another support reference, Soil Support Value (*SSV*), which is expressed by a number. With all these soil support references, *GI, CBR, SSV,* and *k,* it was becoming more and more confusing as to which support value to use and what, if any, relationship there was between these references. The Ohio Department of Transportation (ODOT) developed a correlation chart for referencing these soil

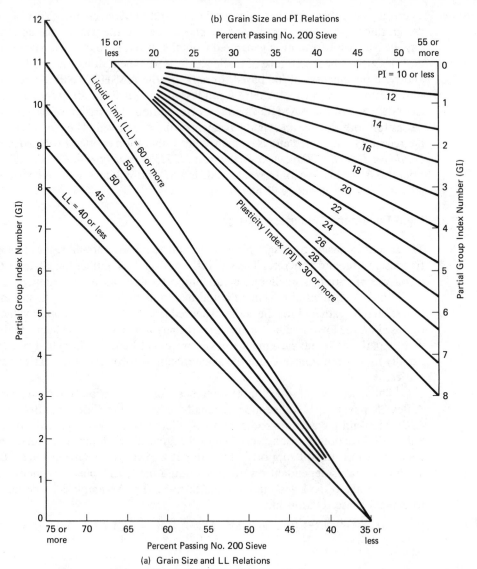

Figure 10-6 Group index charts. (Reprinted with permission of the Ohio Department of Transportation.)

support references. See Fig. 10–7. This chart enables one to read corresponding values for a known support value. For example, a k of 100 pounds per cubic inch (pci) would have the following corresponding values: $SSV = 2.4$; $CBR = 3.0-$; $GI = 19$. This soil would have poor soil support qualities. The subgrade's support value, for rigid pavements, will be expressed in terms of k. This value is expressed in pounds per cubic inch. The values of k range from 50 pci, poor support, to 200+ pci, good support.

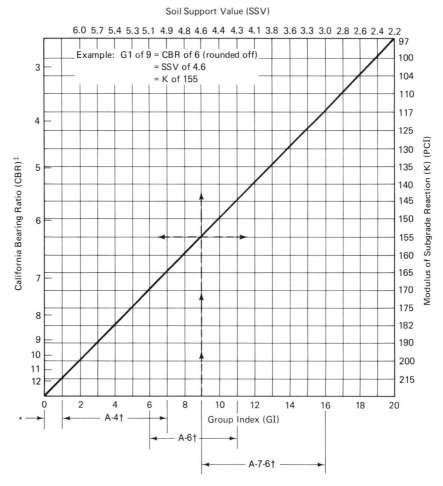

Figure 10–7   Subgrade correlation chart. (From *Location and Design Manual*, Feb. 1978, Ohio Department of Transportation. Reprinted with permission.)

The AASHO Road test resulted in the development of an expression for the pavement's existing condition. The pavement's serviceability (p_t) was a number (0–5) that expressed this serviceability condition. The value of 5 was excellent and 0 failure. The test revealed that if a pavement's p_t became 1.5 or lower, the pavement had to be rebuilt from the subgrade up. For residential pavements, the projected p_t will be 2.0 for the design life of the pavement. When the pavement reaches, $p_t = 2.0$, maintenance must be performed on the pavement. This maintenance will increase the p_t value and the pavement's useful life will be extended. The design life of a pavement is based on the design engineer's estimated time to lower the p_t value to 2.0. This estimate must include considerations for traffic loads, traffic frequencies, paving materials, design thicknesses, and the contractor's ability to build a quality pavement. On the AASHO Road test none of the pavements received a 5.0 serviceability rating for their initial construction. The design life for residential pavements is usually 20 to 35 years.

Another input that is needed is the amount, load, and frequency of traffic. The AASHO Road test related all traffic to an 18,000 pound (18 kip) axle load. See Fig. 10–8. Equivalent axle load configurations were developed for all traffic load combinations. This means that all traffic load combinations are expressed as "how many" 18 kip loads. These are expressed as E18s. For example, for traffic axle and load configurations as shown in Table 10–1, the resulting E18s could be calculated by use of equivalence factor tables. See Table 10–2. Note that the axle breakdown for the different weights and the number of axle loads per day will be different for different proposed pavements. Table 10–2 is for $p_t = 2.0$ and for rigid pavements. A different table will be used for flexible pavements. The equivalence factors are read from Table 10–2 and recorded as shown in Table 10–3. See Table 10–3.

The equivalence factors are multiplied by the number of axles per day and recorded as E18s. Note how little effect the lower axle loads have in regard to equivalent E18s. The E18s are then totaled. In this example, there are 85.32 equivalent E18s per day. This would not necessarily be a residential pavement since most residential

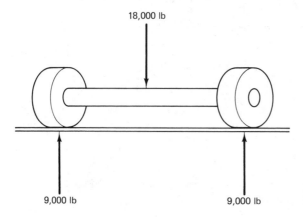

18,000 lb

9,000 lb   9,000 lb

Figure 10-8 Example—18-kip axle load.

TABLE 10-1 AXLE LOAD DISTRIBUTION

Axle load (kips)	Number of axles per day	Equivalence factors	E18s
Single axles			
4	5		
8	10		
10	7		
12	16		
18	7		
20	10		
24	5		
26	6		
Tandem axles			
10	5		
14	7		
16	8		
22	5		
28	4		
36	3		

pavements have equivalent daily E18s in the range of 2 to 6. The total number of E18s for the design life, *D.L.,* period of 20 years can now be calculated:

$$D.L. \ (20) = 85.32 \times 365 \times 20 = 622{,}834 \text{ E18s}$$

The strength of the rigid pavement's material (concrete) must also be considered. The AASHO Road test references the concrete's strength in terms of the concrete's modulus of rupture, *MR*. This value, *MR,* for the concrete is determined by making a $6'' \times 6'' \times 40''$ concrete beam and breaking the beam in flexure. Care must be

TABLE 10-2 AASHO EQUIVALENCE FACTORS (RIGID PAVEMENT)

Axle load (kips)	D—Slab thickness (in.)					
	6	7	8	9	10	11
2	0.0002	0.0002	0.0002	0.0002	0.0002	0.0002
4	0.002	0.002	0.002	0.002	0.002	0.002
6	0.01	0.01	0.01	0.01	0.01	0.01
8	0.03	0.03	0.03	0.03	0.03	0.03
10	0.09	0.08	0.08	0.08	0.08	0.08
12	0.19	0.18	0.18	0.18	0.17	0.17
14	0.35	0.35	0.34	0.34	0.34	0.34
16	0.61	0.61	0.60	0.60	0.60	0.60
18	1.00	1.00	1.00	1.00	1.00	1.00
20	1.55	1.56	1.57	1.58	1.58	1.59
22	2.32	2.32	2.35	2.38	2.40	2.41
24	3.37	3.34	3.40	3.47	3.51	3.53
26	4.76	4.69	4.77	4.88	4.97	5.02
28	6.59	6.44	6.52	6.70	6.85	6.94
30	8.92	8.68	8.74	8.98	9.23	9.39
32	11.87	11.49	11.51	11.82	12.17	12.44
34	15.55	15.00	14.95	15.30	15.78	16.18
36	20.07	19.30	19.16	19.53	20.14	20.71
38	25.56	34.54	24.26	24.63	25.36	26.14
40	32.18	30.85	30.41	30.75	31.58	32.57

Single axles ($p_t = 2.0$)

Axle load (kips)	D—Slab thickness (in.)					
	6	7	8	9	10	11
10	0.01	0.01	0.01	0.01	0.01	0.01
12	0.03	0.03	0.03	0.03	0.03	0.03
14	0.05	0.05	0.05	0.05	0.05	0.05
16	0.09	0.08	0.08	0.08	0.08	0.08
18	0.14	0.14	0.13	0.13	0.13	0.13
20	0.22	0.21	0.21	0.20	0.20	0.20
22	0.32	0.31	0.31	0.30	0.30	0.30
24	0.45	0.45	0.44	0.44	0.44	0.44
26	0.63	0.64	0.62	0.62	0.62	0.62
28	0.85	0.85	0.85	0.85	0.85	0.85
30	1.13	1.13	1.14	1.14	1.14	1.14
32	1.48	1.45	1.49	1.50	1.51	1.51
34	1.91	1.90	1.93	1.95	1.96	1.97
36	2.42	2.41	2.45	2.49	2.51	2.52
38	3.04	3.02	3.07	3.13	3.17	3.19
40	3.79	3.74	3.80	3.89	3.95	3.98
42	4.67	4.59	4.66	4.78	4.87	4.93
44	5.72	5.59	5.67	5.82	5.95	6.03
46	6.94	6.76	6.83	7.02	7.20	7.31
48	8.36	8.12	8.17	8.40	8.63	8.79

(b) Tandem axles ($p_t = 2.0$)

Source: Transportation Research Board Special Report #61, © 1960. Used with permission of Transportation Research Board, Wash., D.C.

TABLE 10-3 E18s RIGID

Axle load (kips)	Number of axles per day	Equivalence (p_t = 2.0) Factors (D = 6 in.)	Rigid E18s
Single axles			
4	5	0.002	0.01
8	10	0.03	0.30
10	7	0.09	0.63
12	16	0.19	3.04
18	7	1.00	7.00
20	10	1.55	15.55
24	5	3.37	16.85
26	6	4.76	28.56
Tandem axles			71.94
10	5	0.01	0.05
14	7	0.05	0.35
16	8	0.09	0.72
22	5	0.32	1.60
28	4	0.85	3.40
36	3	2.42	7.26
			13.38
			85.32

exercised in regard to which flexural test is being used—cantilever, center-point, or third-point. See Fig. 10-9. The third-point flexural test will result in the most conservative results. The break information will be used to determine the *working stress, f_t,* of the concrete by the following equation:

$$f_t = 0.75 \, MR$$

This equation has been adjusted in recent years to reflect a more conservative use design for rigid pavements. The adjusted equation is

$$f_t = 0.50 \, MR$$

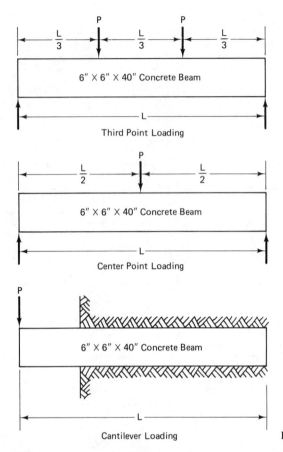

Third Point Loading

Center Point Loading

Cantilever Loading

Figure 10-9 Types of beam breaks.

The original equation will be used in this text since our prime concern will be for residential pavement with a low number of tandem axles.

Now, knowing the soil's k value, estimated E18s per day or E18s for 20 years, and the MR for the concrete, the pavement thickness for the rigid pavement can now be determined. The AASHO Road test developed design nomographs to help in this design procedure. See Fig. 10-10. For example, given the following values:

$$
\begin{aligned}
p_t &= 2.0 \\
\frac{E18s}{20 \text{ years}} &= 9,000,000 \\
MR &= 653 \\
k &= 100
\end{aligned}
$$

Then the pavement's thickness would be 9.6 inches. A 10-inch section would be designed in most cases.

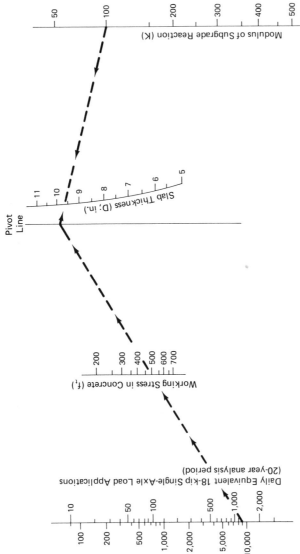

Figure 10-10 Design chart for rigid pavements (p_t = 2.0). (From Transportation Research Board Special Report #61, © 1960. Used with permission of Transportation Research Board, Wash., D.C.)

TABLE 10-4 AASHO EQUIVALENCE FACTORS (FLEXIBLE PAVEMENT)

Axle load (kips)	Structural number (SN)					
	1	2	3	4	5	6
2	0.0002	0.0002	0.0002	0.0002	0.0002	0.0002
4	0.002	0.003	0.002	0.002	0.002	0.002
6	0.01	0.01	0.01	0.01	0.01	0.01
8	0.03	0.04	0.04	0.03	0.03	0.03
10	0.08	0.08	0.09	0.08	0.08	0.08
12	0.16	0.18	0.19	0.18	0.17	0.17
14	0.32	0.34	0.35	0.35	0.34	0.33
16	0.59	0.60	0.61	0.61	0.60	0.60
18	1.00	1.00	1.00	1.00	1.00	1.00
20	1.61	1.59	1.56	1.55	1.57	1.60
22	2.49	2.44	2.35	2.31	2.35	2.41
24	3.71	3.62	3.43	3.33	3.40	3.51
26	5.36	5.21	4.88	4.68	4.77	4.96
28	7.54	7.31	6.78	6.42	6.52	6.83
30	10.38	10.03	9.24	8.65	8.73	9.17
32	14.00	13.51	12.37	11.46	11.48	12.17
34	18.55	17.87	16.30	14.97	14.87	15.63
36	24.20	23.30	21.16	19.28	19.02	19.93
38	31.14	29.95	27.12	24.55	24.03	25.10
40	39.57	38.02	34.34	30.92	30.04	31.25

Single axles ($p_t = 2.0$)

Axle load (kips)	Structural number (SN)					
	1	2	3	4	5	6
10	0.01	0.01	0.01	0.01	0.01	0.01
12	0.01	0.02	0.02	0.01	0.01	0.01
14	0.02	0.03	0.03	0.03	0.02	0.02
16	0.04	0.05	0.05	0.05	0.04	0.04
18	0.07	0.08	0.08	0.08	0.07	0.07
20	0.10	0.12	0.12	0.12	0.11	0.10
22	0.16	0.17	0.18	0.17	0.16	0.16
24	0.23	0.24	0.26	0.25	0.24	0.23
26	0.32	0.34	0.36	0.35	0.34	0.33
28	0.45	0.46	0.49	0.48	0.47	0.46
30	0.61	0.62	0.65	0.64	0.63	0.62
32	0.81	0.82	0.84	0.84	0.83	0.82
34	1.06	1.07	1.08	1.08	1.08	1.07
36	1.38	1.38	1.38	1.38	1.38	1.38
38	1.76	1.75	1.73	1.72	1.73	1.74
40	2.22	2.19	2.15	2.13	2.16	2.18
42	2.77	2.73	2.64	2.62	2.66	2.70
44	3.42	3.36	3.23	3.18	3.24	3.31
46	4.20	4.11	3.92	3.83	3.91	4.02
48	5.10	4.98	4.72	4.58	4.68	4.83

(b) Tandem axles ($p_t = 2.0$)

Source: Transportation Research Board Special Report #61, © 1960. Used with permission of Transportation Research Board, Wash., D.C.

Flexible Pavement Thickness Design

There are many similarities in the thickness design of a flexible pavement when based on the AASHTO method. These similarities are soil support information, traffic (E18s), and serviceability, p_t. In addition to this information, materials considerations are required and a *regional factor,* R, is incorporated into the design.

The soil's support value will be SSV and has been previously discussed in the rigid pavement's design. A correlation between *SSV, k, GI,* and *CBR* is shown in Fig. 10-7.

The amount of traffic is determined as in the rigid design example. However, *different* equivalence E18 tables will be used. See Table 10-4. Different tables are required because single and tandem axle loads affect rigid and flexible pavements differently in regard to their serviceability. Consider the values as shown in Table 10-1. Using Table 10-4, determine the total design E18s for the data as listed in Table 10-1. See Table 10-5.

The daily E18s equal 78.55. This is less than the rigid pavement's E18s of 85.32, but the difference in the values should not confuse the reader since they are values that will be used in *different* design equations. The final pavement evaluation will be based on economics and will be discussed in Chapter 11. Table 10-4 also references a term known as the *Structural Number, SN.* This references the material and course thicknesses of the flexible pavement section.

The flexible pavement section can be made up of different material courses with different thicknesses. See Fig. 10-3. Each material in the system has the ability to spread the wheel load out, which reduces the per square inch load on the material course directly under the material course being considered. See Fig. 10-5. This load transfer is referenced as the material's *structural coefficient, a.* For the AASHO Road test, the structural coefficients for the different materials are shown in Table 10-6. These values are referenced as a_1, or a_2, or a_3 and represent the surface, base, and subbase courses respectively. They are incorporated into an equation for determining the adequacy of the flexible section for carrying traffic. This equation is expressed by

$$SN = a_1 D1 + a_2 D2 + a_3 D3$$

where,

SN	= structural number
a_1, a_2, a_3	= the respective structural coefficients
D1	= thickness of the surface course (in.)
D2	= thickness of the base course (in.)
D3	= thickness of the subbase (in.)

This equation is very useful for comparing the structural adequacy of one flexible pavement section with another.

The *Regional Factor, R,* references the estimated quality of materials, construction capability, and climate in regard to the AASHO Road test. Governmental agencies have set *R,* for their political subdivisions, and the value has ranged from 0.5 to 5.0.

TABLE 10-5 E18s FLEXIBLE (TT)

Axle Load (kips)	Number of axles per day	Equivalence factors	Flexible E18s
Single axles			
4	5	0.002	0.01
8	10	0.03	0.3
10	7	0.08	0.56
12	16	0.18	2.88
18	7	1.00	7.00
20	10	1.55	15.50
24	5	3.33	16.65
26	6	4.68	28.08
Tandem axles			70.98
10	5	0.01	0.05
14	7	0.03	0.21
16	8	0.05	0.40
22	5	0.17	0.85
28	4	0.48	1.92
36	3	1.38	4.14
			7.57
			78.55

Now consider these following conditions:

$$p_t \qquad\qquad = 2.0$$
$$SSV \qquad\qquad = 3.0$$
$$\text{E18s (20 yr.)} = 7,500,000$$
$$R \qquad\qquad\;\; = 1.5$$

See Fig. 10-11. This figure is a nomograph for flexible pavement design. Using the values previously stated, the final, weighted SN will equal 5.2. Weighted values are used and noted since a large number of flexible sections, on the AASHO Road Test, went out of service during the first spring thaw.

TABLE 10-6 STRUCTURAL COEFFICIENTS

Pavement components	Other requirements	Coefficients		
		a_1	a_2*	a_3
Surface course				
Road mix (low stability)	Marshall stability 500–1000	0.20	—	—
Plant mix (high stability)	Marshall stability 2000	0.44†	—	—
Sand asphalt	Marshall stability 1000–1200	0.40	—	—
Base Course				
Sand gravel	CBR 20–30	—	0.07*	—
Crushed stone	CBR 105–110	—	0.14*	—
Water bound macadam		—	0.15–0.20	—
Lime treated	CBR	—	0.15–0.30	—
Sand asphalt	Marshall stability	—	0.30	—
Bituminous treated				
(coarse-gravel)	Marshall stability	—	0.34*	—
Cement treated	650 psi 7-day compressive strength	—	0.23*	—
	Less than 400 psi 7-day	—	0.15	—
	400–650 psi 7-day	—	0.20	—
Old bituminous conc. surface	Undisturbed	—	0.24	—
Old bituminous conc. surface	Scarified and mixed with old base	—	0.14	—
Portland cement conc. surface				
Old		—	0.40	—
New		—	0.50	—
Subbase				
Sandy gravel	CBR 20–30	—	—	0.11†
Sandy or sandy-clay		—	—	0.05–0.10

*Also a'_1 for resurfaced pavement.

†Based on AASHO Road test data.

Source: Transportation Research Board Special Report #61, © 1960. Used with permission of Transportation Research Board, Wash., D.C.

This SN = 5.2 references a pavement section where $a_1D1 + a_2D2 + a_3D3$ equals 5.2. Such a section, using the AASHTO values for a_1, a_2, and a_3 could be

$$
\begin{aligned}
\text{Surface} \quad & a_1D1 = 0.44 \times 5'' = 2.20 \\
\text{Base} \quad & a_2D2 = 0.14 \times 15'' = 2.10 \\
\text{Subbase} \quad & a_3D3 = 0.11 \times 8'' = \underline{0.88} \\
& SN = \overline{5.18}
\end{aligned}
$$

The 5.18 would be considered adequate for the 5.20 requirement. If material substitutions for surface, base, or subbase are considered, the final SN must be equal to the required 5.20.

As discussed earlier in this chapter, there are many methods being used for the design of pavement sections. Each governmental agency has some written policy or referenced procedure that it requires all land planners and subdividers to follow. If

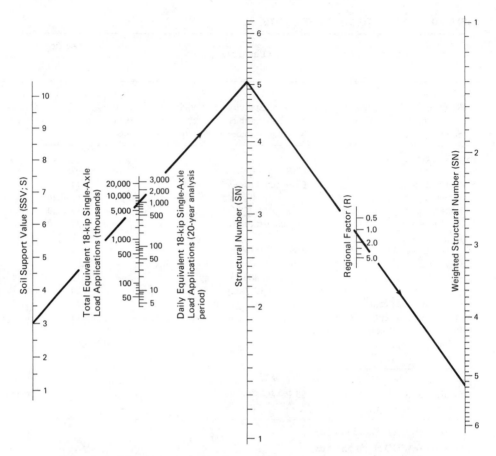

Figure 10–11 Design chart for flexible pavements (p_t = 2.0). (From Transportation Research Special Report #61, © 1960. Used with permission of Transportation Research Board, Wash., D.C.)

a political subdivision does not have a policy, the AASHTO method is highly recommended.

CONSTRUCTION TECHNIQUES

Either type of pavement section, rigid or flexible, requires the existing ground to be excavated for drainage and proper subgrade profile. It is very important to install the stormwater drainage system as soon as possible during the initial construction stages. This installation will lower the ground water elevation and allow for easier and quicker road construction. The stormwater structures, which include inlets, catch basins, and manholes, are not built to their final grade until after the pavement structure is completed. These structures are *boxed out* for final pavement grade adjustment.

Once the subgrade elevation has been established, usually with the use of a road grader, the curb sections are slipped formed for the flexible pavement. The preferred curb section for residential pavements is the *mountable curb*. See Fig. 10-12. This curb section eliminates the need for curb cuts or curb drops. At intersections the barrier straight 6-inch curb section should be used. The mountable curb is transitioned into the straight 6-inch curb over a distance of 10 feet, which usually starts at the beginning of the radius point for the intersection. See Fig. 10-13. The base and surface courses are then placed after the curbs have been slipped or conventionally constructed. Each pavement course requires the proper compaction to achieve the required specified density.

For the rigid pavement section, the pavement could be either full-width or half-width slip formed. It could also be built using forms along each edge. The specific method is usually a decision by the paving contractor. The mountable curb, in this case, is an integral part of the pavement's section. The concrete pavement, for residential use, will contain *no* reinforcement. The pavement's shrinkage will be controlled by placing (sawing) control joints, with a depth of one quarter of the slab's thickness, approximately every 17 feet. (Actual contraction joint placement is a function of the supporting soil and the type of concrete aggregate being used.) For pavements 25 feet wide, a longitudinal joint will also be required. This joint will be on the center line of the pavement. See Fig. 10-14.

Once the subgrade has been properly prepared, the specified concrete mix is placed directly on the subgrade to the required thickness. Following the proper place-

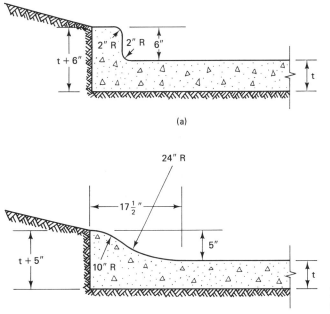

Figure 10-12 Curb sections (a) straight 6-inch curb section, (b) mountable curb section.

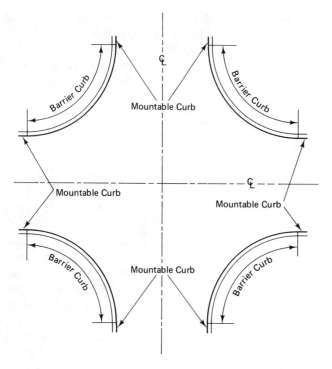

Figure 10-13 Transition curb detail.

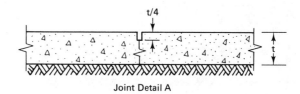

Joint Detail A

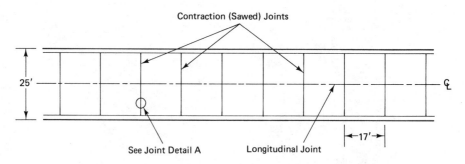

Figure 10-14 Contraction joint details.

ment of the concrete, the concrete should be cured using a chemical or mechanical method of curing to lock in the necessary moisture to assure adequate hydration of the portland cement. The concrete contraction joints should be sawed, as soon as possible, to relieve any shrinkage stresses in the slab. Traffic should not be allowed on the pavement until approximately 5 to 7 days after the placement. This initial traffic loading is a function of slab strength and this strength can be accelerated by changes in the concrete mixture.

With either pavement system, the final requirement is proper earth grading to the top of the curb section. The street serves two purposes in a subdivision: (1) traffic flow and (2) stormwater drainage.

PROBLEMS

10-1. Define the following terms:
   (a) AASHO
   (b) AASHTO
   (c) test roads
   (d) Bates Experimental road
   (e) AASHO Test road

10-2. What is meant by flexible and rigid pavement types?

10-3. Name three basic information inputs required for good pavement design.

10-4. Define the following terms:
   (a) Westergaard's Modulus of Subgrade Reaction, k
   (b) soil support value, SSV
   (c) group index, GI
   (d) California Bearing Ratio, CBR

10-5. What is meant by: E18, design life, and equivalent E18s?

10-6. Explain the calculation of the structural number, $SN,$ as used in flexible pavement design.

10-7. Describe the three types of portland cement concrete beam breaks.

10-8. What is meant by the term *mountable curb*?

10-9. Design both a rigid and flexible pavement section using the following information and the nomographs as provided in Figs. 10-10 and 10-11. The flexible pavement should be a three-layer system consisting of asphalt surface (a_1), stone base (a_2), and a granular subbase (a_3).
   $k = 100$ pci
   $D.L.$ (design life) $= 20$ years
   E18s/day $= 10$
   $MR = 700$ psi
   $a_1 = 0.40$ (4″ maximum)
   $a_2 = 0.14$
   $a_3 = 0.11$ (6″ maximum)

10-10. Design both a rigid and flexible pavement section using the following information and the nomographs as provided in Figs. 10-10 and 10-11. The flexbile pavement should be a three-layer system consisting of asphalt surface (a_1), stone base (a_2), and a granular subbase (a_3).

$CBR = 4$

$D.L.$ (design life) $= 20$ years

E18s/day $= 100$

$MR = 600$ psi

$a_1 = 0.35$

$a_2 = 0.15$

$a_3 = 0.09$

Chapter 11

Economics—
Project Cost
Feasibility

INTRODUCTION

A project cost feasibility study should be conducted on all proposed land development and construction projects. This type of study will encompass all expenditures—land and construction costs, engineering and legal fees. Developers have used so called *cost feasibility studies* in many forms. Some were nothing more than a wild guess as to the projects' costs based on the size of the parcel of land being considered. At the heart of the study is the acquisition of good reliable information and the use of this information in a logical manner to arrive at some conclusions. This chapter will deal with the need for and methods of conducting such studies. It will also include actual examples of different cost feasibility studies. The reader is referred to other texts with questions as to marketing and business strategies.

NEED FOR COST FEASIBILITY STUDIES

With the many rapid changes in technology and the high interest rates for borrowed money, cost feasibility studies for every type of development or construction project, or both, become imperative. It is through the use of thorough cost feasibility studies that the final "go ahead" should be given. Projects have been started without a cost feasibility study and these projects have resulted in a profit for the developer. However, projects that lose money are usually the result of a lack of a feasibility study or an incomplete study. A thorough cost feasibility study should resolve the question of going ahead with the project. This study will also serve in the development of the project's construction budget if the project is constructed.

New technology creates changes in how one does things. Political subdivisions are finding it more and more difficult to stay current with changes in technology. During the planning of a subdivision, a developer may discover a new construction process or material that could result in less expense while resulting in an improved product. The political subdivision, in which the property is located, may not be aware of these new technical developments. In this case, the developer will have to propose these changes to the political subdivision authorities. A cost feasibility study will be required to achieve successful results.

The reverse is also true. The political subdivision may have experienced poor results with a product or construction method and have changed their standards to reflect this change. The expense of these changes will be revealed in a thorough cost study.

The study is also needed to maximize the economical use of a land parcel. If the development costs are too high, maybe a different planning scheme (more lots) could result in a more profitable use by the developer. Another approach is to study the cost feasibility of enlarging the required lot sizes and thereby requiring larger houses to be built. The development has now been changed and is being aimed at a different type of clientele. In all caes, the cost study becomes part of a marketing strategy for selling the lots within the subdivision. The study provides the cost information needed for the establishment of the cost of the individual lots.

When considering the purchase of a parcel of land for a subdivision development, the final "go ahead" decision will rest on *all costs* for the project. Many times the property must be rezoned to allow for the proposed land use. In this case, the developer would seek an "option to purchase" based on zoning changes and a cost feasibility study. The project could be shelved because of zoning requirements or poor projected profits, or both.

METHOD FOR COST FEASIBILITY STUDY

Developers and planners have used various methods for making cost feasibility studies. The method prescribed here has been successfully used by engineers, developers, and planners. This method includes all costs that would be incurred in the development and construction of a project. Typically, these costs and their respective measure of payment are

(1) land (acre, A)
(2) pavement (square yard, sq yd)
(3) sidewalks (square yard, sq yd)
(4) storm sewers (lineal feet, l.f.)
(5) sanitary sewers (lineal feet, l.f.)
(6) utilities (lineal feet, l.f.)
(7) engineering design (percent of total costs)

(8) legal fees (flat rate or percent)

(9) finances (percent of money borrowed)

Each one of these items offers a developer the opportunity to reduce development costs through knowledge of construction practices and engineering design procedures.

In a cost feasibility study, each cost item is calculated based on current (local) cost information. This information is then tabulated and totalled to arrive at the final estimated total cost of the development. Before the use of computers, this information was recorded and kept in file form by the designer and developer. The use of computers for this function will be discussed in Chapter 12. Following is a breakdown on the cost for each referenced category.

1. Land.   Land costs are referenced in dollars per acres. ($/A). This fact highlights the need for a property boundary survey to establish the number of acres within a parcel. The land should be purchased based on the actual number of acres in the field—not as written on a deed. The land costs will vary depending on location. Real estate agencies keep telling developers: "When purchasing land for development, always remember three simple rules: location, location, and location."

2. Pavement.   Street costs can be expressed in dollars per square yard ($/sq yd) or dollars per lineal foot ($/l.f.). In the example section of this chapter the conversion from lineal feet to square yard costs will be reviewed. Pavement cost can be considerable and the planner must seek ways to minimize the amount of pavement required. The planner must also consider all the alternative ways, flexible or rigid, to build a quality pavement. Many political subdivisions have not kept current with technical changes in regard to either pavement design or construction, or both.

3. Sidewalks.   The cost for sidewalks is expressed in dollars per square yard. Subdivision regulations should be reviewed as to the requirements for sidewalks. Some regulations require sidewalks for specific lot widths. Therefore, a developer might be able to eliminate sidewalk costs by designing lot sizes that would not require sidewalks.

4. Storm Sewers.   Storm sewer costs are expressed dollars per lineal foot of pipe and can include the cost of drainage structures. It also includes the cost of the excavation, the pipe, backfilling, seeding, and so on. A reduction in costs will result in the use of less pipe, smaller diameter pipe, shallower trenches, and a reduction in the number of drainage structures. The contractor should also consider construction practices that will help reduce construction costs.

5. Sanitary Sewers.   Sanitary sewer costs are expressed the same as storm sewer costs, dollars per lineal foot. Their costs can be reduced, as with storm sewers, by using less pipe, smaller diameter pipe, shallower trenches, and reducing the number of structures. Some developments will require that a sewer line be extended. The extension cost is sometimes shared by the adjacent property owners or future land developers for the adjacent land. Sanitary sewer costs for a project can be as high as one third of the total cost of the development.

6. Utilities (gas, electric, water).   The cost of extending these facilities into a subdivision will certainly vary depending on the location of the land and the utility company that has jurisdiction for that location. Cost can be expressed as dollars per foot ($/ft) or lump sum.

7. Engineering Fees.   The design engineer usually charges a fee based on a percentage of the project's construction cost. The engineer can also be hired on an hourly or project basis. Experienced development engineers can help reduce design and construction costs through their technical knowledge.

8. Legal Fees.   The legal fees for a project will vary based on the required services. This figure can be estimated as a percentage of the project's cost or as a lump sum per project.

9. Finances.   Finance charges will be based on a percentage of the money borrowed over a certain period of time for the project's development. Different banking institutions charge different interest rates. This is an item that should be thoroughly investigated before agreeing to borrow from a banking institution.

If the estimated total cost was more than planned for in the project's initial concept, alternatives to the original plan should be studied. These alternatives could include breaking the development into smaller parcels, different street patterns, reduced sewer line lengths, different pavement section, acquiring venture capital. If after restudying *all* possible cost reduction methods the project is still too costly, then the project should be dropped. The cost feasibility study is the tool that is used to acquire this information.

Examples of Cost Feasibility Studies

A cost feasibility study can be done for a proposed land development project or a proposed construction material alternative. Two examples will be referenced: (1) a land development project study, and (2) a pavement section study.

1. Land Development Study
For this example, see the given values as shown in Table 11-1. These values were obtained *after* the preliminary planning and preliminary design stages of the project were completed. The average cost per lot is $9,098.71. The project, before any profits can be considered, must yield $9,098.71 per lot. The final decision to proceed with the project will be based on the marketing capability to *sell* the lots for this amount or to include this amount into the cost of houses that will be built on these lots.

2. Pavement Section Study
Alternative pavement sections can result in a savings to the developer. However, the political subdivision must approve any alternatives to their design standards. The following is an example of how to perform an alternative pavement cost feasibility study. Consider the flexible and rigid pavement sections as shown in Fig. 11-1. The lineal feet of curb, in each case, is 2 feet per lineal foot of pavement. (One foot of curb on each side of the street.) The square yardage of pavement is different because the flexible section uses a curb and gutter section thus reducing the amount of paving material between

TABLE 11-1 PROJECT COST BREAKDOWN

Item	Quantity	Unit cost ($)	Cost ($)	Project cost (%)
Land	30.52 A	3,750/A	114,450.00	22.46
Pavement	5,100 sq yd	12.52/sq yd	63,852.00	12.53
Sidewalks	2,100 sq yd	9.00/sq yd	18,900.00	3.71
Storm sewers* (includes all structures)	2,343 ft	27.52/ft	64,479.36	12.66
Sanitary sewers* (includes all structures)	3,873 ft	45.43/ft	175,950.39	34.53
Utilities				
Water	3,873 ft	8.75/ft	33,888.75	6.65
Electric	—	—	—	—
Gas	—	—	—	—
Engineer's fee	Construction cost	10%	35,707.05	7.01
Legal fees	Per project	2,300.00	2,300.00	0.45
			509,527.55	100.00

Number of lots = 56 $\dfrac{\text{Cost}}{\text{Lot}} = 9{,}098.71$

*Actual sewer costs would be broken down by pipe sizes and activities such as excavation, laying of pipe, and so on. Unit costs reflected here are average costs per length of pipe.

the curbs. The square yards of required pavement per lineal foot of pavement are 2.78 and 2.34 for the rigid and flexible sections respectively. The 2.78 sq yd is calculated by

$$\text{No. sq yd} = \frac{25\text{-ft wide} \times 1 \text{ ft in length}}{9 \text{ sq ft/sq yd}}$$

For cost comparisons the pavement sections as shown in Table 11-2 will be considered. Note that all flexible sections have approximately the same SN value of 3.60. The material costs will be as referenced in Table 11-3. These are example costs only and do not reflect current or actual cost information.

The cost for two pavement sections will be studied. These two sections will be the rigid section and the case I flexible section. These cost studies are as follows:

Rigid

6 in. concrete	2.78 × $9.00	= $25.02
Curb	2 × $1.25	= 2.50
	Cost/l.f.	= $27.52
	Cost/sq yd	= $ 9.90

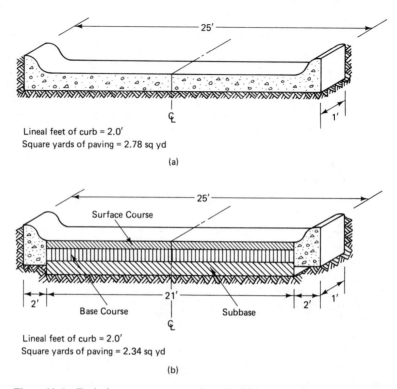

Figure 11-1 Typical pavement cross sections (a) rigid section, (b) flexible section.

TABLE 11-2 EQUIVALENT PAVEMENT SECTIONS

Pavement type	Thickness (in.)	SN
Rigid, plain concrete	6	(Equivalence to $0.60 \times 6 = 3.60$)
Flexible case I		
Asphaltic concrete	3	$3'' \times 0.44^* = 1.32$
Stone base	12	$12'' \times 0.14 = 1.68$
Subbase	6	$6'' \times 0.11 = \underline{0.66}$
Thickness =	21	$SN = 3.16$
Flexible case II		
Asphaltic concrete	3½	$3\frac{1}{2}'' \times 0.44 = 1.54$
Waterproof base	5	$5'' \times 0.30 = 1.50$
Stone base	5	$5'' \times 0.14 = \underline{0.70}$
Thickness =	13½	$SN = 3.78$
Flexible case III		
Asphaltic concrete	4	$4'' \times 0.44 = 1.76$
Waterproof base	4½	$4\frac{1}{2}'' \times 0.30 = 1.35$
Subbase	6	$6'' \times 0.11 = \underline{0.66}$
Thickness =	14½	$SN = 3.77$

*AASHO Road test coefficients.

TABLE 11-3 MATERIAL COSTS FOR PAVEMENT

Item	Method of payment	Cost/unit ($)
Plain concrete pavement (6 in.)	sq yd	9.00
Integral curb	l.f.	1.25
Asphaltic concrete	cu yd	30.00
Stone base	cu yd	10.00
Waterproof base	cu yd	22.00
Subbase	cu yd	7.00
Combination curb and gutter (2.0 ft)	l.f.	4.60
Excavation (addition)	cu yd	1.50

Case I—flexible

3 in. asphalt $\dfrac{3}{36} \times 2.34 \times \$30.00$ = $ 5.84

12 in. base $\dfrac{12}{36} \times 2.34 \times \$10.00$ =   7.77

6 in. subbase $\dfrac{6}{36} \times 2.34 \times \$7.00$ =   2.73

Curb $2 \times \$4.60$ =   9.20

15 in. additional

excavation:

$\dfrac{15}{36} \times 2.34 \times \$1.50$ =   1.46

Cost/l.f.   = \$27.00

Cost/sq yd   = $ 9.71

These calculations show that the rigid section costs \$27.52/l.f. or \$9.90/sq yd. The flexible section costs \$27.00/l.f. or \$9.71/sq yd. At first glance one might consider the flexible section a better buy. To determine the best buy, loads (E18s) must be considered with the construction costs. For the flexible section's estimated total E18s (20 years), see Fig. 10–11. Using this figure and the data, $R = 1.5$, $SSV = 3.0$, $SN = 3.60$, $p_t = 2.0$, the number of E18s that will be carried by this pavement section totals 80,000. In the case of the rigid section ($ft = 525$, $p_t = 2.0$, $k = 117$) in Fig. 10–10, the E18s for 20 years is also 80,000. Now, to compare the pavement sections, compare the number of E18s that can be carried for each dollar spent for the life of the project. If the pavement is 1 mile long, the total pavement cost would be $145,305.60 for the rigid section and $142,560.00 for the flexible section. The loads per dollars spent (L/D) would be equal to

$$\text{Rigid } L/D \quad = \frac{80,000}{\$145,305.60} = 0.55$$

$$\text{Flexible } L/D = \frac{80,000}{\$142,560.00} = 0.56$$

The flexible section is more economical. In this case it just happened that the E18s came out equal. This was because the concrete surface has an estimated (a_1) of 0.60, thus making the pavement section very similar. This concept of L/D has proven very effective when considering multiple pavement sections and this concept will be discussed further in Chapter 12, *Computer Applications.*

REVIEW

The use of a cost feasibility study is vital to the development of a project. If, for example, the project as referenced in Table 11-1 was considered feasible, the values calculated would now become part of the construction budget and project cost-control records. These estimated values would be analyzed for future projects for cost overruns, alternative construction methods, contractor and subcontractor performance, engineering accuracy, and actual project profits.

PROBLEMS

11-1. What is meant by *cost feasibility?*

11-2. List the components that should be included in a cost feasibility study for a proposed property development.

11-3. For the pavement costs for rigid and flexible pavements, as provided in Table 11-3, calculate the estimated pavement costs for Prob. 10-9. (Each pavement section has a curb section as shown in Fig. 11-1.)

11-4. For the pavement costs for rigid and flexible pavements, as provided in Table 11-3, calculate the estimated pavement costs for Prob. 10-10. (Each pavement section has a curb section as shown in Fig. 11-1.)

11-5. For the following information, calculate the estimated cost per lot. See Table 11-1.

Land	52 acres @ $4250/A
Pavement	8840 sq yd @ $11.52/sq yd
Sidewalks	3640 sq yd @ $8.50/sq yd
Storm sewers	4061 @ $32.00/ft
Sanitary sewers	6731 @ $47.81/ft
Utilities—water	6731 @ $7.52/ft
Engineer's fee	9.5% of the construction cost
Legal fees	$4000 for entire project

Chapter 12

Computer Applications

INTRODUCTION

The use of calculating equipment in regard to land planning has changed rapidly in the last twenty years. Prior to 1970, land planning calculations were made using an adding machine or a mechanical calculator, and logarithm and trigonometric tables. Calculations required a considerable amount of time because of the great number of steps required—looking up trigonometric functions for angles, looking up logarithms, and finally using a mechanical calculator. These varied operations also encouraged errors in calculations and in recording the results of the calculations.

In 1970, hand-held calculators were introduced into the market. These early models sold for approximately $400.00. Similar models today sell for around $25.00. These small calculators reduced calculating time and helped eliminate errors. Their use also allowed for the calculating of more complex expressions. Previous calculating methods would have been too time consuming to attempt.

In 1980, the microcomputer became more available to businesses, schools, and the general public. If the hand-held calculator was a major breakthrough for the calculating of land planning requirements, then the microcomputer could be considered as a major breakthrough over the use of the hand-held calculator. The development of the hand-held calculator and the microcomputer has changed not only the way one computes land planning calculations but also one's approach to all problems, both complex and simple.

This chapter will introduce several different possible uses for the microcomputer in regard to land planning. This chapter is not intended to teach the use of a microcomputer but to demonstrate the advantages of a microcomputer for calculations discussed in previous chapters.

HARDWARE AVAILABILITY

Computer *hardware* includes the semiconductor-integrated circuits. Think of hardware as things actually seen. It includes the video, keyboard, printer, disk drives, plotters, and so on. There are many hardware manufacturers; selection will depend on personal preference and needs. Today there is hardware available in almost every price range. Hardware used for the programs referenced in this chapter is an Apple IIe.

If microcomputer hardware is not available for land planning use, then the hand-held calculator could be used. Without the hand-held calculator, then it's back to the logarithm tables. The advantages of the microcomputer are: accuracy, speed, and the opportunity to take on more complex decision-making problems.

SOFTWARE

The *software* is program information that is placed into the computer. Software must be compatible to the hardware that will be used. For land planning calculations, there are a number of software programs that will handle the majority of the required calculations. The software is advertised as being compatible with the type of hardware needed to run the program. To use any of these purchased software programs still requires study on the part of the user. The majority of software programs include written reference material as to their use and applications.

Rapid advances have also been made in computer graphics with the use of a microcomputer. While this graphic equipment is not necessary for the study of land planning techniques, it is becoming very popular with engineering and surveying firms. A brief description and review of this equipment should help the reader understand this application of the microcomputer.

There are now several CAD (computer-aided drafting) software packages that will run on MS-DOS compatible personal computer (PC) hardware. These CAD software packages bring the benefits of extremely expensive mainframe based computer-aided design systems to even the smallest engineering or construction offices. One of the leading PC-CAD software packages is produced by Autodesk Inc. and is called AutoCAD. AutoCAD is a computer-aided drafting and design system that runs on most significant business microcomputers. Most often the software is used with an enhanced IBM-AT computer. The general-purpose AutoCAD system is used world wide by engineers and designers of every discipline—architects, land planners, developers—to produce virtually every type of drawing—mechanical, architectural, topographical maps, and site plans.

AutoCAD is actually a complete, professional CAD system with mini and main-frame system features. Their use requires no prior computer knowledge and the program is easy to tailor to user-specified requirements. Screen and tablet menus are available for a host of uses.

One extremely valuable feature of AutoCAD for site planners, land developers, and real estate personnel is the variables and expressions capability. This allows the user to set variables, perform mathematics and trigonometric functions, and create macro programs that can be used to tailor the system for a specific application or the users' needs. For example, AutoCAD can be programmed to handle horizontal and vertical curves, drainage calculations, pavement design, and so on. AutoCAD handles drawings the way a word processor would handle text. Drawings of any size can be created and edited interactively. The information can be stored on a floppy or hard disk. Drawings can then be plotted to any scale. In this chapter, the microcomputer will be discussed in regard to applicational uses of software for land planning computations.

Creating tailor-made programs can be very time consuming and expensive. However, the application of computer programming techniques to specific application needs can yield rewarding results in terms of long-range time savings, accuracy of work, and improved design results. Included in Appendices A through C are several specially created computer programs that will be reviewed in regard to land planning applications and needs. Their application and results should be studied to indicate what microcomputers are capable of doing for the land planner. These programs are written in Applesoft BASIC and can be run on most Apple IIc or Apple IIe computers. (A disk containing these programs can be ordered from the authors.) These programs have been written for the individual with limited microcomputer knowledge and are designed to help the reader understand basic computer applications.

TYPES OF COMPUTER SOFTWARE METHODS

There are three types of computer software methods that will be used in this chapter as related to land planning. These three software methods are: (1) data systems, (2) spreadsheets, and (3) programs. The first two methods are computer-application methods that can be purchased as a software package and are referred to by such names as Wordstar, Appleworks, Jazz, Lotus 1-2-3, and Jeeves. Naturally, the software purchased would have to be compatible with the hardware that was to be used. Some programs also include word processing as part of the system.

Data systems allow the user to assemble information (data) in a number of ways for comparing, organizing, and sorting. Table 12–1 shows horizontal curve informa-

TABLE 12–1 DATA SYSTEMS SHEET

Curve number	Sta. *PI*	*I* and Θ	*T*	*R*	*S*	*LC*	Sta. *PC*	Sta. *PT*
1	10 + 24.16	16.32917	128.05	892.52	254.36	896.11	8 + 96.11	11 + 50.47
2	9 + 58.93	12.98765	200.67	1762.96	399.62	398.77	7 + 58.26	11 + 57.88
3	15 + 00.67	32.78910	325.78	1107.30	633.68	625.07	11 + 74.89	18 + 08.57
4	17 + 09.09	5.55556	751.52	15489.15	1501.86	1501.27	9 + 57.57	24 + 59.43
5	7 + 81.93	21.90876	55.98	289.22	110.59	109.92	7 + 25.95	8 + 36.54
6	21 + 98.65	12.38765	155.55	1433.31	309.89	309.28	20 + 43.10	23 + 52.99
7	50 + 00.00	20.00000	100.00	567.13	197.97	196.96	49 + 00.00	50 + 97.97
8	50 + 00.00	10.00000	100.00	1143.01	199.49	199.24	49 + 00.00	50 + 99.49
9	50 + 00.00	5.00000	100.00	2290.39	199.87	199.81	49 + 00.00	50 + 99.87
10	50 + 00.00	1.00000	100.00	11458.93	199.99	199.99	49 + 00.00	50 + 99.99

	A	B	C	D	E	F	G	H
1								
2								
3								
4								
5								
6								
7								
8								
9								
10								
11								
12								
13								
14								
15								
16								
17								
18								

Figure 12-1 Spreadsheet form.

TABLE 12-2 DATA SYSTEMS SHEET

Curve number	Sta. PI	I and Θ	T	R	S	LC	Sta. PC	Sta. PT
4	17 + 09.09	5.55556	751.52	15489.15	1501.86	1501.27	9 + 57.57	24 + 59.43
10	50 + 00.00	1.00000	100.00	11458.93	199.99	199.99	49 + 00.00	50 + 99.99
9	50 + 00.00	5.00000	100.00	2290.39	199.87	199.81	49 + 00.00	50 + 99.87
2	9 + 58.93	12.98765	200.67	1762.96	399.62	389.77	7 + 58.26	11 + 57.88
6	21 + 98.65	12.38765	155.55	1433.31	309.89	309.28	20 + 43.10	23 + 52.99
8	50 + 00.00	10.00000	100.00	1143.01	199.49	199.24	49 + 00.00	50 + 99.49
3	15 + 00.67	32.78910	325.78	1107.30	633.68	625.07	11 + 74.89	18 + 08.57
1	10 + 24.16	16.32917	128.05	892.52	254.36	896.11	8 + 96.11	11 + 50.47
7	50 + 00.00	20.00000	100.00	567.13	197.97	196.96	49 + 00.00	50 + 97.97
5	7 + 81.93	21.90876	55.98	289.22	110.59	109.92	7 + 25.95	8 + 36.54

tion printed in data form as to curve reference number order. (Lowest curve reference number first.) Table 12-2 shows the same information printed with the longest radius distance listed first. This information can be rearranged very quickly with the use of data system software.

	A	B	C	D	E	F	G	H
1	34.58	56.89		68027.71				
2								
3								
4								
5								
6								
7								
8								
9								
10								
11								
12								
13								
14								
15								
16								
17								
18								

$D1$: (Value) + $(A1^2 * B1)$

Figure 12–2 Spreadsheet example.

Spreadsheets offer the land planner a tool for doing a number of land planning calculations such as horizontal curves, vertical curves, drainage networks, earth (excavation), and calculations. The Appleworks spreadsheet consists of 99 rows and 127 columns as references for cells or blocks within a grid. See Fig. 12–1. These 12,573 blocks within the grid can contain labels, values, or equations relating to information stored in other blocks.

In Fig. 12–2, the value in the block referenced as $D1$ is the value of block $A1$ squared and multiplied by the value in block $B1$. Note that the contents of block $D1$ state that it is equal to $(A1^2) * B1$. This means that for each value change in the blocks $A1$ or $B1$, the value of $D1$ will also change. Spreadsheets are a very powerful tool for any designer. Specific examples will be shown later in regard to the use of spreadsheets and horizontal and vertical curves.

Specialized computer programs can be written to tailor a program to meet specific needs. There are a number of good software writing books available and most schools now offer computer classes in either their curriculum or their continuing-education programs, or both. Program writing consists of understanding the requirements for communicating with the microcomputer. The program documentation consists of reference *line numbers* and the program instructions to the computer. See Fig. 12–3.

```
500   PRINT "_____"
510   PRINT "PAVEMENT THICKNESS IN INCHES  = ": INPUT T1
520   IF P  =  16 GOTO 630
530   IF P  =  67 GOTO 560
540   PRINT "PAVEMENT WIDTH  =": INPUT W1
550   IF P  =  16 GOTO 630
560   PRINT "COST OF CONCRETE PER SQ.YD. FOR THE THICKNESS OF "T1"
        INCHES"
570   PRINT "FINISHED AND CURED IN FIELD  = ": INPUT C1
580   IF P  =  16 GOTO 630
590   IF P  =  67 GOTO 630
600   PRINT "COST OF INTEGRAL CURB PER LINEAL FOOT  = ": INPUT L1
610   IF P  =  16 GOTO 630
620   PRINT "COST OF EXCAVATION PER CUBIC YARD  = ": INPUT E1
630   X1  =  ( (W1 * C1) / 9) + (L1 * 2) + ( (T1 /   36) * (W1 / 9) * E1)
640   Y1  =  X1 / (W1 / 9)
650   GOSUB 4230
660   PRINT "            "
670   PRINT "THE COST PER LINEAL FOOT  = $ "X1
680   PRINT "THE COST PER SQUARE YARD  = $ "Y1
690   PRINT "          "
700   PRINT "DO YOU WANT HARDCOPY OF DATA  ? (YES OR NO)": INPUT
        H$
```

Figure 12–3 Example—line numbers.

Three programs have been written for this text: (1) solution of any triangle, (2) calculation of a line's bearing and distance knowing the coordinates of two points, and (3) a program regarding pavement cost analysis. These three programs have been written in Applesoft (BASIC) and are listed in Appendices A–C along with the run for each program. The limits to any possible program are the memory capacity of the hardware, the writer's knowledge of a given subject, and the writer's training in computer programming.

EXAMPLES—SPREADSHEETS

Two spreadsheet examples will be presented: horizontal curve and vertical curve calculations. This spreadsheet form is part of the software package in Appleworks.

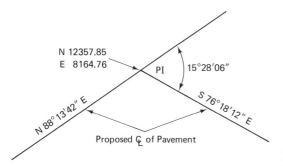

Figure 12-4 Horizontal curve layout.

The horizontal curve will be analyzed in the same manner that a designer would approach the problem. The designer of a horizontal curve would have established the curve's point of intersection, *PI*, station location and would know the intersecting angle, *I*. The tangent distance, *T*, is then set for the layout desired. See Fig. 12-4. Once the values for *PI* and *I* are known, then different tangent distances can be set to see what effect they have on all the other curve components—radius, *R*, arc length, *S*, central angle, Θ, long chord, *LC*, point of curve, *PC*, and the point of tangent, *PT*. See Fig. 12-5. Once the spreadsheet is formatted properly, it allows any number of horizontal curve investigations.

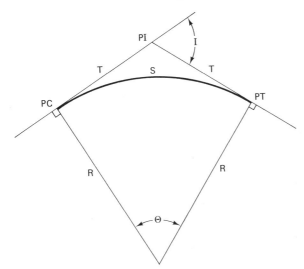

Figure 12-5 Horizontal curve labels.

Table 12-3 shows the solution for ten horizontal curves where initially the *PI* station, *I*, and the tangent length were known. The blocks for each row and column must be set for the unknown being sought. For example, to calculate *R* knowing *T* and *I*, the block would be set up to calculate *R* using the following equation:

$$R = \frac{T}{\tan\left(\dfrac{\Theta}{2}\right)}$$

TABLE 12-3 SPREADSHEET HORIZONTAL CURVE

Given					Solutions					
Curve number	Sta. *P.I.*	Int. Ang.	*T*	*I* (RAD)	*R*	*S*	*Θ*	*LC*	*PC*	*PT*
1	1024.16	16.32917	128.05	.142498	892.52	254.36	16.32917	253.50	896.11	1150.47
2	958.93	12.98765	200.67	.113338	1762.96	399.62	12.98765	398.77	758.26	1157.88
3	1500.67	32.78910	325.78	.286137	1107.30	633.68	32.78910	625.07	1174.89	1808.57
4	1709.09	5.55556	751.52	.048481	15489.15	1501.86	5.55556	1501.27	957.57	2459.43
5	781.93	21.90876	55.98	.191189	289.22	110.59	21.90876	109.92	725.95	836.54
6	2198.65	12.38765	155.55	.108102	1433.31	309.89	12.38765	309.28	2043.10	2352.99
7	5000.00	20.00000	100.00	.174532	567.13	197.97	20.00000	196.96	4900.00	5097.97
8	5000.00	10.00000	100.00	.087266	1143.01	199.49	10.00000	199.24	4900.00	5099.49
9	5000.00	5.00000	100.00	.043633	2290.39	199.87	5.00000	199.81	4900.00	5099.87
10	5000.00	1.00000	100.00	.008727	11458.93	199.99	1.00000	199.99	4900.00	5099.99

For each block, in the *R* column, this equation would be used to calculate *R*. Note that curves 7, 8, 9, and 10 all have the same *PI* location and tangent length, *T,* with different values for the intersection angle, *I.* The equations for the blocks in the other columns are

$$S = R * \Theta * \frac{\pi}{180}$$

$$S = R * I * \frac{\pi}{180}$$

$$LC = 2 * R * \sin\left(\frac{\Theta}{2}\right)$$

$$PC = PI - T$$

$$PT = PC + S$$

Since some spreadsheets do not contain trigonometric functions, a power series should be used for these required values. This is the case with Appleworks.

The values for columns *M* and *N* in Table 12-4 represent the power series for the trigonometric functions of tan Θ, which is

$$\tan \Theta = \Theta + \frac{\Theta^3}{3} + \frac{2\,\Theta^5}{15} + \frac{17\,\Theta^7}{315} + \frac{69\,\Theta^9}{2835}$$

where Θ must be in radians. Since the Appleworks' spreadsheet can only be used to seven places, col. *N* is used for additional places as calculated using the power series. In Table 12-4, the value computation for blocks in col. *M* are as shown in the lower left-hand corner. This represents the value in block *M*4, which is equal to the value in block *E*4, which is *I;* plus the value of *E*4 cubed and divided by 3; plus two times the value of Θ raised to the fifth power divided by 15. This is the first three parts of the power series equation for tan Θ. See Table 12-5.

TABLE 12-4 POWER SERIES

	G	H	I	J	K	L	M	N
1								
2			Solution					
3	S	Θ	LC	PC	PT		Work	Values
4	254.36	16.32917	253.50	896.11	1150.47		.1434705	.0000001
5	399.62	12.98765	398.77	758.26	1157.88		.1138258	.0000000
6	633.68	32.78910	625.07	1174.89	1808.57		.2942022	.0000088
7	1501.86	5.55556	1501.27	957.57	2459.43		.0485191	.0000000
8	110.59	21.90876	109.92	725.95	836.54		.1935526	.0000005
9	309.89	12.38765	309.28	2043.10	2352.99		.1085251	.0000000
10	197.97	20.00000	196.96	4900.00	5097.97		.1763258	.0000003
11	199.49	10.00000	199.24	4900.00	5099.49		.0874882	.0000000
12	199.87	5.00000	199.81	4900.00	5099.87		.0436607	.0000000
13	199.99	1.00000	199.99	4900.00	5099.99		.0087268	.0000000
14								
15								
16								
17								
18								

$$M4: \text{(Value)} + \text{(E4)} + \frac{E4^3}{3} + 2 * \frac{E4^5}{15}$$

TABLE 12-5 POWER SERIES

	G	H	I	J	K	L	M	N
1								
2			Solution					
3	S	Θ	LC	PC	PT		Work	Values
4	254.36	16.32917	253.50	896.11	1150.47		.1434705	.0000001
5	399.62	12.98765	398.77	758.26	1157.88		.1138258	.0000000
6	633.68	32.78910	625.07	1174.89	1808.57		.2942022	.0000088
7	1501.86	5.55556	1501.27	957.57	2459.43		.0485191	.0000000
8	110.59	21.90876	109.92	725.95	836.54		.1935526	.0000005
9	309.89	12.38765	309.28	2043.10	2352.99		.1085251	.0000000
10	197.97	20.00000	196.96	4900.00	5097.97		.1763258	.0000003
11	199.49	10.00000	199.24	4900.00	5099.49		.0874882	.0000000
12	199.87	5.00000	199.81	4900.00	5099.87		.0436607	.0000000
13	199.99	1.00000	199.99	4900.00	5099.99		.0087268	.0000000
14								
15								
16								
17								
18								

$$N4: \text{(Value)} + 17 * \frac{E4^7}{315} + 62 * \frac{E4^9}{2835}$$

TABLE 12–6 VERTICAL CURVE SPREADSHEET

Reference	Given	Ref. sta.	Station 600.00	Tan. elev.	Vertical curve elev.	Ref. sta.	Station 500.00	Tan. elev.	Curve elev.	Ref. sta.	Station 400.00	Tan. elev.	Curve elev.	Station 300.00	Tan. elev.	Curve elev.
Sta. PVI	2397.63	PVC	2097.63	783.85	783.85	PVC	2147.63	785.13	785.13	PVC	2197.63	786.41	786.41	2247.63	787.69	787.69
Elev. PVI	791.53		2100.00	783.91	783.91		2150.00	785.19	785.19		2200.00	786.47	786.47	2250.00	787.75	787.75
S1	2.56		2125.00	784.55	784.52		2175.00	785.83	785.80		2225.00	787.11	787.07	2275.00	788.39	788.33
S2	–1.93		2150.00	785.19	785.09		2200.00	786.47	786.35		2250.00	787.75	787.60	2300.00	789.03	788.83
			2175.00	785.83	785.61		2225.00	787.11	786.84		2275.00	788.39	788.05	2325.00	789.67	789.22
N	25.00		2200.00	786.47	786.08		2250.00	787.75	787.28		2300.00	789.03	788.44	2350.00	790.31	789.53
			2225.00	787.11	786.50		2275.00	788.39	787.66		2325.00	789.67	788.76	2375.00	790.95	789.74
			2250.00	787.75	786.88		2300.00	789.03	787.99		2350.00	790.31	789.01	2400.00	791.48	789.85
			2275.00	788.39	787.21		2325.00	789.67	788.26		2375.00	790.95	789.18	2425.00	791.00	789.88
			2300.00	789.03	787.50		2350.00	790.31	788.47		2400.00	791.48	789.29	2450.00	790.52	789.81
			2325.00	789.67	787.74		2375.00	790.95	788.63		2425.00	791.00	789.33	2475.00	790.04	789.64
			2350.00	790.31	787.93		2400.00	791.48	788.73		2450.00	790.52	789.30	2500.00	789.55	789.38
			2375.00	790.95	788.07		2425.00	791.00	788.78		2475.00	790.04	789.19	2525.00	789.07	789.03
			2400.00	791.48	788.17		2450.00	790.52	788.77		2500.00	789.55	789.02	2547.63	788.63	788.63
			2425.00	791.00	788.22		2475.00	790.04	788.70		2525.00	789.07	788.78			
			2450.00	790.52	788.22		2500.00	789.55	788.58		2550.00	788.59	788.46			
			2475.00	790.04	788.18		2525.00	789.07	788.40		2575.00	788.11	788.08			
			2500.00	789.55	788.09		2550.00	788.59	788.16	PVT	2597.63	787.67	787.67			
			2525.00	789.07	787.96		2575.00	788.11	787.87							
			2550.00	788.59	787.77		2600.00	787.62	787.52							
			2575.00	788.11	787.54		2625.00	787.14	787.12							
			2600.00	787.62	787.27	PVT	2647.63	786.70	786.70							
			2625.00	787.14	786.94											
			2650.00	786.66	786.57											
			2675.00	786.18	786.16											
		PVT	2697.63	785.74	785.74											

Curve length = 600′
Sta. H/L = 2439.72

For any point
Sta.? = 2345.63

H/L PT = 788.23   H/L PT = 787.90   H/L PT = 788.22

Max. elev. = 788.22   Max. elev. = 788.78   Max. elev. = 789.33   Max. elev. = 789.88
Min. elev = 783.85   785.13   Min. elev. = 786.41   Min. elev. = 787.69

Table 12–5 shows values similar to Table 12–4 except the lower left-hand corner shows the value for block $N4$ and it is equal to the !ast two components of the power series. The tan Θ for the different rows is equal to the sum of the respective blocks in col. M and col. N. For example,

$$\tan\left(\frac{\Theta}{2}\right), \text{ reference line } \#7 = M10 + N10$$

$$\tan 10.00000 = 0.1763258 + .0000003$$
$$\tan 10.00000 = 0.1763261$$

The use of a power series is very helpful when using a spreadsheet program that does not contain trigonometric functions. The power series for sine and cosine are

$$\sin\Theta = \Theta - \frac{\Theta^3}{3!} + \frac{\Theta^5}{5!} - \frac{\Theta^7}{7!} + \ldots$$
$$\cos\Theta = 1 - \frac{\Theta^2}{2!} + \frac{\Theta^4}{4!} - \frac{\Theta^6}{6!} + \ldots$$

Another example of spreadsheet use is shown in Table 12–6. This table shows computation of a vertical curve when the initial data consist of the point of the vertical curve, PVI, the proposed slopes for the curve, the length of curve, and the station intervals desired for the curve. Table 12–6 shows the results where the initial values are as shown in Fig. 12–6.

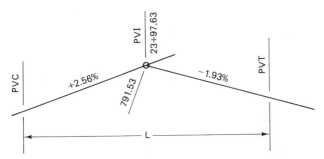

Figure 12–6 Vertical curve positive slope.

Table 12–6 presents the results for four possible curve lengths: 600, 500, 400, and 300 feet with the requested intervals of 25 feet. The table shows the stationing at 25-foot intervals, the tangent elevation, the curve elevation, the station for the highest or lowest point of the curve, and the corresponding curve elevation. It also shows the curve elevation for any requested station on the curve for the 600-foot curve. These values for station $23 + 00.00$ are shown as

- tangent elevation = 789.03
- curve elevation = 787.50
- the highest point on the curve is at sta. $24 + 39.72$
- elevation at sta. $24 + 39.72 = 788.23$
- if the elevation of sta. $23 + 45.63$ was required, the spreadsheet program yields an elevation = 787.90

This type of program proves to be very valuable when calculating earthwork, pavement, and drainage information. Consider another vertical curve with the first slope being negative. See Fig. 12–7.

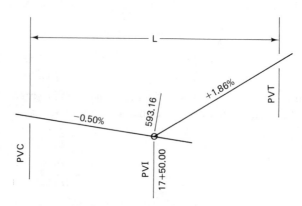

Figure 12-7   Vertical curve negative slope.

Table 12–7 shows the spreadsheet results for the computation of this vertical curve at 25-foot intervals. If the curve length was 600 feet, then the low point is at sta. 15 + 77.12 with a curve elevation of 594.34. As a program check, the curve elevation for station 19 + 00.00 was requested. The resulting elevation is 596.39, which is the same as that as listed in the table.

Table 12–8 illustrates the block content for the calculations of the station column and the tangent elevation column. Consider row 8 in Table 12–8. Since the spreadsheet allows for the use of *if* statements, one can set up the following *if* condition: If the value of contents $(D7 + B10)$ is greater than $(B5 + D3/2)$, then the value would be $(B5 + D3/2)$; if not, then the value will be $D7 + B10$.

$$+ @IF \left[D7 + B10 > B5 + \left(\frac{D3}{2}\right), B5 + \left(\frac{D3}{2}\right), D7 + B10 \right]$$

Similarly, the tangent elevation is found by subtracting the contents of $D7$ from $D8$ and multiplying by $B7/100$ and then adding $E7$.

$$+ \quad (D8 - D7) * \left(\frac{B7}{100}\right) + (E7)$$

It is not necessary to know all this information to run the spreadsheet programs. It is presented to give the reader some idea of spreadsheet development and possible applications for other related land development calculations.

TABLE 12–7 VERTICAL CURVE SPREADSHEET

Reference	Given	Ref. sta.	Station 600.00	Tan. elev.	Vertical Curve elev.	Ref. sta.	Station 500.00	Tan. elev.	Curve elev.	Ref. sta.	Station 400.00	Tan. elev.	Curve elev.	Ref. sta.	Station 300.00	Tan. elev.	Curve elev.
Sta. PVI	1750.00	PVC	1450.00	594.66	594.66	PVC	1500.00	594.41	594.41	PVC	1550.00	594.16	594.16	PVC	1600.00	593.91	593.91
Elev. PVI	593.16		1475.00	594.53	594.55		1525.00	594.28	594.30		1575.00	594.03	594.05		1625.00	593.78	593.81
S1	−.50		1500.00	594.41	594.46		1550.00	594.16	594.22		1600.00	593.91	593.98		1650.00	593.66	593.76
S2	1.86		1525.00	594.28	594.40		1575.00	594.03	594.17		1625.00	593.78	593.95		1675.00	593.53	593.76
			1550.00	594.16	594.36		1600.00	593.91	594.15		1650.00	593.66	593.95		1700.00	593.41	593.80
N	25.00		1575.00	594.03	594.34		1625.00	593.78	594.15		1675.00	593.53	594.00		1725.00	593.28	593.90
			1600.00	593.91	594.34		1650.00	593.66	594.19		1700.00	593.41	594.07		1750.00	593.16	594.04
			1625.00	593.78	594.35		1675.00	593.53	594.26		1725.00	593.28	594.19		1775.00	593.62	594.24
			1650.00	593.66	594.39		1700.00	593.41	594.35		1750.00	593.16	594.34		1800.00	594.09	594.48
			1675.00	593.53	594.45		1725.00	593.28	594.48		1775.00	593.62	594.53		1825.00	594.55	594.78
			1700.00	593.41	594.53		1750.00	593.16	594.63		1800.00	594.09	594.75		1850.00	595.02	595.12
			1725.00	593.28	594.64		1775.00	593.62	594.82		1825.00	594.55	595.02		1875.00	595.49	595.51
			1750.00	593.16	594.77		1800.00	594.09	595.03		1850.00	595.02	595.31		1900.00	595.95	595.95
			1775.00	593.62	594.93		1825.00	594.55	595.28		1875.00	595.49	595.65	PVT	1900.00	595.95	595.95
			1800.00	594.09	595.11		1850.00	595.02	595.55		1900.00	595.95	596.02				
			1825.00	594.55	595.32		1875.00	595.49	595.85		1925.00	596.41	596.43				
			1850.00	595.02	595.55		1900.00	595.95	596.19		1950.00	596.88	596.88				
			1875.00	595.49	595.81		1925.00	596.41	596.55	PVT	1950.00	596.88	596.88				
			1900.00	595.95	596.09		1950.00	596.88	596.94								
			1925.00	596.41	596.39		1975.00	597.34	597.36								
			1950.00	596.88	596.72		2000.00	597.81	597.81								
			1975.00	597.34	597.08	PVT	2000.00	597.81	597.81								
			2000.00	597.81	597.46												
			2025.00	598.27	597.86												
			2050.00	598.74	598.29												
PVT		PVT	2050.00	598.74	598.74												

Curve length = 600'
Sta. H/L = 1577.12

For any point
Sta.? = 1900.00

H/L PT = 594.34   H/L PT = 596.39   H/L PT = 596.39

	600.00	500.00	400.00	300.00
Max. elev. =	598.74	597.81	596.88	595.95
Min. elev. =	594.34	594.15	593.95	593.76

171

TABLE 12-8   SPREADSHEET CELL CONSTANT

	D	Tan. Elev.
1		
2	Station	Tan. Elev.
3	+600	
4		
5	+B5−(D3/2)	+(B6−((+B7/100)*D3/2))
6	+(@INT(D5/B10)+1)*B10	+((D6−D5)*B7/100+(E5))
7	+@IF(D6+B10>B5+(D3/2),B5+(D3/2),D6+B10)	+((D7−D6)*B7/100+(E6))
8	+@IF(D7+B10>B5+(D3/2),B5+(D3/2),D7+B10)	+((D8−D7)*B7/100+(E7))
9	+@IF(D8+B10>B5+(D3/2),B5+(D3/2),D8+B10)	+((D9−D8)*B7/100+(E8))
10	+@IF(D9+B10>B5+(D3/2),B5+(D3/2),D9+B10)	+((D10−D9)*B7/100+(E9))
11	+@IF(D10+B10>B5+(D3/2),B5+(D3/2),D10+B10)	+((D11−D10)*B7/100+(E10))
12	+@IF(D11+B10>B5+(D3/2),B5+(D3/2),D11+B10)	+((D12−D11)*B7/100+(E11))
13	+@IF(D12+B10>B5+(D3/2),B5+(D3/2),D12+B10)	+((D13−D12)*B7/100+(E12))
14	+@IF(D13+B10>B5+(D3/2),B5+(D3/2),D13+B10)	+((D14−D13)*B7/100+(E13))
15	+@IF(D14+B10>B5+(D3/2),B5+(D3/2),D14+B10)	+((D15−D14)*B7/100+(E14))
16	+@IF(D15+B10>B5+(D3/2),B5+(D3/2),D15+B10)	+((D16−D15)*B7/100+(E15))
17	+@IF(D16+B10>B5+(D3/2),B5+(D3/2),D16+B10)	+((D17−D16)*B7/100+(E16))
18	+@IF(D17+B10>B5+(D3/2),B5+(D3/2),D17+B10)	+((D18−B5)*B8/100+(B6))
19	+@IF(D18+B10>B5+(D3/2),B5+(D3/2),D18+B10)	+((D19−B5)*B8/100+(B6))
20	+@IF(D19+B10>B5+(D3/2),B5+(D3/2),D19+B10)	+((D20−B5)*B8/100+(B6))
21	+@IF(D20+B10>B5+(D3/2),B5+(D3/2),D20+B10)	+((D21−B5)*B8/100+(B6))
22	+@IF(D21+B10>B5+(D3/2),B5+(D3/2),D21+B10)	+((D22−B5)*B8/100+(B6))
23	+@IF(D22+B10>B5+(D3/2),B5+(D3/2),D22+B10)	+((D23−B5)*B8/100+(B6))
24	+@IF(D23+B10>B5+(D3/2),B5+(D3/2),D23+B10)	+((D24−B5)*B8/100+(B6))
25	+@IF(D24+B10>B5+(D3/2),B5+(D3/2),D24+B10)	+((D25−B5)*B8/100+(B6))
26	+@IF(D25+B10>B5+(D3/2),B5+(D3/2),D25+B10)	+((D26−B5)*B8/100+(B6))
27	+@IF(D26+B10>B5+(D3/2),B5+(D3/2),D26+B10)	+((D27−B5)*B8/100+(B6))
28	+@IF(D27+B10>B5+(D3/2),B5+(D3/2),D27+B10)	+((D28−B5)*B8/100+(B6))
29	+@IF(D28+B10>B5+(D3/2),B5+(D3/2),D28+B10)	+((D29−B5)*B8/100+(B6))
30	+@IF(D29+B10>B5+(D3/2),B5+(D3/2),D29+B10)	+((D30−B5)*B8/100+(B6))
31		
32	Curve len	
33	Sta.*H/L* =	
34		
35		

D18: (Value, Layout-F2) +@IF(D17+B10>B5+(D3/2),B5+(D3/2),D17+B10)

EXAMPLES—COMPUTER PROGRAMS

As previously noted, three computer programs have been created specifically for this text

- solution for parts of a triangle

- calculation of the bearing and distance between two points knowing the points' coordinates

- pavement cost analysis

While each one of these programs will assist with land planning calculations, they are presented here as examples of how effective the microcomputer can be in the solution of land planning problems. To fully understand these computer programs, it is assumed the reader has already read the proceeding chapters or has a knowledge of trigonometry and pavement design.

The computer program for the solution of any triangle is listed in Appendix A. This program will solve for all parts of a triangle when three parts of the triangle are given. See Fig. 12–8.

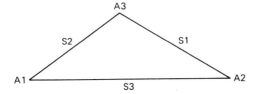

Figure 12–8 Triangle layout.

The program will also indicate whether there is more than one triangle developed from the data given or if no triangle is developed. In addition to this information, the program will calculate the area of each triangle developed. In the example run, Appendix A, of this program the values that were used for the different components of the triangles are as listed in Table 12–9.

TABLE 12–9 TRIANGLE VALUES—GIVEN

Triangle reference number	$S1$	$S2$	$S3$	$A1$	$A2$	$A3$
1	35.62	43.95	55.92	?	?	?
2	?	?	?	35	45	100
3	3	4	5	?	?	?
4	?	43.95	52.11	32	?	?
5	37.9865	43.7896	?	32.7865	?	?
6	35	35	35	?	?	?

Review Appendix A for the program run information. Note that the values for the angles are listed in decimal form. If the angles were needed in degrees, minutes, and seconds, this could be easily done by adding a subroutine to the program. This will be discussed further in the next program dealing with bearings and distances.

In the reference triangle #2 of the program run, the given information has three angles. Naturally, there could be many solutions and the program informs the user of this fact. In reference triangle #5, the data submitted could result in two triangles. The first triangle is as shown in Fig. 12–9 and the second solution is as shown in Fig. 12–10. Many times the second solution will be overlooked. The computer will *not* overlook any possible solution if it is programmed properly.

The program for the calculation for distance and the bearing between two points requires the input of the coordinates for the points in question. See Appendix B for

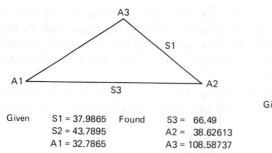

Given   S1 = 37.9865   Found   S3 =   66.49
         S2 = 43.7895   A2 =   38.62613
         A1 = 32.7865   A3 = 108.58737

Figure 12-9   Triangle for first solution.

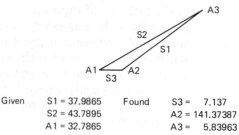

Given   S1 = 37.9865   Found   S3 =   7.137
         S2 = 43.7895   A2 = 141.37387
         A1 = 32.7865   A3 =   5.83963

Figure 12-10   Triangle for second solution.

a listing and run of this program. The computer run is for the figure shown in Fig.
12-11. This figure was selected since it is not a traditional land closure figure. The
program prints values for the side reference number, coordinates as entered, bearing
angle and direction, and the distance between the points in question. When the last
side in the figure is reached, the program requests the coordinates of the first point.

Note that the bearing angle, in this program, is listed in degrees, minutes, and
seconds. To accomplish this, the angle in decimal form is run through the brief
subroutine as listed in lines 1370 to 1440 of the program. This program will speed
up the calculation of distances and bearing angles and result in better accuracy when
compared to hand-held calculator results. There are sophisticated software programs
available for the calculation of bearings, distance, areas, and property closure. The
program, as listed in Appendix B, should give some idea of how extensive such programs could be.

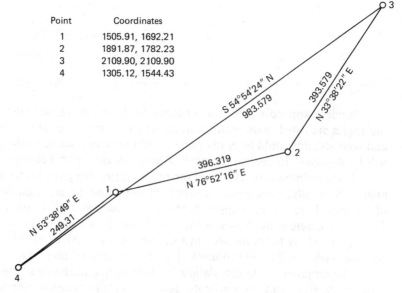

Point	Coordinates
1	1505.91, 1692.21
2	1891.87, 1782.23
3	2109.90, 2109.90
4	1305.12, 1544.43

Figure 12-11   Figure for bearings and distances.

Finally, the third and last computer program deals with cost analysis of pavement sections and types. In Chapter 11, procedures for the calculation of pavement costs were outlined. These same procedures will be used in the computer program. See Fig. 11-1. This figure shows the pavement cross section that is 1 foot in length. The pavement's cross sectional width in this program can vary, but it will always be considered being 1 foot in length. Appendix C lists the pavement cost-analysis program. This program is longer than the first two programs because of the large number of options contained in the program:

- different pavement sections
- different materials
- different costs
- different pavement geometry

This type of program allows the land planner to design the most economical pavement section by comparing costs of different pavement types, materials, and material costs. While the program results in a cost for each proposed section with the data given in cost per lineal foot and cost per square yard, the actual cost comparisons for pavement types should be as presented in Chapter 11. The loads (E18s) that a pavement will carry to some estimated serviceability level must be included in the cost comparison.

The run of this program shows the five pavement sections that can be analyzed

1. rigid concrete pavement with integral curbs
2. flexible pavement, 3-layer system with curb and gutter
3. flexible pavement, 2-layer system with curb and gutter
4. rigid pavement with no curbs
5. flexible pavement, 3-layer system with no curbs

The curb and gutter section for categories 2 and 3 is a curb section 2 feet wide as shown in Fig. 11-1. If a wider curb and gutter section is used, a cost adjustment will have to be made for this wider selection.

The concrete for category 1 is a concrete that would have a modulus of rupture, *MR,* or third-point loading, of at least 700 psi in 28 days. As with the curb and gutter section's width, if different concrete strength criteria are used then different costs should be considered.

The first run of this program is for a flexible pavement section using the AASHO Road test structural coefficient data for *A*1, *A*2, *A*3 with *SN* equal to 3.6. The program's cost estimate, for the pavement section in question, is an estimated cost of $24.60/l.f. or $10.22/sq yd. When asked to change input, *SN* was reduced from 3.6 to 3.0. This resulted in a thinner pavement section and, naturally, a reduction in estimated cost—$24.00/l.f. and $8.86/sq yd.

The second run of this program was for a rigid concrete section. The program's cost estimate for the pavement section in question was an estimated cost of $31.80/l.f.

or $11.45/sq yd. Both runs take into account the amount of excavation required for the pavement section. The excavation is figured for the total thickness of the pavement. Hardcopy for the program results in the printing of the input values and the cost estimate results.

The review of these programs, horizontal curve, vertical curve, solution of a triangle, bearing angle and distance, and the pavement cost analysis, should suggest other possible programs that could be developed for the microcomputer and subject areas other than land planning.

PROBLEMS

12-1. Define the following:
  (a) computer hardware
  (b) computer software
  (c) video
  (d) keyboard
  (e) printer

12-2. Define the following:
  (a) disk drive
  (b) CAD
  (c) AutoCAD
  (d) spreadsheet
  (e) data base

12-3. In Table 12-1, how does the radius, R, change for decreases in I and Θ? (See curves 6 to 10.)

12-4. In Table 12-6, as the vertical curve is lengthened, what happens to the maximum curve elevation? List maximum curve elevations for curves with lengths, L, of 600, 500, 400, and 300 feet.

12-5. In Table 12-8, what is meant by: $+B5 - (D3/2)$ for cell $D5$?

12-6. If a computer is available, try to run the reference program as listed in Appendix A.

12-7. If a computer is available, try to run the reference program as listed in Appendix B.

12-8. If a computer is available, try to run the reference program as listed in Appendix C.

Appendix A

Program for the Solution of Any Triangle

```
50   REM  ******   THE SOLUTION FOR ANY TRIANGLE  *************
60   PRINT "    "
70   REM  ******   CREATED BY WILLIAM E. BREWER   *************
80   PRINT "     "
90   REM  ***************  COPYRIGHTED - 1986 ********************
100  PRINT "    "
110  REM -  THE PROGRAM WILL ACCEPT ANY THREE (3) UNKNOWNS; SIDES
120  REM -  OR ANGLES.
130  HOME
140  PRINT "'TRIANGLE', A PROGRAM FOR SOLVING TRIANGLES"
150  PRINT "      "
160  PRINT  TAB( 37);"A3"
170  PRINT "    "
180  PRINT "    "
190  PRINT "     "
200  PRINT  TAB( 10);"A1"; TAB( 55);"A2"
210  PRINT "    "
220  PRINT "    "
230  PRINT "GENERAL LAYOUT WITH S1, S2, AND S3 OPPOSITE ANGLES A1, A2 AND
     A3."
240  PRINT "DO YOU WANT TO SEE PROGRAM ? YES OR NO": INPUT W$
250  IF W$ = "YES" THEN 270
260  HOME : PRINT "SORRY THAT YOU DIDN'T WANT TO SEE THE PROGRAM": END
270  PRINT "THIS PROGRAM WILL SOLVE ANY TRIANGLE IF YOU KNOW AT LEAST THRE
     E"
280  PRINT "(3) COMPONENTS OF THE TRIANGLE.  THE PROGRAM WILL ALSO INFORM
     YOU"
290  PRINT "IF THE VALUES DO NOT FORM A TRIANGLE"
300  PRINT "    "
310  PRINT "ENTER VALUES KNOWN: S1, S2, S3, A1, A2, OR A3 IN THIS ORDER."
320  PRINT "    "
330  PRINT "NOTE ::::: ALL ANGLES MUST BE IN DECIMAL FORM !!!
340  PRINT "    "
350  PRINT "IF VALUE IS UNKNOWN, ENTER A ZERO (0)."
360  PRINT "S1= ": INPUT S1
```

```
370   PRINT "S2= ": INPUT S2
380   PRINT "S3= ": INPUT S3
390   PRINT "A1= ": INPUT A1
400   PRINT "A2= ": INPUT A2
410   PRINT "A3= ": INPUT A3
420 P = P + 1
430   IF A1 + A2 + A3 = 0 THEN 630
440   IF S3 + A2 + A3 = 0 THEN 780
450   IF S3 + A1 + A3 = 0 THEN 890
460   IF S3 + A1 + A2 = 0 THEN 1000
470   IF S2 + A2 + A3 = 0 THEN 2920
480   IF S2 + A1 + A3 = 0 THEN 1060
490   IF S2 + A1 + A2 = 0 THEN 1130
500   IF S1 + A2 + A3 = 0 THEN 1230
510   IF S1 + A1 + A3 = 0 THEN 1300
520   IF S1 + A1 + A2 = 0 THEN 1360
530   IF S2 + S3 + A3 = 0 THEN 1460
540   IF S2 + S3 + A2 = 0 THEN 1510
550   IF S2 + S3 + A1 = 0 THEN 1560
560   IF S1 + S3 + A3 = 0 THEN 1610
570   IF S1 + S3 + A2 = 0 THEN 1660
580   IF S1 + S3 + A1 = 0 THEN 1710
590   IF S1 + S2 + A3 = 0 THEN 1760
600   IF S1 + S2 + A2 = 0 THEN 1810
610   IF S1 + S2 + A1 = 0 THEN 1860
620   IF S1 + S2 + S3 = 0 THEN 1910
630   IF S3 =  > (S2 + S1) THEN 1940
640 H1 = (S2 ^ 2 + S3 ^ 2 - S1 ^ 2) / (2 * S2 * S3)
650   IF  ABS (H1) > 1 THEN 1940
660 H2 = (1 - H1 ^ 2) ^ .5
670 A1 =  ATN (H2 / H1) * 57.29578
680 H1 = (S1 ^ 2 + S3 ^ 2 - S2 ^ 2) / (2 * S1 * S3)
690 H2 = (1 - H1 ^ 2) ^ .5
700 A2 =  ATN (H2 / H1) * 57.29578
710 H1 = (S1 ^ 2 + S2 ^ 2 - S3 ^ 2) / (2 * S1 * S2)
720   IF H1 = 0 THEN A3 = 90
730   IF A3 = 90 GOTO 1960
740 H2 = (1 - H1 ^ 2) ^ .5
750 A3 =  ATN (H2 / H1) * 57.29578
760   IF A3 < 0 THEN A3 = 180 + A3
770   GOTO 1960
780 Y1 = ( SIN (A1 * .01745329) / S1) * S2
790   IF Y1 > 1 THEN 1940
800 Y2 = (1 - Y1 ^ 2) ^ .5
810 A2 =  ATN (Y1 / Y2) * 57.29578
820 A3 = (180 - (A1 + A2))
830 S3 = ((S2 ^ 2 + S1 ^ 2) - (2 * S2 * S1 *  COS (A3 * .01745329))) ^ .5
840   IF S1 =  > S2 THEN  GOTO 1960
850   PRINT "THERE ARE TWO POSSIBLE SOLUTIONS."
860   PRINT "THIS IS THE FIRST SOLUTION".
870   GOSUB 2800
880   GOTO 2990
890 Y1 = ( SIN (A2 * .01745329) / S2) * S1
900   IF Y1 > 1 THEN 1940
910 Y2 = (1 - Y1 ^ 2) ^ .5
920 A1 =  ATN (Y1 / Y2) * 57.29578
930 A3 = (180 - (A1 + A2))
940 S3 = ((S2 ^ 2 + S1 ^ 2) - (2 * S2 * S1 *  COS (A3 * .01745329))) ^ .5
950   IF S2 =  > S1 GOTO 1960
960   PRINT "THERE ARE TWO POSSIBLE SOLUTIONS."
970   PRINT "THIS IS THE FIRST SOLUTION."
980   GOSUB 2800
990   GOTO 3050
1000 S3 = ((S2 ^ 2 + S1 ^ 2) - (2 * S2 * S1 *  COS (A3 * .01745329))) ^ .5
```

```
1010 H1 = (S2 ^ 2 + S3 ^ 2 - S1 ^ 2) / (2 * S2 * S3)
1020 H2 = (1 - H1 ^ 2) ^ .5
1030 A1 =  ATN (H2 / H1) * 57.29578
1040 A2 = (180 - (A1 + A3))
1050  GOTO 1960
1060 S2 = ((S1 ^ 2 + S3 ^ 2) - (2 * S1 * S3 *  COS (A2 * .01745329))) ^ .5

1070 H1 = (S2 ^ 2 + S3 ^ 2 - S1 ^ 2) / (2 * S2 * S3)
1080 H1 =  ABS (H1)
1090 H2 = (1 - H1 ^ 2) ^ .5
1100 A1 =  ATN (H2 / H1) * 57.29576
1110 A3 = 180 - (A1 + A2)
1120  GOTO 1960
1130 Y1 = ( SIN (A3 * .01745329) / S3) * S1
1140  IF Y1 > 1 THEN 1940
1150 Y2 = (1 - Y1 ^ 2) ^ .5
1160 A1 =  ATN (Y1 / Y2) * 57.29578
1170 A2 = 180 - (A3 + A1)
1180 S2 = ((S3 ^ 2 + S1 ^ 2) - (2 * S3 * S1 *  COS (A2 * .01745329))) ^ .5

1190  IF S3 = > S1 THEN 1960
1200  PRINT "THERE ARE TWO SOLUTIONS."
1210  GOSUB 2800
1220  GOTO 3130
1230 S1 = ((S2 ^ 2 + S3 ^ 2) - (2 * S2 * S3 *  COS (A1 * .01745329))) ^ .5

1240 Y1 = ( SIN (A1 * .01745329) / S1) * S2
1250  IF Y1 > 1 THEN 1940
1260 Y2 = (1 - Y1 ^ 2) ^ .5
1270 A2 =  ATN (Y1 / Y2) * 57.29578
1280 A3 = 180 - (A1 + A2)
1290  GOTO 1960
1300  IF S2 = > S3 THEN 2520
1310 S4 = ( SIN (A2 * .01745329) * S3)
1320  IF  ABS (S2 - S4) < .00001 THEN 2590
1330  IF S2 < S4 THEN 2780
1340  IF S2 > S4 THEN 2640
1350  IF Y1 > 1 THEN 1940
1360 Y1 = ( SIN (A3 * .01745329) / S3) * S2
1370 Y2 = (1 - Y1 ^ 2) ^ .5
1380 A2 =  ATN (Y1 / Y2) * 57.29578
1390 A1 = 180 - (A3 + A2)
1400 S1 = ((S3 ^ 2 + S2 ^ 2) - (2 * S3 * S2 *  COS (A1 * .01745329))) ^ .5

1410  IF S3 > S2 THEN 1960
1420  PRINT "THERE ARE TWO SOLUTIONS."
1430  PRINT "THIS IS THE FIRST SOLUTION."
1440  GOSUB 2800
1450  GOTO 3090
1460 A3 = 180 - (A1 + A2)
1470  IF A3 < 1 THEN 1940
1480 S2 = (S1 /  SIN (A1 * .01745329)) *  SIN (A2 * .01745329)
1490 S3 = (S1 /  SIN (A1 * .01745329)) *  SIN (A3 * .01745329)
1500  GOTO 1960
1510 A2 = 180 - (A1 + A3)
1520  IF A2 < 1 THEN 1940
1530 S2 = (S1 /  SIN (A1 * .01745329)) *  SIN (A2 * .01745329)
1540 S3 = (S1 /  SIN (A1 * .01745329)) *  SIN (A3 * .01745329)
1550  GOTO 1960
1560 A1 = 180 - (A2 + A3)
1570  IF A1 < 1 THEN 1940
1580 S2 = (S1 /  SIN (A1 * .01745329)) *  SIN (A2 * .01745329)
1590 S3 = (S1 /  SIN (A1 * .01745329)) +  SIN (A3 * .01745329)
1600  GOTO 1960
```

```
1610 A3 = 180 - (A1 + A2)
1620  IF A3 < 1 THEN 1940
1630 S1 = (S2 /  SIN (A2 * .01745329)) *  SIN (A1 * .01745329)
1640 S3 = (S2 /  SIN (A2 * .01745329)) *  SIN (A3 * .01745329)
1650  GOTO 1960
1660 A2 = 180 - (A1 + A3)
1670  IF A2 < 1 THEN 1940
1680 S1 = (S2 /  SIN (A2 * .01745329)) *  SIN (A1 * .01745329)
1690 S3 = (S2 /  SIN (A2 * .01745329)) *  SIN (A3 * .01745329)
1700  GOTO 1960
1710 A1 = 180 - (A2 + A3)
1720  IF A1 < 1 THEN 1940
1730 S1 = (S2 /  SIN (A2 * .01745329)) *  SIN (A1 * .01745329)
1740 S3 = (S2 /  SIN (A2 * .01745329)) *  SIN (A3 * .01745329)
1750  GOTO 1960
1760 A3 = 180 - (A1 + A2)
1770  IF A3 < 1 THEN 1940
1780 S1 = (S3 /  SIN (A3 * .01745329)) *  SIN (A1 * .01745329)
1790 S2 = (S3 /  SIN (A3 * .01745329)) *  SIN (A2 * .01745329)
1800  GOTO 1960
1810 A2 = 180 - (A1 + A3)
1820  IF A2 < 1 THEN 1940
1830 S1 = (S3 /  SIN (A3 * .01745329)) *  SIN (A1 * .01745329)
1840 S2 = (S3 /  SIN (A3 * .01745329)) *  SIN (A1 * .01745329)
1850  GOTO 1960
1860 A1 = 180 - (A2 + A3)
1870  IF A1 < 1 THEN 1940
1880 S1 = (S3 /  SIN (A3 * .01745329)) *  SIN (A1 * .01745329)
1890 S2 = (S3 /  SIN (A3 * .01745329)) *  SIN (A2 * .01745329)
1900  GOTO 1960
1910  IF (A1 + A2 + A3) <  > 180 THEN 2500
1920  PRINT "THERE ARE MANY SOLUTIONS, SET A SIDE VALUE !!!"
1930  GOTO 2030
1940  PRINT "NOT A TRIANGLE, TRY AGAIN BUDDY !!!"
1950  GOTO 2030


]LIST 1960-2430

1960  PRINT "TRIANGLE REFERENCE NUMBER "P
1970  GOSUB 3180
1980  PRINT "S1= "G1,"A1= "A1: PRINT "S2= "G2,"A2= "A2: PRINT "S3= "G3,"A3
      = "A3
1990  GOTO 2080
2000  PRINT "DO YOU WANT HARD COPY ? YES OR NO": INPUT X$
2010  IF X$ = "YES" THEN  GOSUB 2150
2020  PRINT "  "
2030  PRINT "DO YOU HAVE ANOTHER TRIANGLE TO RUN ? YES OR NO": INPUT X$
2040  HOME
2050  IF X$ = "YES" THEN 310
2060  PRINT "THIS CONCLUDES THIS PROGRAM."
2070  END
2080  PRINT "DO YOU WANT THE AREA ? YES OR NO": INPUT X$
2090 M = (S1 + S2 + S3) * .5
2100 N = (M * (M - S1) * (M - S2) * (M - S3)) ^ .5
2110  GOSUB 3310
2120  IF X$ = "NO" THEN 2000
2130  PRINT "THE AREA OF THE TRIANGLE = "N1
2140  GOTO 2000
2150 D$ =  CHR$ (4)
2151  PRINT D$;"PR#1"
2160  PRINT "  "
2170  PRINT "TRIANGLE REFERENCE NUMBER "P
2180  PRINT "  "
2190  PRINT "S1= "G1,"A1= "A1: PRINT "S2= "G2,"A2= "A2: PRINT "S3= "G3,"A3
      = "A3
```

```
2200   PRINT "THE AREA OF THIS TRIANGLE = "N1
2210   PRINT "    "
2220   PRINT D$;"PR#3"
2230   RETURN
2240   PRINT "THERE IS ONLY ONE SOLUTION !"
2250 Y1 = ( SIN (A1 * .01745329) / S1) * S3
2260   IF Y1 > 1 THEN 1940
2270   Y2 = (1 - Y1 ^ 2) ^ .5
2280   A3 =  ATN (Y1 / Y2) * 57.29578
2290   A2 = 180 - (A1 + A3)
2300   S2 = ( SIN (A2 * .01745329) * S1) /  SIN (A1 * .01745329)
2310   GOTO 1960
2320   PRINT "THERE IS ONLY ONE SOLUTION AND A3 = 90 DEGREES."
2330 A2 = 90 - A1
2340 S2 = ( COS (A1 * .01745329)) * S3
2350 A3 = 90
2360   GOTO 1960
2370   PRINT "THERE ARE TWO SOLUTIONS !!!"
2380 Y1 = ( SIN (A1 * .01745329) / S1) * S3
2390 Y2 = (1 - Y1 ^ 2) ^ .5
2400 A3 =  ATN (Y1 / Y2) * 57.29578
2410 A2 = 180 - (A1 + A3)
2420 S2 = ( SIN (A2 * .01745329) * S1) /  SIN (A1 * .01745329)
2430   PRINT "THIS IS THE FIRST OF TWO POSSIBLE SOLUTIONS."
2440   GOSUB 2800
2450   PRINT "THIS IS THE SECOND SOLUTION AND 'A2' IS ACUTE."
2460 A3 = 180 - A3
2470 A2 = 180 - (A1 + A3)
2480 S2 = ( SIN (A2 * .01745329) * S1) /  SIN (A1 * .01745329)
2490   GOTO 1960
2500   PRINT "THERE IS NO SOLUTION, NOT A TRIANGLE !!!"
2510   GOTO 2030
2520   PRINT "THERE IS ONLY ONE SOLUTION AND A2 IS OBTUSE."
2530 Y1 = ( SIN (A2 * .01745329) / S2) * S3
2540 Y2 = (1 - Y1 ^ 2) ^ .5
2550 A3 =  ATN (Y1 / Y2) * 57.29578
2560 A1 = 180 - (A2 + A3)
2570 S1 = ( SIN (A1 * .01745329) * S2) /  SIN (A2 * .01745329)
2580   GOTO 1960
2590   PRINT "THERE IS ONLY ONE SOLUTION AND A3 = 90 DEGREES."
2600 A1 = 90 - A2
2610 S1 = ( COS (A2 * .01745329)) * S3
2620 A3 = 90
2630   GOTO 1960
2640   PRINT "THERE ARE TWO SOLUTIONS !!!"
2650 Y1 = ( SIN (A2 * .01745329) / S2) * S3
2660 Y2 = (1 - Y1 ^ 2) ^ .5
2670 A3 =  ATN (Y1 / Y2) * 57.29578
2680 A1 = 180 - (A2 + A3)
2690 S1 = ( SIN (A1 * .01745329) * S2) /  SIN (A2 * .01745329)
2700   PRINT "THIS IS THE FIRST OF TWO SOLUTIONS !"
2710   GOSUB 2800
2720   PRINT "THIS IS THE SECOND SOLUTION, A2 IS ACUTE."
2730 A3 = 180 - A3
2740 A1 = 180 - (A2 + A3)
2750 S1 = ( SIN (A1 * .01745329) * S2) /  SIN (A2 * .01745329)
2760   PRINT "THIS IS THE SECOND POSSIBLE SOLUTION !"
2770   GOTO 1960
2780   PRINT "THERE IS NO SOLUTION, NOT A TRIANGLE !!!"
2790   GOTO 2030
2800   PRINT "TRIANGLE REFERENCE NUMBER "P
2810   GOSUB 3180
2820   PRINT "S1= "G1,"A1= "A1: PRINT "S2= "G2,"A2= "A2: PRINT "S3= "G3,"A3
     = "A3
2830   PRINT "DO YOU WANT THE AREA ? , YES OR NO": INPUT X$
```

```
2840 M = (S1 + S2 + S3) * .5
2850 N = (M * (M - S1) * (M - S2) * (M - S3)) ^ .5
2860  GOSUB 3310
2870  IF X$ = "NO" THEN 2890
2880  PRINT "THE AREA OF THE TRIANGLE = "N1
2890  PRINT "DO YOU WANT HARD COPY ? YES OR NO": INPUT X$
2900  IF X$ = "YES" THEN  GOSUB 2150
2910  RETURN
2920  IF  ABS (S1 - S3) < .00001 THEN 2240
2930  IF S1 =  > S3 THEN 2240
2940 S4 = ( SIN (A1 * .01745329) * S3)
2950  IF  ABS (S1 - S4) < .00001 THEN 2320
2960  IF S1 < S4 THEN 2500
2970  IF S1 > S4 THEN 2370
2980  GOTO 1960
2990  PRINT "THIS IS THE SECOND SOLUTION."
3000 A2 = 180 - A2
3010 A3 = 180 - (A1 + A2)
3020 S3 = ( SIN (A3 * .01745329) * S1) /  SIN (A1 * .01745329)
3030  GOTO 1960
3040  PRINT "THIS IS THE SECOND  SOLUTION."
3050 A1 = 180 - A1
3060 A3 = 180 - (A1 + A2)
3070 S3 = ( SIN (A3 * .01745329) * S2) /  SIN (A2 * .01745329)
3080  GOTO 1960
3090 A2 = 180 - A2
3100 A1 = 180 - (A2 + A3)
3110 S1 = ( SIN (A1 * .01745329) * S3) /  SIN (A3 * .01745329)
3120  GOTO 1960
3130  PRINT "THIS IS THE SECOND SOLUTION."
3140 A2 = 180 - A2
3150 A1 = 180 - (A3 + A2)
3160 S2 = ( SIN (A2 * .01745329) * S1) /  SIN (A1 * .01745329)
3170  GOTO 1960
3180 G1 =  INT (1000 * S1)
3190  IF 1000 * S1 - G1 < .5 GOTO 3210
3200 G1 = G1 + 1
3210 G1 = G1 / 1000
3220 G2 =  INT (1000 * S2)
3230  IF 1000 * S2 - G2 < .5 GOTO 3250
3240 G2 = G2 + 1
3250 G2 = G2 / 1000
3260 G3 =  INT (1000 * S3)
3270  IF 1000 * S3 - G3 < .5 GOTO 3290
3280 G3 = G3 + 1
3290 G3 = G3 / 1000
3300  RETURN
3310 N1 =  INT (1000 * N)
3320  IF 1000 * N - N1 < .5 GOTO 3340
3330 N1 = N1 + 1
3340 N1 = N1 / 1000
3350  RETURN


]RUN


'TRIANGLE', A PROGRAM FOR SOLVING TRIANGLES

                         A3

        A1

                                          A2
```

GENERAL LAYOUT WITH S1, S2, AND S3 OPPOSITE ANGLES A1, A2 AND A3.
DO YOU WANT TO SEE PROGRAM ? YES OR NO
?YES
THIS PROGRAM WILL SOLVE ANY TRIANGLE IF YOU KNOW AT LEAST THREE
(3) COMPONENTS OF THE TRIANGLE. THE PROGRAM WILL ALSO INFORM YOU
IF THE VALUES DO NOT FORM A TRIANGLE

ENTER VALUES KNOWN: S1, S2, S3, A1, A2, OR A3 IN THIS ORDER.

NOTE :::: ALL ANGLES MUST BE IN DECIMAL FORM ! ! !

IF VALUE IS UNKNOWN, ENTER A ZER0 (0).
S1=
?35.62
S2=
?43.95
S3=
?55.92
A1=
?0
A2=
?0
A3=
?0
TRIANGLE REFERENCE NUMBER 1
S1= 35.62   A1= 39.554108
S2= 43.95   A2= 51.7881117
S3= 55.92   A3= 88.6577816
DO YOU WANT THE AREA ? YES OR NO
?YES
THE AREA OF THE TRIANGLE = 782.535
DO YOU WANT HARD COPY ? YES OR NO
?NO

DO YOU HAVE ANOTHER TRIANGLE TO RUN ? YES OR NO
?YES
ENTER VALUES KNOWN: S1, S2, S3, A1, A2, OR A3 IN THIS ORDER.

NOTE :::: ALL ANGLES MUST BE IN DECIMAL FORM ! ! !

IF VALUE IS UNKNOWN, ENTER A ZER0 (0).
S1=
?0
S2=
?0
S3=
?0
A1=
?35
A2=
?45
A3=
?100
THERE ARE MANY SOLUTIONS, SET A SIDE VALUE ! ! !
DO YOU HAVE ANOTHER TRIANGLE TO RUN ? YES OR NO
?YES
ENTER VALUES KNOWN: S1, S2, S3, A1, A2, OR A3 IN THIS ORDER.

NOTE :::: ALL ANGLES MUST BE IN DECIMAL FORM ! ! !

IF VALUE IS UNKNOWN, ENTER A ZER0 (0).
S1=
?3
S2=
?4

```
S3=
?5
A1=
?0
A2=
?0
A3=
?0
TRIANGLE REFERENCE NUMBER 3
S1= 3            A1= 36.8698979
S2= 4            A2= 53.1301028
S3= 5            A3= 90
DO YOU WANT THE AREA ? YES OR NO
?YES
THE AREA OF THE TRIANGLE = 6
DO YOU WANT HARD COPY ? YES OR NO

?NO

DO YOU HAVE ANOTHER TRIANGLE TO RUN ? YES OR NO
?YES
ENTER VALUES KNOWN: S1, S2, S3, A1, A2, OR A3 IN THIS ORDER.

NOTE ::::: ALL ANGLES MUST BE IN DECIMAL FORM !!!

IF VALUE IS UNKNOWN, ENTER A ZERO (0).
S1=
?0
S2=
?43.95
S3=
?52.11
A1=
?32
A2=
?0
A3=
?0
TRIANGLE REFERENCE NUMBER 4
S1= 27.615       A1= 32
S2= 43.95        A2= 57.4983369
S3= 52.11        A3= 90.5016632
DO YOU WANT THE AREA ? YES OR NO
?NO
DO YOU WANT HARD COPY ? YES OR NO
?NO

DO YOU HAVE ANOTHER TRIANGLE TO RUN ? YES OR NO
?YES
ENTER VALUES KNOWN: S1, S2, S3, A1, A2, OR A3 IN THIS ORDER.

NOTE :::: ALL ANGLES MUST BE IN DECIMAL FORM !!!

IF VALUE IS UNKNOWN, ENTER A ZERO (0).
S1=
?37.9865
S2=
?43.789654
S3=
?0
A1=
?32.7865
A2=
?0
A3=
?0
```

```
THERE ARE TWO POSSIBLE SOLUTIONS.
THIS IS THE FIRST SOLUTION.
TRIANGLE REFERENCE NUMBER 1
S1= 37.987      A1= 32.7865
S2= 43.79       A2= 38.6261301
S3= 66.49       A3= 108.58737
DO YOU WANT THE AREA ? , YES OR NO
?YES
THE AREA OF THE TRIANGLE = 788.325
DO YOU WANT HARD COPY ? YES OR NO
?NO
THIS IS THE SECOND SOLUTION.
TRIANGLE REFERENCE NUMBER 5
S1= 37.987      A1= 32.7865
S2= 43.79       A2= 141.37387
S3= 7.137       A3= 5.83963004
DO YOU WANT THE AREA ? YES OR NO
?YES
THE AREA OF THE TRIANGLE = 84.621
DO YOU WANT HARD COPY ? YES OR NO
?NO

DO YOU HAVE ANOTHER TRIANGLE TO RUN ? YES OR NO
?YES
ENTER VALUES KNOWN: S1, S2, S3, A1, A2, OR A3 IN THIS ORDER.

NOTE ::::: ALL ANGLES MUST BE IN DECIMAL FORM !!!

IF VALUE IS UNKNOWN, ENTER A ZERO (0).
S1=
?35
S2=
?35
S3=
?35
A1=
?0
A2=
?0
A3=
?0
TRIANGLE REFERENCE NUMBER 6
S1= 35          A1= 60.0000005
S2= 35          A2= 60.0000005
S3= 35          A3= 60.0000005
DO YOU WANT THE AREA ? YES OR NO
?YES
THE AREA OF THE TRIANGLE = 530.441
DO YOU WANT HARD COPY ? YES OR NO
?NO

DO YOU HAVE ANOTHER TRIANGLE TO RUN ? YES OR NO
?NO
THIS CONCLUDES THIS PROGRAM.
```

Appendix B

Bearing
and Distance Program

```
50   REM  ******  BEARING AND DISTANCE PROGRAM  ********
60   PRINT "    "
70   REM  ******  CREATED BY WILLIAM E. BREWER, P.E. ******
80   PRINT "      "
90   REM  *******        COPYRIGHTED - 1986      *********
100  PRINT "      "
110  REM   THIS PROGRAM WILL CALCULATE THE BEARING ANGLE AND
120  REM   THE DISTANCE BETWEEN ANY TWO POINTS IF THE COORDINATES
130  REM   OF THE POINTS ARE KNOWN.
140  HOME
150  PRINT "COMPUTER PROGRAM FOR DETERMINING THE BEARING AND THE"
160  PRINT "DISTANCE BETWEEN TWO KNOWN POINTS.  THE COORDINATES"
170  PRINT "MUST BE KNOWN TO USE THIS PROGRAM."
180  PRINT "  "
190  PRINT "WILL YOU WANT A HARDCOPY ? (YES OR NO)": INPUT Q$
200  IF Q$ = "YES" THEN 1310
210  PRINT "    "
220  PRINT "ENTER THE NUMBER OF SIDES IN THE FIGURE."
230  INPUT S1
240  PRINT "    "
250  PRINT "ENTER THE COORDINATES FOR THE FIRST POINT AS X1, Y1"
260  PRINT "AND THE COORDINATES FOR THE SECOND POINT AS X2, Y2."
270  PRINT "        "
280 N = N + 1
290  PRINT "INPUT THE COORDINATES FOR THE POINTS."
300  PRINT "X"N"= ": INPUT X1
310  PRINT "Y"N"= ": INPUT Y1
320  PRINT "X"N + 1"= ": INPUT X2
330  PRINT "Y"N + 1"= ": INPUT Y2
340  IF X1 = X2 AND Y1 > Y2 THEN 420
350  IF X1 < X2 AND Y1 > Y2 THEN 570
360  IF X1 < X2 AND Y1 = Y2 THEN 620
370  IF X1 < X2 AND Y1 < Y2 THEN 660
380  IF X1 = X2 AND Y1 < Y2 THEN 710
390  IF X1 > X2 AND Y1 < Y2 THEN 750
```

```
400   IF X1 > X2 AND Y1 = Y2 THEN 800
410   IF X1 > X2 AND Y1 > Y2 THEN 840
420 A$ = "SOUTH"
430 Z1 = 0
440 D2 = Y1 - Y2
450   PRINT "THE DISTANCE= "D2
460   PRINT "THE BEARING ANGLE= "Z1
470   GOTO 910
480   PRINT "  "
490   PRINT "DO YOU HAVE ANOTHER FIGURE TO RUN ? (YES OR NO)": INPUT G$
500 N = 0
510 S1 = 0
520 K = 0
530   IF P = 12 GOTO 1350
540   HOME
550   IF G$ = "YES" THEN 190
560   GOTO 890
570 A$ = "SOUTH EAST"
580 B = (X2 - X1) / (Y1 - Y2)
590 Z1 =   ATN (B) * 57.29578
600 D2 = ((X2 - X1) ^ 2 + (Y1 - Y2) ^ 2) ^ .5
610   GOTO 910
620 A$ = "EAST"
630 Z1 = 90
640 D2 = X2 - X1
650   GOTO 910
660 A$ = "NORTH EAST"
670 B = (X2 - X1) / (Y2 - Y1)
680 Z1 =   ATN (B) * 57.29578
690 D2 = ((X2 - X1) ^ 2 + (Y2 - Y1) ^ 2) ^ .5
700   GOTO 910
710 A$ = "NORTH"
720 Z1 = 0
730 D2 = Y2 - Y1
740   GOTO 910
750 A$ = "NORTH WEST"
760 B = (X1 - X2) / (Y2 - Y1)
770 Z1 =   ATN (B) * 57.29578
780 D2 = ((X1 - X2) ^ 2 + (Y2 - Y1) ^ 2) ^ .5
790   GOTO 910
800 A$ = "WEST"
810 Z1 = 90
820 D2 = X1 - X2
830   GOTO 910
840 A$ = "SOUTH WEST"
850 B = (X1 - X2) / (Y1 - Y2)
860 Z1 =   ATN (B) * 57.29578
870 D2 = ((X1 - X2) ^ 2 + (Y1 - Y2) ^ 2) ^ .5
880   GOTO 910
890   PRINT "THIS CONCLUDES THIS PROGRAM."
900   END
910   PRINT "REFERENCE SIDE NUMBER "N
920   PRINT "    "
930   PRINT "LINE REFERENCE COORDINATES:"
940   IF K = 12 THEN 1160
950   GOSUB 1370
960   PRINT "X"N"= "X1,"X"N + 1"= "X2: PRINT "Y"N"= "Y1,"Y"N + 1"= "Y2
970   PRINT "   "
980   PRINT "BEARING ANGLE= "
990   PRINT T1"-"T3"-"T5,A$
1000   PRINT "BEARING ANGLE (DECIMAL FORM)= "
1010   PRINT Z1,A$
1020   LET Y1 = Y2
1030 X1 = X2
1040   GOSUB 1460
```

```
1050   PRINT "DISTANCE= "D1
1060   IF N = (S1 - 1) THEN 1090
1070   IF N = > S1 THEN 490
1080   GOTO 1260
1090 N = N + 1
1100   PRINT "INPUT THE COORDINATES FOR THE BEGINNING POINT."
1110   PRINT "X1= ": INPUT X2
1120   PRINT "Y1= ": INPUT Y2
1130 K = 12
1140   GOTO 340
1150   PRINT "    "
1160   PRINT "X"N"= "X1,"X1= "X2: PRINT "Y"N"= "Y1,"Y1= "Y2"
1170   GOSUB 1370
1180   PRINT "BEARING ANGLE= "
1190   PRINT T1"-"T3"-"T5,A$
1200   PRINT "BEARING ANGLE (DECIMAL FORM)= "
1210   PRINT Z1,A$
1220   GOSUB 1460
1230   PRINT "DISTANCE= "D1
1240 S1 = 0
1250   GOTO 490
1260   PRINT "INPUT THE COORDINATES FOR THE POINT."
1270 N = N + 1
1280   PRINT "X"N + 1"= ": INPUT X2
1290   PRINT "Y"N + 1"= ": INPUT Y2
1300   GOTO 340
1310 D$ =   CHR$ (4)
1320 P = 12
1330   PRINT D$;"PR#1"
1340   GOTO 220
1350   PRINT D$;"PR#3"
1360   GOTO 550
1370 T1 =   INT (Z1)
1380 T2 = (Z1 - T1) * 60
1390 T3 =   INT (T2)
1400 T4 = (T2 - T3) * 60
1410 T5 =   INT (100 * T4)
1420   IF 100 * T4 - T5 < .5 GOTO 1440
1430 T5 = T5 + 1
1440 T5 = T5 / 100
1450   RETURN
1460 D1 =   INT (1000 * D2)
1470   IF 1000 * D2 - D1 < .5 GOTO 1490
1480 D1 = D1 + 1
1490 D1 = D1 / 1000
1500   RETURN


]RUN


COMPUTER PROGRAM FOR DETERMINING THE BEARING AND THE
DISTANCE BETWEEN TWO KNOWN POINTS.  THE COORDINATES
MUST BE KNOWN TO USE THIS PROGRAM.

WILL YOU WANT A HARDCOPY ? (YES OR NO)
?YES
ENTER THE NUMBER OF SIDES IN THE FIGURE.
?4

ENTER THE COORDINATES FOR THE FIRST POINT AS X1, Y1
AND THE COORDINATES FOR THE SECOND POINT AS X2, Y2.

INPUT THE COORDINATES FOR THE POINTS.
X1=
?1505.91
```

```
Y1=
?1692.21
X2=
?1891.87
Y2=
?1782.23
REFERENCE SIDE NUMBER 1

LINE REFERENCE COORDINATES:
X1= 1505.91     X2= 1891.87
Y1= 1692.21     Y2= 1782.23


BEARING ANGLE=
76-52-16.44        NORTH EAST
BEARING ANGLE (DECIMAL FORM)=
76.8712344         NORTH EAST
DISTANCE= 396.319
INPUT THE COORDINATES FOR THE POINT.
X3=
?2109.90
Y3=
?2109.90
REFERENCE SIDE NUMBER 2

LINE REFERENCE COORDINATES:
X2= 1891.87     X3= 2109.9
Y2= 1782.23     Y3= 2109.9


BEARING ANGLE=
33-38-22.55        NORTH EAST
BEARING ANGLE (DECIMAL FORM)=
33.6395984         NORTH EAST
DISTANCE= 393.579
INPUT THE COORDINATES FOR THE POINT.
X4=
?1305.12
Y4=
?1544.43
REFERENCE SIDE NUMBER 3

LINE REFERENCE COORDINATES:
X3= 2109.9      X4= 1305.12
Y3= 2109.9      Y4= 1544.43


BEARING ANGLE=
54-54-23.83        SOUTH WEST
BEARING ANGLE (DECIMAL FORM)=
54.9066183         SOUTH WEST
DISTANCE= 983.579
INPUT THE COORDINATES FOR THE BEGINNING POINT.
X1=
?1505.91
Y1=
?1692.21
REFERENCE SIDE NUMBER 4

LINE REFERENCE COORDINATES:
X4= 1305.12     X1= 1505.91
Y4= 1544.43     Y1= 1692.21
BEARING ANGLE=
53-38-49.92        NORTH EAST
BEARING ANGLE (DECIMAL FORM)=
53.6471986         NORTH EAST            .
DISTANCE= 249.31
DO YOU HAVE ANOTHER FIGURE TO RUN ? (YES OR NO)
?NO
```

Appendix C

Pavement Cost-Analysis Program

```
50   REM  ********     PAVEMENT COST-ANALYSIS PROGRAM     ************
60   PRINT "      "
70   REM  ******     CREATED BY WILLIAM E. BREWER, P.E.   ************
80   PRINT "      "
90   REM  **********
100  PRINT "            "
110  REM      THIS PROGRAM WILL CALCULATE THE COST PER LINEAL FOOT AND
120  REM      COST PER SQUARE YARD FOR PAVEMENT WITH AND WITHOUT CURBS
130  REM      AND FOR FIVE (5) DIFFERENT PAVEMENT TYPE SITUATIONS.
140  HOME
150  PRINT "*****************************************************************
     ****"
160  PRINT "     "
170  PRINT  TAB( 20);"PAVEMENT COST ANALYSIS PROGRAM"
180  PRINT "     "
190  PRINT "*****************************************************************
     ****"
200  PRINT "THIS PROGRAM WILL COMPUTE THE COST PER SQUARE YARD OR"
210  PRINT "COST PER LINEAL FOOT FOR NEW PAVEMENT CONSTRUCTION."
220  PRINT "      "
230  PRINT "THE USER CAN USE AASHTO COEFFICIENTS OR ASSIGN VALUES"
240  PRINT "FOR THE COEFFICIENTS.  THE PROGRAM REQUIRES THE INPUT"
250  PRINT "OF PAVEMENT MATERIAL COST ($/CU.YD.) AND ($/L.F.) FOR CURBING"
260  PRINT "WITH SPECIFIC INFORMATION REGARDING THE PAVEMENT'S WIDTH AND"
270  PRINT "DEPTHS OF MATERIALS BEING CONSIDERED."
280  PRINT "      "
290  PRINT "DESCRIBE THE PAVEMENT SECTION BEING CONSIDERED."
300  PRINT "SELECT PAVEMENT TYPE FROM THE FOLLOWING LIST:"
310  PRINT "-----------------------------------------------------------"
320  CLEAR
330  PRINT "<1>   RIGID CONCRETE PAVEMENT WITH INTEGRAL CURBS."
340  PRINT "<2>   FLEXIBLE PAVEMENT, 3 LAYER SYSTEM WITH CURB AND GUTTER."
350  PRINT "<3>   FLEXIBLE PAVEMENT, 2 LAYER SYSTEM WITH CURB AND GUTTER."
360  PRINT "<4>   RIGID PAVEMENT WITH NO CURBS."
370  PRINT "<5>   FLEXIBLE PAVEMENT, 3 LAYER SYSTEM WITH NO CURBS."
```

```
380    PRINT "        "
390    PRINT "INPUT THE PAVEMENT SYSTEM BEING CONSIDERED -"
400    INPUT J
410    HOME
420    ON J GOTO 430,850,1640,2290,2760
430    PRINT "RIGID CONCRETE PAVEMENT WITH INTEGRAL CURBS."
440    PRINT "--------------------------------------------------------------"

450 N = 1
460    PRINT "PLEASE SUPPLY THE INFORMATION REQUESTED;"
470    PRINT "        "
480    PRINT "THIS ESTIMATE IS BASED ON CONCRETE WITH A MR = 700 PSI."
490    PRINT "PAVEMENT GEOMETRY -"
500    PRINT "--------------------------------"
510    PRINT "PAVEMENT THICKNESS IN INCHES = ": INPUT T1
520    IF P = 16 GOTO 630
530    IF P = 67 GOTO 560
540    PRINT "PAVEMENT WIDTH =": INPUT W1
550    IF P = 16 GOTO 630
560    PRINT "COST OF CONCRETE PER SQ.YD. FOR THE THICKNESS OF "T1" INCHES"
570    PRINT "FINISHED AND CURED IN FIELD = ": INPUT C1
580    IF P = 16 GOTO 630
590    IF P = 67 GOTO 630
600    PRINT "COST OF INTEGRAL CURB PER LINEAL FOOT = ": INPUT L1
610    IF P = 16 GOTO 630
620    PRINT "COST OF EXCAVATION PER CUBIC YARD = ": INPUT E1
630 X1 = ((W1 * C1) / 9) + (L1 * 2) + ((T1 / 36) * (W1 / 9) * E1)
640 Y1 = X1 / (W1 / 9)
650    GOSUB 4230
660    PRINT "            "
670    PRINT "THE COST PER LINEAL FOOT = $ "X1
680    PRINT "THE COST PER SQUARE YARD = $ "Y1
690    PRINT "        "
700    PRINT "DO YOU WANT HARDCOPY OF DATA ? (YES OR NO)": INPUT H$
710    IF H$ = "YES" THEN  GOSUB 3470
720    PRINT "DO YOU WANT TO CHANGE ANY INPUT ? (YES OR NO)": INPUT V$
730    IF V$ = "NO" THEN 1560
740    PRINT "       . "
750    PRINT "WHICH CATEGORY:": PRINT  TAB( 12);"<1> PAVEMENT THICKNESS": PRINT
       TAB( 12);"<2> PAVEMENT WIDTH": PRINT  TAB( 12);"<3> COST OF CONCRETE
       ": PRINT  TAB( 12);"<4> COST OF CURB": PRINT  TAB( 12);"<5> COST OF E
       XCAVATION": PRINT  TAB( 12)"<6> ALL CATEGORIES": INPUT I
760 P = 16
770    ON I GOTO 800,540,560,600,620,780
780 P = 10
790    GOTO 510
800    PRINT "A CHANGE IN THICKNESS REQUIRES A CHANGE IN COST OF CONCRETE !"

810    PRINT "THE CURRENT LISTED CONCRETE COST IS $ "C1" PER SQUARE YARD FOR
       "
820    PRINT "A SLAB THICKNESS OF "T1" INCHES."
830 P = 67
840    GOTO 510
850    PRINT "FLEXIBLE PAVEMENT, 3 LAYER SYSTEM WITH CURB AND GUTTER."
860    PRINT "-------------------------------------------------------------
       --"
870    PRINT "     "
880 N = 2
890    PRINT "PLEASE SUPPLY THE INFORMATION REQUESTED;"
900    PRINT "     "
910    PRINT "THIS ESTIMATE IS BASED ON THE AASHO ROAD TEST GENERAL"
920    PRINT "EQUATION; SN = A1*D1 + A2*D2 + A3*D3"
930    PRINT "     "
940    PRINT "DO YOU HAVE VALUES FOR A1, A2, A3 OR SHOULD AASHO VALUES"
950    PRINT "BE USED ? (YES IF YOU WANT TO INPUT VALUES, NO IF NOT.)": INPUT
       V$
```

```
960    IF V$ = "YES" GOTO 1540
970    PRINT "PAVEMENT GEOMETRY -";
980    PRINT "PAVEMENT STRUCTURAL NUMBER (SN) = ": INPUT S1
990    IF P = 35 GOTO 1190
1000   PRINT "PAVEMENT SURFACE COURSE THICKNESS IN INCHES = ": INPUT B1
1010   IF P = 35 GOTO 1190
1020   PRINT "PAVEMENT SUBBASE THICKNESS IN INCHES = ": INPUT B3
1030   IF P = 35 GOTO 1190
1040   PRINT "PAVEMENT WIDTH, WITHOUT CURB AND GUTTER =": INPUT W2
1050   IF P = 35 GOTO 1190
1060   IF P = 30 GOTO 1190
1070   PRINT "COST OF SURFACE MATERIAL IN CUBIC YARDS = ": INPUT C2
1080   IF P = 35 GOTO 1190
1090   PRINT "COST OF BASE MATERIAL IN CUBIC YARDS = ": INPUT C3
1100   IF P = 35 GOTO 1190
1110   PRINT "COST OF SUBBASE MATERIAL IN CUBIC YARDS = ": INPUT C4
1120   IF P = 35 GOTO 1190
1130   PRINT "COST OF THE CURB AND GUTTER PER LINEAL FOOT = ": INPUT L2
1140   IF P = 35 GOTO 1190
1150   PRINT "COST OF EXCAVATION IN CUBIC YARDS = ": INPUT E2
1160   IF P = 35 GOTO 1190
1170   IF P = 13 GOTO 1190
1180   A1 = .44:A2 = .14:A3 = .11
1190   B2 = (S1 - (B1 * A1 + B3 * A3)) / A2
1200   IF B2 < 0 THEN 4400
1210   X2 = (((B1 * W2 * C2) / 9) / 36) + (((B2 * W2 * C3) / 9) / 36) + (((B
       3 * W2 * C4) / 9) / 36) + (((B1 + B2 + B3) * (W2 / 9) * E2) / 36)
1220   X3 = (X2 + 2 * L2) + ((6 * 4 * E2) / 9) / 36
1230   Y2 = X3 / ((W2 + 4) / 9)
1240   X1 = X3
1250   Y1 = Y2
1260   GOSUB 4230
1270   X3 = X1
1280   Y2 = Y1
1290   PRINT "      "
1300   PRINT "THE COST PER LINEAL FOOT = $ "X3
1310   PRINT "THE COST PER SQUARE YARD = $ "Y2
1320   PRINT "      "
1330   PRINT "DO YOU WANT HARDCOPY OF DATA ? (YES OR NO)": INPUT H$
1340   IF H$ = "YES" THEN   GOSUB 3470
1350   PRINT "DO YOU WANT TO CHANGE ANY INPUT ? (YES OR NO)": INPUT V$
1360   IF V$ = "NO" THEN 1560
1370   PRINT "WHICH CATEGORY:": PRINT  TAB( 12);"<1> STRUCTURAL COEFFICIENT
       S": PRINT  TAB( 12);"<2> STRUCTURAL NUMBER": PRINT  TAB( 12);"<3> PAV
       EMENT GEOMETRY": PRINT  TAB( 12);"<4> COST INFORMATION": PRINT  TAB(
       12);"<5> ALL CATEGORIES": INPUT I
1380   P = 35
1390   ON I GOTO 1520,980,1470,1420,1400
1400   P = 0
1410   GOTO 940
1420   PRINT "WHICH VALUE:": PRINT  TAB( 20);"<1> SURFACE": PRINT  TAB( 20)
       ;"<2> BASE": PRINT  TAB( 20);"<3> SUBBASE": PRINT  TAB( 20);"<4> CURB
       AND GUTTER": PRINT  TAB( 20);"<5> EXCAVATION": PRINT  TAB( 20);"<6>
       ALL FIVE CATEGORIES": INPUT J
1430   P = 35
1440   ON J GOTO 1070,1090,1110,1130,1150,1450
1450   P = 13
1460   GOTO 1070
1470   PRINT "WHICH CATEGORY: <1> SURFACE, <2> SUBBASE, <3> WIDTH OR <4> AL
       L THREE ?"
1480   INPUT U
1490   ON U GOTO 1000,1020,1040,1500
1500   P = 30
1510   GOTO 1000
1520   PRINT "INPUT VALUES FOR A1,A2,AND A3 IN THIS ORDER.": INPUT A1,A2,A3
```

```
1530   GOTO 1190
1540   PRINT "INPUT VALUES FOR A1,A2, AND A3 IN THIS ORDER.": INPUT A1,A2,A
       3
1550   GOTO 970
1560   PRINT "DO YOU HAVE ANOTHER PAVEMENT SECTION TO REVIEW ? (YES OR NO)"
       : INPUT R$
1570   IF R$ = "YES" THEN 1590
1580   IF R$ = "NO" THEN 1610
1590   HOME
1600   GOTO 300
1610   HOME
1620   PRINT "THIS CONCLUDES THIS PROGRAM !"
1630   END
1640   PRINT "FLEXIBLE PAVEMENT, 2 LAYER SYSTEM WITH CURB AND GUTTER."
1650   PRINT "-------------------------------------------------------------
       -"
1660   PRINT "         "
1670 N = 3
1680   PRINT "PLEASE SUPPLY THE INFORMATION REQUESTED;"
1690   PRINT "         "
1700   PRINT "THIS ESTIMATE IS BASED ON THE AASHO ROAD TEST GENERAL"
1710   PRINT "EQUATION; SN = A1*D1 + A2*D2 + A3*D3 WHERE THE A3*D3"
1720   PRINT "COMPONENT WILL NOT BE CONSIDERED."
1730   PRINT "         "
1740   PRINT "DO YOU HAVE VALUES FOR A1 AND A2 OR SHOULD AASHO VALUES"
1750   PRINT "BE USED ? (YES IF YOU WANT TO INPUT VALUES, NO IF NOT.)": INPUT
       V$
1760   IF V$ = "YES" GOTO 2140
1770   PRINT "PAVEMENT GEOMETRY -"
1780   PRINT "PAVEMENT STRUCTURAL NUMBER (SN) = ": INPUT S2
1790   IF P = 21 GOTO 1950
1800   PRINT "PAVEMENT SURFACE COURSE THICKNESS IN INCHES = ": INPUT D1
1810   IF P = 21 GOTO 1950
1820   PRINT "PAVEMENT WIDTH, WITHOUT CURB AND GUTTER = ": INPUT W3
1830   IF P = 21 GOTO 1950
1840   IF P = 25 GOTO 1950
1850   PRINT "COST OF SURFACE MATERIAL IN CUBIC YARDS = ": INPUT C5
1860   IF P = 21 GOTO 1950
1870   PRINT "COST OF BASE MATERIAL IN CUBIC YARDS = ": INPUT C6
1880   IF P = 21 GOTO 1950
1890   PRINT "COST OF THE CURB AND GUTTER PER LINEAL FOOT =": INPUT L3
1900   IF P = 21 GOTO 1950
1910   PRINT "COST OF EXCAVATION IN CUBIC YARDS = ": INPUT E3
1920   IF P = 21 GOTO 1950
1930   IF P = 25 GOTO 1950
1940 A1 = .44:A2 = .14
1950 D2 = ((S2 - (A1 * D1)) / A2)
1960 X4 = ((D1 * C5 * W3 / 9) + (D2 * C6 * W3 / 9) + ((D1 + D2) * E3 * W3
       9)) / 36 + (2 * L3) + (6 * 4 * E3 / 9) / 36
1970 Y3 = X4 / ((W3 + 4) / 9)
1980 X1 = X4
1990 Y1 = Y3
2000   GOSUB 4230
2010 X4 = X1
2020 Y3 = Y1
2030   PRINT "         "
2040   PRINT "THE COST PER LINEAL FOOT = $ "X4
2050   PRINT "COST PER SQUARE YARD = $ "Y3
2060   PRINT "         "
2070   PRINT "DO YOU WANT HARDCOPY OF DATA ? (YES OR NO)": INPUT H$
2080   IF H$ = "YES" THEN  GOSUB 3470
2090   PRINT "DO YOU WANT TO CHANGE ANY INPUT ? (YES OR NO)": INPUT V$
2100   IF V$ = "NO" THEN 1560
2110   PRINT "WHICH CATEGORY:": PRINT  TAB( 12);"<1> STRUCTURAL COEFFICIENT
       S": PRINT  TAB( 12);"<2> STRUCTURAL NUMBER": PRINT  TAB( 12);"<3> PAV
```

```
     EMENT GEOMETRY": PRINT  TAB( 12);"<4> COST INFORMATION": PRINT  TAB(
     12)"<5> ALL CATEGORIES": INPUT I
2120 P = 21
2130  ON I GOTO 2180,1780,2200,2250,2160
2140  PRINT "INPUT VALUES FOR A1 AND A2 IN THIS ORDER.": INPUT A1,A2
2150  GOTO 1770
2160 P = 0
2170  GOTO 1740
2180  PRINT "INPUT VALUES FOR A1 AND A2 IN THIS ORDER.": INPUT A1,A2
2190  GOTO 1950
2200  PRINT "WHICH CATEGORY: <1> SURFACE, <2> WIDTH OR <3> BOTH ?"
2210  INPUT U
2220  ON U GOTO 1800,1820,2230
2230 P = 25
2240  GOTO 1800
2250  PRINT "WHICH VALUE:": PRINT  TAB( 20);"<1> SURFACE": PRINT  TAB( 20)
     ;"<2> BASE": PRINT  TAB( 20);"<3> CURB AND GUTTER": PRINT  TAB( 20);"
     <4> EXCAVATION": PRINT  TAB( 20);"<5> ALL FOUR CATEGORIES": INPUT J
2260  ON J GOTO 1850,1870,1890,1910,2270
2270 P = 25
2280  GOTO 1850
2290  PRINT "RIGID PAVEMENT WITH NO CURBS."
2300  PRINT "-----------------------------------"
2310  PRINT "         "
2320 N = 4
2330  PRINT "THIS TYPE OF PAVEMENT ANALYSIS COULD BE USED FOR A PARKING LO
     T"
2340  PRINT "OR DRIVEWAY."
2350  PRINT "         "
2360  PRINT "PLEASE SUPPLY THE INFORMATION REQUESTED;"
2370  PRINT "         "
2380  PRINT "THIS ESTIMATE IS BASED ON CONCRETE WITH A MR = 700 PSI."
2390  PRINT "PAVEMENT GEOMETRY -"
2400  PRINT "PAVEMENT THICKNESS IN INCHES = ": INPUT T2
2410  IF P = 16 GOTO 2500
2420  IF P = 67 GOTO 2450
2430  PRINT "LOT WIDTH =": INPUT W4
2440  IF P = 16 GOTO 2500
2450  PRINT "COST OF CONCRETE PER SQ. YD. FOR THE THICKNESS OF "T2" INCHES
     "
2460  PRINT "FINISHED AND CURED IN FIELD = ": INPUT C7
2470  IF P = 16 GOTO 2500
2480  IF P = 67 GOTO 2500
2490  PRINT "COST OF EXCAVATION PER CUBIC YARD = ": INPUT E4
2500 X5 = ((W4 * C7) / 9) + ((T2 / 36) * (W4 / 9) * E4)
2510 Y4 = X5 / (W4 / 9)
2520 X1 = X5
2530 Y1 = Y4
2540  GOSUB 4230
2550 X5 = X1
2560 Y4 = Y1
2570  PRINT "         "
2580  PRINT "THE COST OF THE LOT PER LINEAL FOOT = $ "X5
2590  PRINT "THE COST OF THE LOT PER SQUARE YARD = $ "Y4
2600  PRINT "         "
2610  PRINT "DO YOU WANT HARDCOPY OF DATA ? (YES OR NO)": INPUT H$
2620  PRINT "         "
2630  IF H$ = "YES" THEN  GOSUB 3470
2640  PRINT "DO YOU WANT TO CHANGE ANY INPUT ? (YES OR NO)": INPUT V$
2650  IF V$ = "NO" THEN 1560
2660  PRINT "WHICH CATEGORY:": PRINT  TAB( 20);"<1> PAVEMENT THICKNESS": PRINT
     TAB( 20);"<2> LOT WIDTH": PRINT  TAB( 20);"<3> COST OF CONCRETE": PRINT
     TAB( 20);"<4> COST OF EXCAVATION": PRINT  TAB( 20);"<5> ALL CATEGORI
     ES": INPUT I
2670 P = 16
```

```
2680  ON I GOTO 2710,2430,2450,2490,2690
2690  P = 0
2700  GOTO 2400
2710  PRINT "A CHANGE IN THICKNESS REQUIRES A CHANGE IN COST OF CONCRETE !
      "
2720  PRINT "THE CURRENT LISTED CONCRETE COST IS $ "C7" PER SQUARE YARD FO
      R"
2730  PRINT "A SLAB THICKNESS OF "T2" INCHES."
2740  P = 67
2750  GOTO 2400
2760  PRINT "FLEXIBLE PAVEMENT, 3 LAYER SYSTEM WITH NO CURBS."
2770  PRINT "-------------------------------------------------------------"
2780  PRINT "              "
2790  N = 5
2800  PRINT "THIS TYPE OF PAVEMENT ANALYSIS COULD BE USED FOR A"
2810  PRINT "PARKING LOT OR DRIVEWAY."
2820  PRINT "          "
2830  PRINT "PLEASE SUPPLY THE INFORMATION REQUESTED;"
2840  PRINT "          "
2850  PRINT "THIS ESTIMATE IS BASED ON THE AASHO ROAD TEST VALUES"
2860  PRINT "EQUATION; SN = A1*D1 + A2+D2 + A3*D3"
2870  PRINT "          "
2880  PRINT "DO YOU HAVE VALUES FOR A1, A2, A3 OR SHOULD AASHO VALUES"
2890  PRINT "BE USED ? (YES IF YOU WANT TO INPUT VALUES, NO IF NOT.)": INPUT
      V$
2900  IF V$ = "YES" GOTO 3340
2910  PRINT "PAVEMENT GEOMETRY -"
2920  PRINT "PAVEMENT STRUCTURAL NUMBER (SN) = ": INPUT S1
2930  IF P = 35 GOTO 3110
2940  PRINT "PAVEMENT SURFACE COURSE THICKNESS IN INCHES = ": INPUT B1
2950  IF P = 35 GOTO 3110
2960  PRINT "PAVEMENT SUBBASE THICKNESS IN INCHES = ": INPUT B3
2970  IF P = 35 GOTO 3110
2980  PRINT "PAVEMENT OR LOT WIDTH = ": INPUT W2
2990  IF P = 35 GOTO 3110
3000  IF P = 30 GOTO 3110
3010  PRINT "COST OF SURFACE MATERIAL IN CUBIC YARDS = ": INPUT C2
3020  IF P = 35 GOTO 3110
3030  PRINT "COST OF BASE MATERIAL IN CUBIC YARDS = ": INPUT C3
3040  IF P = 35 GOTO 3110
3050  PRINT "COST OF SUBBASE MATERIAL IN CUBIC YARDS =": INPUT C4
3060  IF P = 35 GOTO 3110
3070  PRINT "COST OF EXCAVATION IN CUBIC YARDS = ": INPUT E2
3080  IF P = 35 GOTO 3110
3090  IF P = 13 GOTO 3110
3100  A1 = .44:A2 = .14:A3 = .11
3110  B2 = (S2 - (B1 * A1 + B3 * A3)) / A2
3120  IF B2 < 0 THEN 4400
3130  X2 = (((B1 * W2 * C2) / 9) / 36) + (((B2 * W2 * C3) / 9) / 36) + (((B
      3 * W2 * C4) / 9) / 36) + (((B1 + B2 + B3) * (W2 / 9) * E2) / 36)
3140  Y2 = X2 / (W2 / 9)
3150  X1 = X2
3160  Y1 = Y2
3170  GOSUB 4230
3180  X2 = X1
3190  Y2 = Y1
3200  PRINT "          "
3210  PRINT "THE COST PER LINEAL FOOT = $ "X2
3220  PRINT "THE COST PER SQUARE YARD = $ "Y2
3230  PRINT "          "
3240  PRINT "DO YOU WANT HARD COPY ? (YES OR N0)": INPUT H$
3250  PRINT "          "
3260  IF H$ = "YES" THEN  GOSUB 3470
3270  PRINT "DO YOU WANT TO CHANGE ANY INPUT ? (YES OR NO)": INPUT V$
3280  IF V$ = "NO" THEN 1560
```

```
3290  PRINT "WHICH CATEGORY:": PRINT  TAB( 12);"<1> STRUCTURAL COEFFICIENT
      S": PRINT  TAB( 12);"<2> STRUCTURAL NUMBER": PRINT  TAB( 12);"<3> PAV
      EMENT GEOMETRY": PRINT  TAB( 12);"<4> COST INFORMATION": PRINT  TAB(
      12);"<5> ALL CATEGORIES": INPUT I
3300  P = 35
3310  ON I GOTO 3360,2920,3420,3380,3320
3320  P = 0
3330  GOTO 2880
3340  PRINT "INPUT VALUES FOR A1, A2, AND A3 IN THIS ORDER.": INPUT A1,A2,
      A3
3350  GOTO 2910
3360  PRINT "INPUT VALUES FOR A1, A2, AND A3 IN THIS ORDER.": INPUT A1,A2,
      A3
3370  GOTO 3110
3380  PRINT "WHICH VALUES:": PRINT  TAB( 20);"<1> SURFACE": PRINT  TAB( 20
      );"<2> BASE": PRINT  TAB( 20);"<3> SUBBASE": PRINT  TAB( 20);"<4> EXC
      AVATION": PRINT  TAB( 20);"<5> ALL FOUR CATEGORIES": INPUT J
3390  ON J GOTO 3010,3030,3050,3070,3400
3400  P = 13
3410  GOTO 3010
3420  PRINT "WHICH CATEGORY: <1> SURFACE, <2> SUBBASE, <3> WIDTH OR <4> AL
      L THREE ?"
3430  INPUT U
3440  ON U GOTO 2940,2960,2980,3450
3450  P = 30
3460  GOTO 2940
3470 D$ =  CHR$ (4)
3480  PRINT D$;"PR#1"
3490  IF N = 1 GOTO 3550
3500  IF N = 2 GOTO 3690
3510  IF N = 3 GOTO 3890
3520  IF N = 4 GOTO 4070
3530  IF N = 5 THEN 4190
3540  RETURN
3550  PRINT "        "
3560  PRINT "RIGID CONCRETE PAVEMENT WITH INTEGRAL CURBS"
3570  PRINT "----------------------------------------------------------
      ---"
3580  PRINT "    "
3590  PRINT "PAVEMENT THICKNESS = "T1" INCHES."
3600  PRINT "PAVEMENT WIDTH = "W1" FEET."
3610  PRINT "COST OF FINISHED CONCRETE PER SQ. YD. = $ "C1
3620  PRINT "COST OF INTEGRAL CURB PER L.F. = $ "L1
3630  PRINT "COST OF EXCAVATION PER C.Y. = $ "E1
3640  PRINT "    "
3650  PRINT "COST PER LINEAL FOOT = $ "X1
3660  PRINT "COST PER SQUARE YARD = $ "Y1
3670  PRINT D$;"PR#3"
3680  RETURN
3690  PRINT "    "
3700  PRINT "FLEXIBLE PAVEMENT, 3 LAYER SYSTEM WITH CURB AND GUTTER."
3710  PRINT "-----------------------------------------------------------"

3720  PRINT "    "
3730  PRINT "STRUCTURAL COEFFICIENTS: A1 ="A1", A2 ="A2", A3 ="A3
3740  PRINT "PAVEMENT STRUCTURAL NUMBER (SN) ="S1
3750  PRINT "SURFACE COURSE = "B1" INCHES"
3760  GOSUB 4340
3770  PRINT "BASE COURSE = "B2" INCHES"
3780  PRINT "SUBBASE COURSE = "B3" INCHES"
3790  PRINT "PAVEMENT WIDTH WITHOUT CURB AND GUTTER = "W2" FEET."
3800  PRINT "COST OF SURFACE, BASE, SUBBASE = $ "C2", "C3", "C4" RESPECTIV
      ELY"
3810  IF N = 5 THEN 3830
3820  PRINT "COST OF CURB AND GUTTER = $ "L2" PER LINEAL FOOT"
```

```
3830  PRINT "COST OF EXCAVATION PER C.Y. = $ "E2
3840  PRINT "    "
3850  PRINT "COST PER LINEAL FOOT = $ "X1
3860  PRINT "COST PER SQUARE YARD = $ "Y1


3870  PRINT D$;"PR#3"
3880  RETURN
3890  PRINT "    "
3900  PRINT "FLEXIBLE PAVEMENT, 2 LAYER SYSTEM WITH CURB AND GUTTER."
3910  PRINT "----------------------------------------------------------"
3920  PRINT "STRUCTURAL COEFFICIENTS: A1 ="A1", A2 ="A2
3930  PRINT "PAVEMENT STRUCTURAL NUMBER (SN) ="S2
3940  PRINT "SURFACE COURSE = "D1" INCHES."
3950  B2 = D2
3960  GOSUB 4340
3970  PRINT "BASE COURSE = "B2" INCHES."
3980  PRINT "PAVEMENT WIDTH WITHOUT  CURB AND GUTTER = "W3" FEET."
3990  PRINT "COST OF SURFACE AND BASE = $ "C5", "C6" RESPECTIVELY"
4000  PRINT "COST OF CURB AND GUTTER = $ "L3" PER LINEAL FOOT"
4010  PRINT "COST OF EXCAVATION PER C.Y. = $ "E3
4020  PRINT "    "
4030  PRINT "COST PER LINEAL FOOT = $ "X1
4040  PRINT "COST PER SQUARE YARD = $ "Y1
4050  PRINT D$;"PR#3"
4060  RETURN
4070  PRINT "    "
4080  PRINT "RIGID PAVEMENT WITH NO CURBS."
4090  PRINT "----------------------------------------------------------"

4100  PRINT "PAVEMENT THICKNESS = "T2" INCHES."
4110  PRINT "PAVEMENT WIDTH = "W4" FEET."
4120  PRINT "COST OF FINISHED CONCRETE PER SQ. YD. = $ "C7
4130  PRINT "COST OF EXCAVATION PER C.Y. = $ "E4
4140  PRINT "    "
4150  PRINT "COST PER LINEAL FOOT = $ "X1
4160  PRINT "COST PER SQUARE YARD = $ "Y1
4170  PRINT D$;"PR#3"
4180  RETURN
4190  PRINT "    "
4200  PRINT "FLEXIBLE PAVEMENT, 3 LAYER SYSTEM WITH NO CURBS."
4210  PRINT "------------------------------------------------------"
4220  GOTO 3730
4230  M1 =  INT (100 * X1)
4240  IF 100 * X1 - M1 < .5 GOTO 4260
4250  M1 = M1 + 1
4260  M1 = M1 / 100
4270  X1 = M1
4280  M2 =  INT (100 * Y1)
4290  IF 100 * Y1 - M2 < .5 GOTO 4310
4300  M2 = M2 + 1
4310  M2 = M2 / 100
4320  Y1 = M2
4330  RETURN
4340  V1 =  INT (100 * B2)
4350  IF 100 * B2 - V1 < .5 GOTO 4370
4360  V1 = V1 + 1
4370  V1 = V1 / 100
4380  B2 = V1
4390  RETURN
4400  PRINT "THE LIMITS ON THE BASE AND SUBBASE THICKNESSES ARE"
4410  PRINT "USUALLY 3 INCHES AND 6 INCHES RESPECTIVELY.  YOU"
4420  PRINT "HAVE EXCEEDED THESE LIMITS AND YOUR A1*D1 + A2*D2 IS"
4430  PRINT "GREATER THAN SN.  PLEASE START OVER !!!"
4440  PRINT "    "
```

```
4450   GOTO 300


] RUN


*********************************************************************
                     PAVEMENT COST-ANALYSIS PROGRAM

*********************************************************************
THIS PROGRAM WILL COMPUTE THE COST PER SQUARE YARD OR
COST PER LINEAL FOOT FOR NEW PAVEMENT CONSTRUCTION.

THE USER CAN USE AASHTO COEFFICIENTS OR ASSIGN VALUES
FOR THE COEFFICIENTS.   THE PROGRAM REQUIRES THE INPUT
OF PAVEMENT MATERIAL COST ($/CU.YD.) AND ($/L.F.) FOR CURBING
WITH SPECIFIC INFORMATION REGARDING THE PAVEMENT'S WIDTH AND
DEPTHS OF MATERIALS BEING CONSIDERED.

DESCRIBE THE PAVEMENT SECTION BEING CONSIDERED.
SELECT PAVEMENT TYPE FROM THE FOLLOWING LIST:
-----------------------------------------------------------------
<1>   RIGID CONCRETE PAVEMENT WITH INTEGRAL CURBS.
<2>   FLEXIBLE PAVEMENT, 3 LAYER SYSTEM WITH CURB AND GUTTER.
<3>   FLEXIBLE PAVEMENT, 2 LAYER SYSTEM WITH CURB AND GUTTER.
<4>   RIGID PAVEMENT WITH NO CURBS.
<5>   FLEXIBLE PAVEMENT, 3 LAYER SYSTEM WITH NO CURBS.

INPUT THE PAVEMENT SYSTEM BEING CONSIDERED -
?2
FLEXIBLE PAVEMENT, 3 LAYER SYSTEM WITH CURB AND GUTTER.
-----------------------------------------------------------------

PLEASE SUPPLY THE INFORMATION REQUESTED;

THIS ESTIMATE IS BASED ON THE AASHO ROAD TEST GENERAL
EQUATION; SN = A1*D1 + A2*D2 + A3*D3

DO YOU HAVE VALUES FOR A1, A2, A3 OR SHOULD AASHO VALUES
BE USED ? (YES IF YOU WANT TO INPUT VALUES, NO IF NOT.)
?NO
PAVEMENT GEOMETRY -
PAVEMENT STRUCTURAL NUMBER (SN) =
?3.6
PAVEMENT SURFACE COURSE THICKNESS IN INCHES =
?3
PAVEMENT SUBBASE THICKNESS IN INCHES =
?6
PAVEMENT WIDTH, WITHOUT CURB AND GUTTER =
?21
COST OF SURFACE MATERIAL IN CUBIC YARDS =
?30
COST OF BASE MATERIAL IN CUBIC YARDS =
?12
COST OF SUBBASE MATERIAL IN CUBIC YARDS =
?7
COST OF THE CURB AND GUTTER PER LINEAL FOOT =
?4.27
COST OF EXCAVATION IN CUBIC YARDS =
?1.63

THE COST PER LINEAL FOOT = $ 28.39
```

```
THE COST PER SQUARE YARD = $ 10.22

DO YOU WANT HARDCOPY OF DATA ? (YES OR NO)
?NO
DO YOU WANT TO CHANGE ANY INPUT ? (YES OR NO)
?YES
WHICH CATEGORY:
              <1> STRUCTURAL COEFFICIENTS
              <2> STRUCTURAL NUMBER
              <3> PAVEMENT GEOMETRY
              <4> COST INFORMATION
              <5> ALL CATEGORIES
?2
PAVEMENT STRUCTURAL NUMBER (SN) =
?3.0

THE COST PER LINEAL FOOT = $ 24.6
THE COST PER SQUARE YARD = $ 8.86

DO YOU WANT HARDCOPY OF DATA ? (YES OR NO)
?NO
DO YOU WANT TO CHANGE ANY INPUT ? (YES OR NO)
?NO
DO YOU HAVE ANOTHER PAVEMENT SECTION TO REVIEW ? (YES OR NO)
?NO
THIS CONCLUDES THIS PROGRAM !




]RUN



********************************************************************

             PAVEMENT COST-ANALYSIS PROGRAM

********************************************************************
THIS PROGRAM WILL COMPUTE THE COST PER SQUARE YARD OR
COST PER LINEAL FOOT FOR NEW PAVEMENT CONSTRUCTION.

THE USER CAN USE AASHTO COEFFICIENTS OR ASSIGN VALUES
FOR THE COEFFICIENTS.  THE PROGRAM REQUIRES THE INPUT
OF PAVEMENT MATERIAL COST ($/CU.YD.) AND ($/L.F.) FOR CURBING
WITH SPECIFIC INFORMATION REGARDING THE PAVEMENT'S WIDTH AND
DEPTHS OF MATERIALS BEING CONSIDERED.

DESCRIBE THE PAVEMENT SECTION BEING CONSIDERED.
SELECT PAVEMENT TYPE FROM THE FOLLOWING LIST:
------------------------------------------------------
<1>  RIGID CONCRETE PAVEMENT WITH INTEGRAL CURBS.
<2>  FLEXIBLE PAVEMENT, 3 LAYER SYSTEM WITH CURB AND GUTTER.
<3>  FLEXIBLE PAVEMENT, 2 LAYER SYSTEM WITH CURB AND GUTTER.
<4>  RIGID PAVEMENT WITH NO CURBS.
<5>  FLEXIBLE PAVEMENT, 3 LAYER SYSTEM WITH NO CURBS.

INPUT THE PAVEMENT SYSTEM BEING CONSIDERED -
?1
RIGID CONCRETE PAVEMENT WITH INTERGRAL CURBS.
------------------------------------------------------------
PLEASE SUPPLY THE INFORMATION REQUESTED;

THIS ESTIMATE IS BASED ON CONCRETE WITH A MR = 700 PSI.
PAVEMENT GEOMETRY -
------------------------------------
```

```
PAVEMENT THICKNESS IN INCHES =
?6
PAVEMENT WIDTH =
?25
COST OF CONCRETE PER SQ.YD. FOR THE THICKNESS OF 6 INCHES
FINISHED AND CURED IN FIELD =
?9.83
COST OF INTEGRAL CURB PER LINEAL FOOT =
?1.87
COST OF EXCAVATION PER CUBIC YARD =
?1.63

THE COST PER LINEAL FOOT = $ 31.8
THE COST PER SQUARE YARD = $ 11.45

DO YOU WANT HARDCOPY OF DATA ?  (YES OR NO)
?YES

RIGID CONCRETE PAVEMENT WITH INTEGRAL CURBS
-----------------------------------------------------------------

PAVEMENT THICKNESS = 6 INCHES.
PAVEMENT WIDTH = 25 FEET.
COST OF FINISHED CONCRETE PER SQ. YD. = $ 9.83
COST OF INTEGRAL CURB PER L.F. = $ 1.87
COST OF EXCAVATION PER C.Y. = $ 1.63

COST PER LINEAL FOOT = $ 31.8
COST PER SQUARE YARD = $ 11.45
```

Appendix D

Mathematics Review

INTRODUCTION

This appendix is designed to serve as a concise reference to the mathematical processes that are indispensable to land planners and site developers. The ability of the site developer and land planner to prepare workable and economical construction drawings is necessary for the success of any project. This appendix provides an easily understood reference that will rapidly recall the basic methods and formulas for solving the mathematical problems encountered in land planning and development. The reader should have a basic understanding of mathematics prior to reading this book.

Contained in this appendix will be an explanation and examples of basic algebra; angular measurements expressed in degrees, minutes, and seconds; and decimal equivalents of these angular measurements. Horizontal and vertical land measurement techniques, and geometric formulas for areas of circles and polygons will be reviewed. Trigonometric functions, their relationships to the parts of a right triangle, and the applications of these relationships will be explained.

BASIC ALGEBRA

Many site problems can be solved by the use of algebraic equations. Basic algebra is quickly forgotten unless it is used frequently. Therefore, a short restatement of some algebraic rules used in solving problems will be discussed.

1. Parentheses and brackets are symbols of aggregation that are used to indicate that some operation is to be extended over the whole expression enclosed by the parentheses or brackets, for example,

$$y = x (a + b)$$

The sum of $(a + b)$ is multiplied by x.

2. In a succession of indicated operations involving addition, subtraction, multiplication, division, powers, and roots when no parentheses are used
   a. All powers and roots are found first.
   b. All multiplications are performed next in order.
   c. All divisions are performed next and these are done in order from left to right.
   d. Additions and subtractions are performed in any order, for example,

$$y = \frac{x (a + b)^2}{x^2 - 1}$$

where, $x = 2$, $a = 3$, $b = 4$

$$y = \frac{2 (3 + 4)^2}{2^2 - 1}$$

$$y = \frac{2 (49)}{4 - 1}$$

$$y = \frac{98}{3}$$

$$y = 32.67$$

3. An algebraic equation is a statement of quality. That which is on the left of the equal sign is equal to that which is on the right of the equal sign. Both sides of an equation may be multiplied or divided by the same number without disturbing the equality of the statement. The same number may be added to or subtracted from both sides of an equation without disturbing the equation's balance.

4. In a statement where one fraction equals another fraction, the equation is referred to as a proportional statement. In this type of equation the product of the *means* equals the product of the *extremes*, e.g.

$$\frac{a}{b} = \frac{c}{x}$$

In this equation a and x are called the *extremes* while b and c are called the *means*. Therefore, in this equation a is to b as c is to x, or $ax = bc$ and $x = bc/a$.

ANGULAR MEASUREMENTS

Degrees are the common measurement form for angles. A full circle contains 360°, a half circle contains 180° and a quarter of a circle contains 90°. A degree is further

divided into 60 parts, each of which is referred to as one minute ('). Each minute is further divided into 60 parts, each of which is called a second (″). The angular measurement 45 degrees, 32 minutes, 29 seconds is expressed in the form 45° 32′ 29″. The symbol (°) refers to degrees, (′) refers to minutes, and (″) refers to seconds. An angle is referred to by the symbol ∠ followed by a letter or a symbol to identify it such as ∠ A or ∠ B. (See Fig. D-1.)

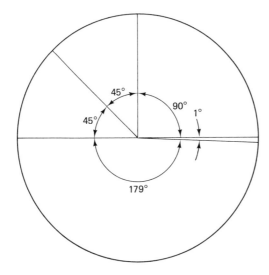

Figure D-1 Circle.

ADDITION AND SUBTRACTION OF ANGLES

When two angles are expressed in degrees, minutes, and seconds and are to be added or subtracted, you need to follow the correct addition or subtraction procedures.

Example D-1 Adding Angles

$$\angle C = \angle A + \angle B$$

$$\angle A = 45°32'\,29''$$
$$\angle B = \underline{56°17'\,13''}$$
$$\angle C = 101°\,49'\,42''$$

This example is a simple addition problem involving angles. However, if the minutes and seconds measurements added together are greater then 60 minutes or 60 seconds, it is necessary to convert these measurements to their actual values.

Example D-2 Adding Angles

$$\angle A = 45°\,32'\,29''$$
$$\angle B = \underline{75°\,38'\,43''}$$
$$\angle C = 120°\,70'\,72'' \qquad \angle C \text{ must be converted}$$
$$\angle C = 121°\,11'\,12''$$

Angle C in this problem must be converted from the form 120° 70′ 72″ because there are only 60 seconds in a minute and 60 minutes in a degree. The 72″ is equal to 1 minute (60 seconds) plus 12 seconds. We add one full minute to the minute measurement. The minute measurement is now 71′ 12″. The minute measurement must now be converted by the same method as used for the second's conversion. The 71′ is equivalent to 1 degree (60 minutes) plus 11 minutes. Thus, the entire angular measurement is now (120° + 1°), or 121° 11′ 12″ when converted into the proper representation.

Subtraction of angles involves the same process used in the addition of angles except it is reversed.

Example D–3 Subtraction of Angles

$$\angle A = 67° \ 47′ \ 12″$$
$$- \ \angle B = 55° \ 12′ \ 05″$$
$$\angle C = 12° \ 35′ \ 07″$$

This example is a relatively simple subtraction problem involving angles expressed in degrees, minutes, and seconds, because this problem does not involve the necessity to convert the angle. The next example will involve converting the largest angle into a form from which the second angle may be subtracted.

Example D–4 Subtraction of Angles with Conversion

$$\angle A = 67° \ 45′ \ 12″ \text{ converts to } 66° \ 104′ \ 72″$$
$$\angle B = 55° \ 47′ \ 21″ \qquad - \quad 55° \quad 47′ \ 21″$$
$$\angle C = 11° \quad 57′ \ 51″$$

CONVERTING ANGLES TO DEGREES AND DECIMAL PARTS

In order to work with angles expressed in degrees, minutes, and seconds in mathematical equations it is often necessary to convert the angle to decimal parts of a degree. This is especially necessary when using some hand calculators and performing trigonometric functions with angular measurements. To convert the angular measurement 11° 57′ 51″ into its decimal equivalent form, the following step by step approach may be used:

1. Convert 11° 57′ 51″ into decimal form.
2. Divide the *second* measurement by 60. (51/60 = 0.850)
3. Add decimal equivalent (0.850) to the minute measurement and again divide by 60. (57 + 0.850)/60 = 0.964167
4. The degree measurement is now expressed as 11.964167°.

Therefore, 11° 57′ 51″ = 11.964167°.

It is now a simple matter to do a variety of trigonometric calculations that include sine, cosine, tangent, and their arc functions with the angular measurement presented in its decimal equivalent using a hand calculator. See Chapter 12 for a computer program for converting angles to decimal form.

CONVERTING DEGREES AND DECIMAL PARTS
INTO DEGREES, MINUTES, AND SECONDS

There will be times when it will be necessary to convert angular measurements from the degree equivalent into degrees, minutes and seconds. Using the angular measurement that was converted into its decimal equivalent in the previous section, the angle will now be converted back to degrees, minutes, and seconds using the following step by step approach:

1. Convert $11.964167°$ into degrees, minutes, and seconds.
2. $11.964167 - 11.0 = 0.964167$ (This represents the minutes and seconds of the angle in decimal form.)
3. $0.964167 \times 60 = 57.850$ (The 57 represents the minutes.)
4. $57.850 - 57 = 0.850$ (This represents the seconds portion of the angle in decimal form.)
5. $0.850 \times 60 = 51.0$ (The 51 represents the seconds.)
6. Therefore, $11.964167° = 11° \, 57' \, 51''$

LAND MEASUREMENTS—DISTANCES

In site development, *horizontal* distances may be measured with the use of a transit and an engineer's measuring tape. When a transit is used with trigonometry, many tape measurements can be eliminated. The measuring tape that is used is an engineer's or surveyor's tape. This tape is graduated into divisions of feet and decimal parts of a foot — tenths and hundredths. The decimal system is more adaptable to computations required in surveying and site development. For professionals involved in site development it is important that they can rapidly convert measurements from feet and inches into feet and decimal parts of a foot. Following are sample problems that will illustrate this procedure.

Example D-5

Convert 12 feet $10\frac{3}{8}$ inches to feet and decimal of feet.

a. $\frac{3}{8} = 0.375$ in. (Divide 3 by 8.)

Therefore, $10\frac{3}{8}$ in. $= 10.375$ in.

b. $\frac{10.375}{12} = 0.8648$ ft (Divide 10.375 by 12.)

Therefore, 12 ft $10\frac{3}{8}$ in. $= 12.8646$ ft.

It is also necessary to be able to convert measurements from feet and decimals back into feet and inches. In order to accomplish this, first multiply the decimal part of the figure by 12 and then convert the decimal part of the answer to a fraction by multiplying this decimal part by the denominator to obtain its numerator.

Example D-6

Convert 125.318 feet to feet and inches expressed to the nearest sixteenth of an inch.

a. 0.318×12 in. $= 3.816$ in.
b. $0.816 \times 16 = 13.05$, therefore $3.816 = 3\frac{13}{16}$ in.

Therefore, 125.318 ft. $= 125$ ft $3\frac{13}{16}$ in.

Stationing is another form of horizontal reference measurement used in site development for roads and sewers. The progression in stationing is from a referenced point of commencement (usually noted as $0+00$) proceeding in a direction that is logical, usually south to north and west to east. The next station, 100 feet from the initial station, is referenced as $1+00$. If a fractional measurement of 275.83 ft, from the initial reference, were to be referenced in stationing, it would be $2+75.83$. A reference point could have two reference stations as noted in Fig. D-2.

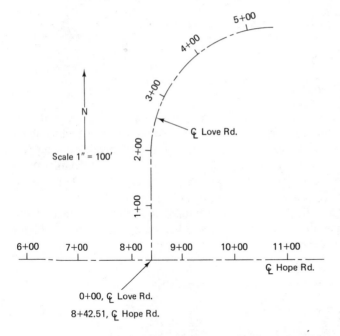

Figure D-2   Stationing.

Vertical distance is described in site planning as elevation. Elevation is expressed in feet and decimal parts of a foot as measured from a known elevation, which is usually sea level. Elevation is measured by using a surveyor's level rod, which is a rod with feet and decimal parts of a foot inscribed on it. This is similar to the engineer's measuring tape. Elevations are required in land planning for the establishment of proper controls for drainage, grading, and street locations. These activities are usually accomplished with the development of a contour map. The development of contour maps (topography) is discussed in Chapter 5.

CIRCLES

It is important for site planners to understand the relationships of the parts of the circle and the applications of these relationships. In site planning the arc distance is of crucial importance and the knowledge of the calculations regarding the arc distance should be a priority with site planners. Figure D–3, illustrates the appropriate parts of a circle. Following is an explanation of the different parts of a circle with specific formulae that will be used in site planning calculations.

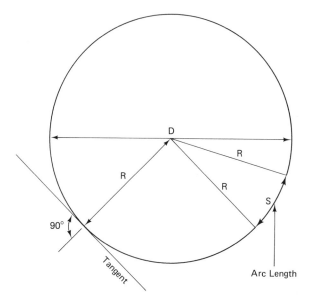

Figure D-3 Circle.

D = Diameter, width of a circle.

R = Radius, one half the diameter's length.

C = Circumference, total arc length around the circle.
   $C = \pi D$ (the numerical value of π will be listed below.) $C = 2\pi R$

T = Tangent, a straight line touching the edge of the circle at only one point. A radius drawn to the point where the tangent touches the circle forms a 90-degree angle with the tangent.

S = Arc length, the length of part of the circle. This is also measured along a section of the circumference. (Land planning applications using S are discussed in Chapter 9.)

π = 3.1416. This is the relationship between the diameter and the circumference of a circle. $\pi = C/D$: this relationship is the same for every circle.

A = Area of the circle. $A = (\pi D^2)/4$ or $A = \pi R^2$.

TRIANGLES

Triangles, when the shape can be identified, make the land planners' work easier. Right, equilateral, isosceles, and oblique triangles will be reviewed in this section. (See Fig. D–4.)

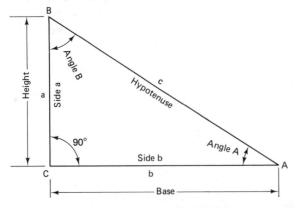

Figure D-4 Right triangle.

Right triangles contain one 90-degree angle and geometrical and trigonometrical relationships that are unique. One such relationship is expressed by the Pythagorean theorem, which states that the length of the hypotenuse (side opposite the 90-degree angle) squared is equal to the sum of the squares of the other two sides.

$$c^2 = a^2 + b^2$$

If $a = 3$, $b = 4$, $c = 5$ then,

$$25 = 9 + 16$$

The sum of the interior angles of any closed figure is equal to

$$\Sigma \text{ Int. } \angle = (N-2)180°$$

where N = number of sides in a figure.
therefore, for a triangle, the sum of the interior angles equals

$$\Sigma \text{ Int. } \angle = (3-2)180° = 180° \text{ degrees}$$

The area of a triangle is found by multiplying the base times the height and then dividing by 2.

$$A = \frac{bh}{2}$$

Equilateral triangles are triangles in which each side is of equal length. In an equilateral triangle each angle is equal to 60°. To find the area of an equilateral triangle it is first necessary to calculate the height (h) as noted in Fig. D–5. The area is then equal to one half the base times the height.

Isosceles triangles are triangles in which two of the sides are of equal length. In Fig. D–6 side AC = side BC. In an isosceles triangle the angles created by the

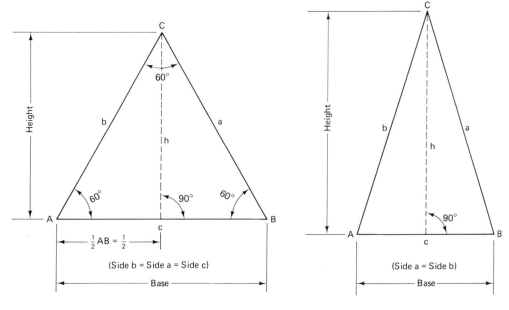

Figure D-5 Equilateral triangle.   **Figure D-6** Isosceles triangle.

sides and the base are equal. To find the area of an isosceles triangle, it is first necessary to find the height of the triangle.

BASIC TRIGONOMETRIC FUNCTIONS

Trigonometric functions are the proportionate ratios of the sides of a right triangle. (See Fig. D-7.) For any angle in a triangle there are six ratios (functions) that are of fundamental importance. For every angle only one value for each trigonometric function exists. In the study of land development, only three of these functions will be used.

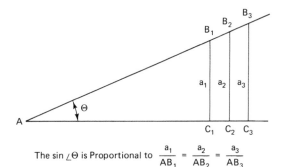

The sin $\angle\Theta$ is Proportional to $\dfrac{a_1}{AB_1} = \dfrac{a_2}{AB_2} = \dfrac{a_3}{AB_3}$

Figure D-7 Trigonometric functions.

Figure D-8 illustrates these three trigonometric functions or ratios, which are

$$\sin \angle A = \text{side opposite/hypotenuse or } \frac{BC}{AB}, \text{ or } \frac{a}{c}$$

$$\cos \angle A = \text{side adjacent/hypotenuse or } \frac{AC}{AB}, \text{ or } \frac{b}{c}$$

$$\tan \angle A = \text{side opposite/side adjacent or } \frac{BC}{AC}, \text{ or } \frac{a}{b}$$

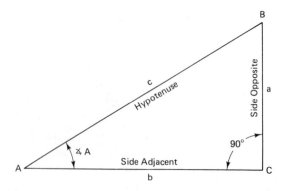

Figure D-8   Trigonometric functions.

Oblique triangles contain no right angles and no two angles are the same. To solve an oblique triangle for unknown angles or sides requires the given values of three unknowns—for example, two sides and one angle, two angles and one side, or all three sides. Knowing the three angles would not allow for the solution of sides since many oblique triangles could be drawn using the three given angles. Methods for solving for the unknown angles or sides involves the use of the sine and cosine laws.

Law of Sines:

$$\frac{a}{\sin A} = \frac{b}{\sin B} = \frac{c}{\sin C}$$

The length of any side of a triangle is to the sine of the angle opposite as another side is to the sine of its angle opposite.

Law of Cosines:

$$c^2 = a^2 + b^2 - 2\,ab\cos C$$

The distance squared is equal to the sum of the squares of the other two sides minus two times the product of the two sides and the angle opposite the side being sought. For example, in Fig. D-9, if

$$\angle B = 35° \, 15' 15''$$
$$c = 35.95'$$
$$a = 25.62'$$

then one could use the Law of Cosines to find the missing components in the triangle.

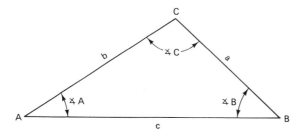

Figure D-9   Oblique triangle.

The Law of Sines would not work since one needs to know an angle and the side opposite.

$$c^2 = a^2 + b^2 - 2\,ab\,\cos C$$

Rewriting this equation for the given values

$$b^2 = a^2 + c^2 - 2\,ac\,\cos B$$

$b^2 = (25.62) + (35.95) - 2 \times 25.62 \times 35.95 \times \cos (35°\,15'15'')$
$b^2 = 656.38 + 1292.40 - (1842.08 \times \cos (35.254167))$
$b^2 = 1948.78 - 1842.08 \times 0.81660$
$b^2 = 444.54$
$b\ \ = 21.084$ ft

Now use the Law of Sines to calculate the angle at A.

$$\frac{a}{\sin A} = \frac{b}{\sin B}$$

$$\frac{25.62}{\sin A} = \frac{21.084}{\sin (35.254167)}$$

$$\sin A = \frac{25.62 \times 0.577204}{21.084} = 0.70138$$

$$\angle A\ \ = 44.53810° = 44°32'17''$$

Now find the last angle, C using the equation $(N - 2)180°$.

$$\angle C = 180 - (\angle A + \angle B) = 180° - (44.5381° + 35.254°)$$
$$\angle C = 100.280° = 100°12'28''$$

PROBLEMS

D-1.   Solve for y in the following expression.
Where, $x = 1$, $a = 5$, $b = 6$

$$y = 2x(a^2 + b)^2$$

D-2.   Solve for y in the following expression when $x = 4$.

$$y = x^2$$

D–3. What is the sum of angles *A, B, C*?

$$A = 47° 16' 12''$$
$$B = 72° 00' 23''$$
$$C = 108° 19' 32''$$

D–4. Subtract angle *B* (36° 38′10″) from angle *A* (91° 16′05″).

D–5. Convert the following angles (degrees, minutes, seconds) to degrees and decimal parts.

$$A = 75° 16' 32''$$
$$B = 81° 09' 12''$$
$$C = \ \ 7° 00' 06''$$
$$D = 15° 15' 15''$$
$$E = 45° 00' 00''$$
$$F = 17° 59' 59''$$

D–6. Convert the following angles (degrees and decimal parts) to degrees, minutes, and seconds.

$$A = \ \ 16.5869514°$$
$$B = \ \ 12.4545454°$$
$$C = \ \ 75.0123456°$$
$$D = \ \ 60.7500000°$$
$$E = 179.4984752°$$
$$F = \ \ 72.5867547°$$

D–7. For a given radius of 14.95 feet find the area and circumference of the circle.

D–8. In a five-sided figure, find the value of the missing interior angle, *E,* knowing the other angles as listed

$$A = \ \ 76° 52' 12''$$
$$B = \ \ 61° 19' 03''$$
$$C = \ \ 93° 15' 19''$$
$$D = 121° 07' 55''$$
$$E = \ \ ? \ \ ? \ \ ?$$

D–9. Find the missing sides or angles for the information listed in Table D–1. See Fig. D–4 for reference.

TABLE D–1

Reference	Sides			Angles		
	a	b	c	A	B	C
a	17.5	61.2	?	?	?	90
b	58.52	58.52	?	?	?	90
c	?	?	100.0	30.00	?	90
d	3.0	4.00	5.00	?	?	?
e	?	?	75.61	28.95	?	90

D-10. Find the missing sides or angles for the information listed in Table D-2. See Fig. D-9
for reference.

TABLE D-2

Reference	Sides			Angles		
	a	b	c	A	B	C
a	60.00	60.00	60.0	?	?	?
b	75.00	89.00	120.0	?	?	?
c	81.59	55.55	?	37.95	?	?
d	52.17	?	100.0	?	?	131.956759
e	71.42	?	?	37.95	41.947567	?

Bibliography

1. Beyer, William H., *Standard Mathematical Tables*. Boca Raton, FL: CRC Press, Inc., 1983.
2. Breed, Charles B., *Surveying*. New York, NY: John Wiley, 1942.
3. *Design and Construction of Sanitary and Storm Sewers*. Washington, D.C.: Water Pollution Control Federation, 1970.
4. *Handbook of Steel Drainage & Highway Construction Products*. New York, NY: American Iron and Steel Institute, 1971.
5. Kissam, Phillip, *Surveying Practice, The Fundamentals of Surveying*. New York, NY: McGraw-Hill, 1978.
6. Luthin, James, *Drainage Engineering*. Huntington, NY: R. E. Dreiger Publishing, 1978.
7. Meacham, D. G., *Structural Design Criteria for Corrugated Steel Culverts*. Columbus, OH: Ohio Department of Transportation, Feb. 1971.
8. Metcalf and Eddy, Inc., *Wastewater Engineering*. New York, NY: McGraw-Hill, 1972.
9. Munson, Albe E., *Construction Design for Landscape Architects*. New York, NY: McGraw-Hill, 1974.
10. Nelson, R.H., *Zoning and Property Rights*. Cambridge, MA: MIT Press, 1977.
11. Nunnally, S. W., *Managing Construction Equipment*. Englewood Cliffs, NJ: Prentice-Hall, 1977.
12. Parker, Home W., *Wastewater Systems Engineering*. Englewood Cliffs, NJ: Prentice-Hall, 1975.
13. Poole, L., M. McNiff, S. Cook, *Apple II User's Guide*. Berkeley, CA: Osborne/McGraw-Hill, 1983.
14. *Recommended Standards for Sewage Works, Great Lakes–Upper Mississippi River Board of Sanitary Engineers*. Albany, NY: Health Education Service, 1972.

15. Reichart, F. E., *Vibrations of Soils and Foundations.* Englewood Cliffs, NJ: Prentice-Hall, 1970.

16. Rubenstein, Harvey M., *Site and Environmental Planning.* New York, NY: John Wiley, 1980.

17. Sowers, George B., *Soil Mechanics and Foundations.* New York, NY: MacMillan, 1951.

18. Steele, R. C., *Modern Topographic Drawing.* Houston, TX: Gulf Publishing Co., 1980.

19. Terzaghi, Karl, *Soil Mechanics In Engineering Practice.* New York, NY: John Wiley, 1967.

20. Tymes, Elna, *Mastering Appleworks.* Berkeley, CA: Sybex, 1984.

21. United States Patent 4,050,261, Brewer et al. *Method of Backfilling,* Sept. 27, 1977.

22. United States Patent 4,050,950, Brewer et al. *Controlled Density Fill Material Containing Fly Ash,* Dec. 13, 1977.

23. Unterman, R. K., *Principles and Practices of Grading, Drainage, and Road Alignment: An Ecologic Approach.* Reston, VA: Reston Publishing Company, 1978.

24. Weaver, C., and R. Babcock, *City Zoning.* Chicago, IL: Planners Press (American Planning Association), 1979.

25. Yoder, E. J. and M. W. Witczak, *Principles of Pavement Design.* New York, NY: John Wiley, 1975.

Index